Christian Responses to Terrorism

McMaster Divinity College Press
McMaster General Studies Series, Volume 10

Christian Responses to Terrorism
The Kenyan Experience

Edited by
GORDON L. HEATH
and
DAVID K. TARUS

PICKWICK *Publications* · Eugene, Oregon

CHRISTIAN RESPONSES TO TERRORISM
The Kenyan Experience

McMaster General Studies Series, Volume 10
McMaster Divinity College Press

Copyright © 2017 Wipf and Stock Publishers. All rights reserved. Except for brief quotations in critical publications or reviews, no part of this book may be reproduced in any manner without prior written permission from the publisher. Write: Permissions, Wipf and Stock Publishers, 199 W. 8th Ave., Suite 3, Eugene, OR 97401.

Pickwick Publications
An Imprint of Wipf and Stock Publishers
199 W. 8th Ave., Suite 3
Eugene, OR 97401

McMaster Divinity College Press
1280 Main Street West
Hamilton, ON, Canada L8S 4K1

www.wipfandstock.com

PAPERBACK ISBN: 978-1-4982-2927-2
HARDCOVER ISBN: 978-1-4982-2929-6
EBOOK ISBN: 978-1-4982-2928-9

Cataloguing-in-Publication data:

Names: Heath, Gordon L., editor. | Tarus, David K., editor.

Title: Christian responses to terrorism : the Kenyan experience / Gordon L. Heath and David K. Tarus, editors

Description: Eugene, OR: Pickwick Publications, 2017 | McMaster General Studies Series, Volume 10 | Includes bibliographical references and index.

Identifiers: ISBN 978-1-4982-2927-2 (paperback) | ISBN 978-1-4982-2929-6 (hardcover) | ISBN 978-1-4982-2928-9 (ebook)

Subjects: LCSH: Terrorism—Kenya | Christianity and politics—Kenya | Islam and politics—Kenya | Violence—Religious aspects | Peace—Religious aspects.

Classification: BL65 V55 C48 2017 (print) | BL65 (ebook)

Manufactured in the U.S.A.   12/15/17

Contents

Acknowledgments | vii

Editors and Contributors | ix

Part 1: Essays

1   Introduction | 3
       —David K. Tarus and Gordon L. Heath

2   A History of Christian–Muslim Relations in Kenya, 1963–2015 | 12
       —Newton Kahumbi Maina

3   Christian Responses to Terror in Kenya | 33
       —Joseph D. Galgalo

4   A Pacifist Response to Terrorism | 50
       —Joseph B. Onyango Okello

5   Evangelicals and Public Life in Kenya | 72
       —Julius Gathogo

6   Being Human in Kenya: Theological Anthropology in the Age of Terror | 88
       —David K. Tarus

7   "We Have No More Cheeks to Turn": Christian and Muslim Responses to Terrorism in Kenya | 106
       —Joseph Wandera

8   Reconciliatory Peace in the Face of Terror: A Personal Appeal for Quaker Peace Building in Kenya | 123
       —Esther M. Mombo

9 Gender, Women, and Children, and Al-Shabaab Terrorism in Kenya: A Christian Response | 132
   —Eunice Karanja Kamaara and Simon Gisege Omare

10 Missions to Muslims: A Kenyan Experience | 151
    —Joseph K. Koech

Part 2: Responses

11 Response to Joseph D. Galgalo and Joseph B. O. Okello | 173
    —Gordon L. Heath

12 A Response to Julius Gathogo | 176
    —Brian Stanley

13 A Response to David K. Tarus | 179
    —Richard J. Gehman

14 A Response to Esther M. Mombo and Joseph Wandera | 183
    —Gregg A. Okesson

15 A Response to Eunice K. Kamaara and Simon G. Omare | 193
    —Cynthia Long Westfall

16 A Response to Joseph K. Koech | 202
    —Wafik Wahba

17 Reading from a Muslim Perspective: Forging the Way Ahead | 205
    —Halkano Abdi Wario

Appendix: Timeline of Some of the Terrorist Attacks in Kenya from 2011 to 2016 | 215

Subject Index | 223

Names Index | 226

Acknowledgments

THE GENESIS OF THIS book was a conversation in a car about the contemporary crisis in Kenya. At the time, we were not thinking of a publishing venture. However, not long after, we sat down to discuss the formation of what would become this book. Since the project's inception a few years ago, many people have helped bring it to fruition, and a few thanks are in order.

McMaster Divinity College is a place where scholarly research and publishing by faculty and doctoral students is encouraged. Thank you to President Stanley Porter and Academic Dean Phil Zylla for fostering such an environment.

Thank you to all the contributors and responders who made this book a unique contribution to global theology in general, and the Kenyan church in particular.

The work of Lois Dow as copy editor was stellar, and thank you as well to Don Springer whose editing is deeply appreciated.

Finally, thank you to our families. Your backing is deeply appreciated, and to you this book is dedicated.

Editors and Contributors

EDITORS

Gordon L. Heath (PhD, St. Michael's College) is Professor of Christian History as well as Centenary Chair in World Christianity at McMaster Divinity College, Hamilton, Ontario, Canada. He also serves as Director of the Canadian Baptist Archives. His research interests rest primarily in the area of Christians and war, or the intersection of church and state. His publications include *The British Nation is Our Nation: The BACSANZ Baptist Press and the South African War, 1899–1902* (Paternoster, 2017); *A War with a Silver Lining: Canadian Protestant Churches and the South African War, 1899–1902* (McGill-Queens University Press, 2009); and *Doing Church History: A User-friendly Introduction to Researching the History of Christianity* (Clements, 2008). He has also edited a number of volumes, such as *American Churches and the First World War* (Pickwick, 2016) and *Canadian Churches and the First World War* (Pickwick, 2014).

David K. Tarus (PhD, McMaster Divinity College) is a graduate of Scott Christian University, Kenya, (BTh), and Wheaton College Graduate School, USA, (MA Historical & Systematic Theology). The title of his dissertation is "A Different Way of Being: Toward a Reformed Theology of Ethnopolitical Cohesion for the Kenyan Context." He has previously worked as the coordinator of Scott Christian University Eldoret Campus. Tarus has published several articles, including "Social Transformation in the Circle of Concerned African Women Theologians" (*AJET*); "The Significance of Intellectual Humility for Theologians Today" (*AJET*); "John Stott and Biblical Preaching in Africa" (*IJAH*); and "Conquering Africa's Second Devil: Ecclesiastical Role in Combating Ethnic Bigotry" (*African Affairs*).

CONTRIBUTORS

Joseph D. Galgalo (PhD, Systematic Theology, from the University of Cambridge) is Associate Professor of Systematic Theology and the Vice Chancellor of St. Paul's University, Limuru, Kenya. He is also an Anglican minister and an honorary canon of All Saints Cathedral, Nairobi. He has served on a number of international commissions, including the Inter-Anglican theological and doctrinal commission of the Anglican Communion (2001–2007). His research interests are in contextual theologies and theological education. He has published widely in refereed journals and book chapters, and is the author of *African Christianity: The Stranger Within* (Zapf Chancery, Eldoret, 2012); and co-edited a number of books including *Theological Education in Africa* (2004) and *God and Disability* (2010).

Julius Gathogo (PhD, University of KwaZulu-Natal) is a Senior Lecturer at Kenyatta University and a Research Fellow at the University of South Africa. He has published extensively in refereed journals and has authored several books. His research interests include contemporary theo-ethical trajectories, African theologies, and mission histories. He is a prolific writer and researcher with a global appeal.

Richard J. Gehman attended Berean Bible School, Wheaton College and Graduate School, Gordon Divinity School (now Gordon Conwell), and Fuller Theological Seminary (School of World Missions). For thirty-six years, beginning in 1966, he and his wife, Florence, served in Kenya with the Africa Inland Church, mostly in theological education at Scott Theological College (now Scott Christian University) and with the Theological Advisory Group, a research and renewal ministry. In 2002, Gehman and his wife retired in the United States where he has continued writing books for the African Church.

Eunice Karanja Kamaara is Professor of Religion at Moi University, Kenya, and International Affiliate of Indiana University Purdue University, Indianapolis (USA). She holds a PhD in African Christian Ethics and an MSc in International Health Research Ethics. Her research expertise is in interpretive methods with inter-disciplinary perspectives: ethical, medical, socio-anthropological, theological, and gender approaches to religion and development in contemporary Africa. She is particularly interested in translating research findings into practical development through policy influence and community research uptake. She is widely published and has consulted in research for national and international organizations, including, but not limited to, the World Bank, Church World Service (CWS), the United States Agency for International Development (USAID), the United Nations Population Fund (UNFPA), the Templeton World Charity Foundation Inc. (TWCF), and the World Council of Churches (WCC). Kamaara currently serves as Director of Church World Service and in the Ethics Review Board of Médecins Sans Frontières (MSF) as a cultural and behavioral expert.

Joseph K. Koech (DPhil, Moi University) is currently the Head of Department and Associate Professor in the Department of Philosophy, Religion and Theology at Moi University, Kenya. His academic interests include New Testament Studies as it relates to the African context, African Independent Churches, Christian leadership, and pastoral care. He has published several articles in academic journals, and a book entitled *The Spirit as Liberator: A Study of Luke 4:14–30 in the African Context*. He is an Editorial Board member of *Journal of Technology and Socio-economic Development* published by the Eldoret National Polytechnic, Kenya, and also Associate Editor of *Contemporary Issues in Philosophy, Religion and Theology, Utafiti*, a Publication of the Department of Philosophy, Religion and Theology, Moi University.

Newton Kahumbi Maina (PhD, Kenyatta University) is a Senior Lecturer and current Chairman of the Department of Philosophy and Religious Studies, Kenyatta University. His areas of research interest are Islamic Studies, Christian–Muslim Relations, Religion, Gender, and Culture. His publications include *Role of Women in Ethnic Conflict Management and Resolution in Kenya* (2015) and *Islamic Influence on Education in Africa* (2011). His articles in journals and books include: "Challenges of Teaching Islamic Studies by Non-Muslims in Kenyan Tertiary Institutions" (2013); "The Interface between Religion & Culture: Constraints to Muslim Girls' Access to Secondary School Education in Kenya" (2007); "Islamophobia among Christians and Its Challenge in Entrenchment of Kadhi Courts in Kenya" (2011); "Historical Roots of Conflicts between Christians and Muslims in Kenya" (2009); "Christian–Muslim Dialogue in Kenya" (2003); "Interpretation of the Qur'an and Its Influence in Girls' Access to Secondary School Education in Kenya" (2007).

Esther M. Mombo (PhD, Edinburgh University) is Associate Professor of Church History at St. Paul's University, Kenya. She also serves as Director, International Partnerships and Alumni Relations in the same University. Her research interests include the growth and development of the church, especially the Quakers in East Africa, women and church leadership, and interfaith relations. Her publications include *Contested Space: Ethnicity and Religion in Kenya* (Limuru: Zaph Chancery, 2013); *Disability, Society and Theology: Voices from Africa* (Limuru: Zapf Chancery, 2011); *If You Have No Voice Just Sing: Narratives of Women's Lives and Theological Education at St. Paul's University* (Limuru: Zapf Chancery, 2011); *A Guide to Leadership* (London: SPCK, 2010).

Joseph B. Onyango Okello is an Associate Professor of Philosophy and Ethics at Asbury Theological Seminary, Dunnam Campus, in Orlando, Florida. He is also the current president of Kenya Christian Fellowship in America, a Christian organization with 26 chapters throughout the United States of America. Okello holds an MA and a PhD, both in philosophy, from the University of Kentucky. He also holds a Master of Divinity and an MA in Church Music from Asbury Theological Seminary. He is the author of *A History and Critique of Methodological Naturalism* (Wipf & Stock, 2016), and *Evil and Pain: A Critique of the Materialistic Account of Pain*. Okello, his wife Sophie, and their son, Sean, live in Oviedo, Florida.

Gregg A. Okesson (PhD, Leeds University, UK) is the Dean of the E. Stanley Jones School of World Mission and Evangelism and Professor of Leadership and Development at Asbury Theological Seminary, USA. His research interests fall within the area of Public Missiology, African Christianity, International Development, and Cross-cultural Leadership. His publications include *Re-Imaging Modernity: A Contextualized Theological Study of Power and Humanity within Akamba Christianity in Kenya* (Pickwick, 2012); *Advocating for Justice: An Evangelical Vision for Transforming Systems and Structures* (Baker Academic, 2016); and he is currently writing a book on public missiology (Baker Academic, forthcoming 2018).

Simon Gisege Omare (PhD, Moi University) is a lecturer at Moi University in the department of Philosophy, Religion and Theology. He lectures in sociology of religion and African religion. He has also published the following books: *Witchcraft Scapegoat: Abagusii Beliefs and Violence against "Witches"* (2015); *Religion and Environment Conservation: The Role of Isukha Religious Beliefs and Practices in the Conservation of Kakamega Forest* (2010). He has also published several articles on various themes regarding how religion influences the environment, politics, science, violence, and the belief in witchcraft.

Brian Stanley (PhD, University of Cambridge) is Professor of World Christianity at the University of Edinburgh, and Director of the Centre for the Study of World Christianity. He has published widely on the history of the modern missionary movement and of world Christianity. He is editor of the journal *Studies in World Christianity* (Edinburgh University Press) and co-editor of the Eerdmans series Studies in the History of Christian Missions. His most recent books are *The World Missionary Conference, Edinburgh 1910* (Eerdmans, 2009) and *The Global Diffusion of Evangelicalism: The Age of Billy Graham and John Stott* (IVP, 2013). His *A World History of Christianity in the Twentieth Century* will be published by Princeton University Press in 2018.

Wafik Wahba (ThM, Princeton; PhD, Northwestern University) is Associate Professor of Global Christianity at Tyndale Seminary in Toronto, Canada. He has taught Theology, Global Christianity, Cultural Contextualization, and Islam in the USA, Middle East, Africa, South East Asia, and South America. He has written several books and articles including his contributions to *The Future of Reformed Theology* (Eerdmans, 1999), *Repentance in Christian Theology* (Liturgical, 2006), *Evangelicals around the World: A Global Handbook for the 21st Century* (Thomas Nelson, 2015), *Christianity and Islam: Global Perspectives* (IVP Academic, 2017). Wahba co-led the unit on "Theological Education for Mission" at the 2004 Forum of the Lausanne Committee in Pattaya, Thailand, and he is one of the authors of *Effective Theological Education for World Evangelization*, Lausanne Occasional Paper No. 57 (May 2005). He serves on the Board of Directors for several International Christian Organizations.

Joseph Wandera is a Senior Lecturer in the Department of Religious Studies and Coordinator, Centre for Christian-Muslim Relations, in Eastleigh, St. Paul's University, Kenya. His teaching and research interests are on the nexus between religion and public life and Christian–Muslim Relations in Africa. Wandera's PhD was obtained at the Department of Religious Studies, University of Cape Town, where he worked on Public Preaching by Muslims and Pentecostal Preachers in Western Kenya and its influence on interfaith relations.

Halkano Abdi Wario is a lecturer in Islamic Studies at the Department of Philosophy, History and Religion, Egerton University. He is also a senior Volkswagen Foundation Humanities Research Fellow at the same university with a research project that explores the nexus of religious knowledge and construction of alternative counter-narrativity in faith-based and donor funded organizations countering violent extremism in Kenya. He completed his doctoral studies in 2012 at Bayreuth International Graduate School of African Studies (BIGSAS), University of Bayreuth, Germany, focusing on localization of a translational Islamic movement called Tablīghī Jamāʿat in Kenya. His research interests include mediation and mediatization of religious knowledge, Muslim print cultures, religious transnationalism, religion and spatiality, religion and security, Islamic reformism in Eastern Africa, and emerging trends in Islamic law in Africa and dynamics of countering violent extremism in the Horn of Africa.

Cynthia Long Westfall (PhD, University of Surrey) is Associate Professor of New Testament at McMaster Divinity College, Hamilton, Ontario, Canada. Her publications include *Paul and Gender: Reclaiming the Apostle's Vision for Men and Women in Christ* (Baker, 2016) and *A Discourse Analysis of the Structure of Hebrews: Relationship between Form and Meaning* (T. & T. Clark, 2006). She has coedited several volumes, including *The Bible and Social Justice: Old Testament and New Testament Foundations for the Church's Urgent Call* (Wipf & Stock, 2016). In addition to teaching, Westfall serves on the steering committee of the SBL Biblical Greek Language and Linguistics section, the ETS Evangelicals and Gender section, and the ETS Hebrews section.

Sketch Map of Kenya and Region

PART 1

Essays

1

Introduction

DAVID K. TARUS AND GORDON L. HEATH

WHILE MANY IN AMERICA automatically think of 9/11, Boston, or Orlando when terrorism is mentioned, Europeans may think of attacks in Madrid, Paris, Brussels, or London. However, religiously inspired terrorism is not solely a Western problem. Asians and Africans have their own memories of horrors inflicted upon their neighbors and nations. One such nation that has had a significant history of religiously inspired terrorism is Kenya.

The *Encyclopedia of Terrorism and Political Violence* provides over sixty possible definitions for terrorism.[1] While there is debate over the actual definition, the word itself comes from the Latin *terrere* "to cause to tremble."[2] In modern political usage the term arose during the days of terror during the French Revolution. The "terror" then was what occurred during the darkest days of fear, unrest, and violence, and it was used as a tactic to eliminate one's enemies and achieve political ends.[3]

Terror and religion—what do they have in common? Sadly, a great deal. As many have noted, terrorism has been, and often is, in part, motivated by religion.[4] As Mark Juergensmeyer writes, religion has "supplied

---

1. Thackrah, *Encyclopedia of Terrorism*, 58–63.

2. For a brief discussion of some of the issues, see Juergensmeyer, *Terror in the Mind*, 7–10.

3. Ibid., 5.

4. For terrorism in general, see Combs, *Terrorism*. For Islamic fundamentalism and terror, see Murphy, *Sword of Islam*; Milton-Edwards, *Islamic Fundamentalism*.

3

not only the ideology but also the motivation and the organizational structure" for many modern-day terrorists.⁵ In fact, Juergensmeyer claims, since the 1980s, religiously motivated terrorism has increased at a phenomenal rate, and one US government official stated that religiously motivated terrorism is "the most important security challenge ... in the wake of the Cold War."⁶ Compounding the dangers associated with the evolution of modern-day religiously inspired terrorism is the new technology available to terrorists. As Walter Laqueur notes, "Science and technology have made enormous progress, but human nature, alas, has not changed. There is as much fanaticism and madness as there ever was, and there are now very powerful weapons of mass destruction available to the terrorist."⁷ Those and other problems faced the government of Kenya during its recent crisis.

Kenya is a multi-ethnic African country with a population of roughly 44 million. Prior to the escalation of terrorism in 2011, Kenya had suffered three major terrorist attacks. The first was the bombing of the Norfolk Hotel in downtown Nairobi on 31 December 1980 that killed twenty people and wounded eighteen others. The Popular Front for the Liberation of Palestine (PFLP) allegedly perpetrated the attack to retaliate against Kenya allowing Israeli troops to refuel in Nairobi before freeing 103 Israeli and Jewish people that were being held hostage in Entebbe, Uganda. The freedom operation, which was successful, was carried out on 4 July 1976.⁸

The second and largest attack was the twin bombings of the American embassies in Nairobi (Kenya) and Dar es Salaam (Tanzania) on 7 August 1998. The al-Qaeda-led attacks resulted in the deaths of 224 people, including twelve Americans, and left more than 4,000 people injured.⁹ A planned attack on the American embassy in Kampala (Uganda) was thwarted on that same day.¹⁰ Samuel Aronson observes that the terrorist attacks on the American embassies marked a shift in US foreign policy, for it alerted the US government to the reality and

---

5. Juergensmeyer, *Terror in the Mind*, 5.
6. Ibid., 6.
7. Laqueur, *New Terrorism*, 4.
8. Davis, *Africa*, 50.
9. Siler, "Kenya and Tanzania."
10. Watts et al., *Al-Qaida's (Mis)Adventures*, 48.

subtle nature of international terrorist cells that could cause massive damage to American properties abroad.[11]

The next major attack occurred on 28 November 2002, with the bombing of the Paradise Hotel in Kikambala, Mombasa. At the same time, terrorists shot a surface-to-air missile at an Israeli commercial airplane departing from Mombasa International airport en route to Tel Aviv. The missile missed the airplane, but twelve people died and eighty were injured in the hotel attack.[12]

Terror attacks have escalated since October 2011 as a response to Kenya's military presence in Somalia. Prior to the Westgate Mall attack, Kenya had suffered at least twenty grenade attacks,[13] probably even more, as some cases, especially in the poor North Eastern counties, are not closely reported by Kenyan media. Al-Shabaab has conducted successive small-scale grenade attacks concentrated in North Eastern (the regions bordering Somalia), Nairobi, and Coastal regions. The attacks have targeted churches, bars, hotels, markets, bus stations, police stations, and public transportation service vehicles. In fact, the Global Terrorism Index of 2014 ranked Kenya twelfth out of 162 countries on terrorism.[14]

On 21 September 2013, a group of four gunmen stormed the Westgate Mall in Westlands, Nairobi, shooting people indiscriminately before specifically killing those who could not recite the Qur'an or say Muslim prayers. The four-day attack left 67 people dead and at least 175 wounded. The mall was considered a prestigious shopping destination to visit, and a landmark of Kenya's progress and development. It was also a major shopping destination for Western dignitaries, tourists, and visitors to Kenya, or those in transit to other East African countries. Hence, by attacking Westgate, al-Shabaab targeted a facility with strong Western connections. The Westgate Mall has since been rebuilt and reopened. The opening of the mall, including four new others such as the Two Rivers Mall, which is East and Central Africa's largest mall, is an indication of the government's resolve to win the war against domestic terror.

Other acts of violence in the recent past are the sporadic attacks in the Coastal regions of Lamu, Mpeketoni, and Tana River, in the months

11. Aronson, "Kenya and the Global War," 27.
12. Davis, *Africa*, 50–51.
13. See the Appendix to this volume, "Chronology of Terrorist Attacks in Kenya."
14. Institute for Economics and Peace, *Global Terrorism Index* 2014.

of June and July 2014. A group of young men, at least fifty in number, repeatedly invaded rural and urban townships over a period of weeks along the Coastal areas mentioned above, and dragged men out of their houses, either slitting their throats or shooting them at close range.[15] The attackers specifically targeted non-Muslim men. This indicates that religion rather than "local political networks" was the cause of the violence.[16] Religion also played a key role in the Garissa University College massacre that occurred on 2 April 2015 where 148 people were executed. Al-Shabaab also claimed responsibility for that attack. The four assailants, who were also killed during the attack, singled out Christians and shot them.

The Kenyan government has sought to put an end to such attacks, while at the same time attempting—not always successfully—to avoid unnecessarily antagonizing the Muslim population at large.[17] The first large-scale response was Kenya's military incursion into Somalia in October 2011, its first-ever regional military mission outside its borders. It sent troops to Somalia to keep the Kenyan border secure, to stop the prevalent al-Shabaab-led kidnappings and extortion of tourists along the North Eastern and the Coastal regions, and to end piracy in the Indian Ocean. The incursion into Somalia, known as *Operation Linda Nchi* (Swahili for Operation Protect the Country), was led by the Kenya Defence Forces (KDF). KDF is now integrated into the United Nations sponsored African Union Mission to Somalia (AMISOM). The incursion into Somalia has resulted in retaliatory attacks by al-Shabaab, which has its base in Somalia. Before the KDF incursion, al-Shabaab had warned that Kenya would suffer massive attacks if it dared send troops to Somalia.[18]

The Kenyan government, through its counter-terrorism tactics, has been accused of carrying out illegal arrests of hundreds of Muslim youths, assassinations of several perceived radical religious leaders, and torture of terrorism suspects.[19] Perceived radical Muslim clerics

15. Okeyo, "Geo-Politics."

16. President Uhuru Kenyatta initially said that local political networks were responsible for the violence.

17. Ndzovu, *Muslims in Kenyan Politics*, 114–27.

18. Odhiambo et al., "Reprisal Attacks," 53.

19. For a comprehensive documentary of the assassination of Muslim clerics in Kenya, see, the al-Jazeera Documentary "Inside Kenya's Death Squads."

who have been assassinated in recent years include Sheikh Mohammed Kassim (2012), Sheikh Aboud Rogo (2012), Sheikh Ibrahim Omar Ismail (2013), and Sheikh Abubakar Shariff, also known as Makaburi (2014).[20] Rather than quelling terrorism, such types of government response often add fuel to the flames of extremism because Muslims are driven to seek spiritual guidance and direction from radical popular literature and militant community leaders. Furthermore, radical Muslims are assassinating conservative mainstream Muslim clerics in retaliation for the deaths of the radical clerics. Many such clerics are forced to leave their mosques, which are then taken over by radicalized youths. Conservative Muslim clerics who have been killed in the recent past include Sheikh Mohammed Idriss (2014) and Sheikh Salim Bakari (2014). As a result of such activities, significant numbers of Kenyan Muslims have increasingly felt marginalized and alienated.[21]

The state has responded, but what of the churches? Kenya is a predominantly Christian nation, with roughly 80 percent Christian and 11 percent Muslim.[22] As Paul Gifford has noted, in the latter half of the twentieth century, Kenyan churches had a less than stellar track record when it came to constructive engagement with the state; oftentimes their otherworldliness, parochial focus, or domestication actually made them part of the problem.[23] But what about their activity in the early twenty-first century? As targets of extremists, many church leaders recently have publicly called for more police protection, and some have even expressed the desire to carry firearms in churches in order to protect themselves and their congregants. The former reaction may seem commonsensical, while the latter too extreme. But what exactly are Kenyan Christians to do when faced with the threat of terrorism, and how are they to think about violence and a Christian's role in its suppression? Is self-defense a legitimate option? What about retaliation? How is the Christian community to respond to the Muslim community at large, and in what way should they speak about those who commit terror in the name of Islam? Finally, what biblical and theological resources should church leaders

20. Botha, "Radicalisation," 3.
21. Ndzovu, *Muslims in Kenyan Politics*.
22. Kenya National Bureau of Statistics, "Population and Housing Census 2009." There is no consensus on percentages, and some argue that the government figures are skewed for political reasons. See Ndzovu, *Muslims in Kenyan Politics*, 8–9.
23. Gifford, *Christianity*.

and members draw upon in order to ensure a wise and pastoral response to the threat and reality of violence?

Over the past few decades there has been a growing recognition that the complexion of the worldwide church has dramatically shifted away from being primarily Western. As Philip Jenkins has so famously stated,

> [T]he center of gravity in the Christian world has shifted inexorably southward, to Africa, Asia, and Latin America. Already today, the largest Christian communities on the planet are to be found in Africa and Latin America. If we want to visualize a "typical" contemporary Christian, we should think of a woman living in a village in Nigeria or in a Brazilian *favela*. As Kenyan scholar John Mbiti has observed, "the centers of the church's universality [are] no longer in Geneva, Rome, Athens, Paris, London, New York, but Kinshasa, Buenos Aires, Addis Ababa and Manila." Whatever Europeans or North Americans may believe, Christianity is doing very well indeed in the global south—not just surviving but expanding.[24]

An important element to that global growth is the ongoing development of non-Western theologies written by and for the various global Christian communities. This book is an attempt to do just that—it is a series of theological reflections to address a specifically Kenyan crisis. The authors of the Essays in this volume are Kenyans, and it seeks to provide instruction by Kenyans for Kenyans. It is a contribution to the development of an African and global Christian response to the threat of terrorism in Kenya. Others have already begun to reflect upon the Kenyan churches' responses, and think theologically about the way forward.[25] This book continues that helpful and necessary trajectory. Bringing the Kenyan reflections into a larger global conversation are the comments by the respondents, one a Muslim, the others Christian. The intention of including Christian respondents from outside of Kenya is

---

24. Jenkins, *Next Christendom*, 2. See also Hastings, *World History*; Hylson-Smith, *To the Ends*; Jenkins, *Lost History*; Isichei, *History of Christianity*; Kim and Kim, *Christianity*; Marty, *Christian World*; Noll, *New Shape*; Rah, *Next Evangelicalism*; Sanneh, *Whose Religion*.

25. Omayio, "Keeping Religion"; Omayio, "Response of the Church"; Kipkoros, "Towards a Christian Response." For churches and reconciliation in general, see Kilonzo, "Silent Religiosity."

to enlarge the conversation partners and engage in a global theological discussion.

Kenyan Muslims have also struggled with how to respond to the heightened tensions, and much of the community's political response has been shaped by "their constant sense of marginalization as a minority."[26] If post-colonialism has taught us anything over the last decades, it has taught us to "listen to the margins." And in that spirit, we included a Muslim response to Christian proposals. The inclusion of a Muslim respondent to this project provides a sense as to how Christian reflections and proposals are being heard from "outside" the church, as well as to model a healthy and goodwill interfaith dialogue—something necessary in the present crisis in Kenya.

The way forward for Kenyans is fraught with danger, and, as Gifford states, "Christianity in Kenya obviously fulfils so many different roles that no simple answer is possible" to the role it is to take in public life.[27] There is no easy solution to the problem of violence in Kenya, and Christians face incredible pressures to act in ways that are contrary to Christian discipleship. Nevertheless, it is hoped that this volume will be one resource that will help forge a constructive and Christian way forward despite such temptations. It is also hoped that this resource for Kenya will inform Christian responses to terrorism in other contexts around the world.

REFERENCES

Al Jazeera. "Inside Kenya's Death Squads." http://interactive.aljazeera.com/aje/Kenya DeathSquads/#film. Accessed 10 December 2014.
Aronson, Samuel L. "Kenya and the Global War on Terror: Neglecting History and Geopolitics in Approaches to Counterterrorism." *African Journal of Criminology and Justice Studies* 7, no. 1/2 (2013) 24–34.
Botha, Anneli. "Radicalisation in Kenya: Recruitment to Al-Shabaab and the Mombasa Republican Council." *Institute for Security Studies* (2014) 1–28.
Combs, Cindy B. *Terrorism in the Twenty-First Century*. 3rd ed. Upper Saddle River, NJ: Prentice Hall, 2003.
Davis, John, ed. *Africa and the War on Terrorism*. Aldershot: Ashgate, 2007.
Gifford, Paul. *Christianity, Politics, and Public Life in Kenya*. London: Hurst, 2009.
Hastings, Adrian, ed. *A World History of Christianity*. Grand Rapids: Eerdmans, 1999.
Hylson-Smith, Kenneth. *To the Ends of the Earth: The Globalization of Christianity*. London: Paternoster, 2007.

---

26. Ndzovu, *Muslims in Kenyan Politics*, 10.

27. Gifford, *Christianity*, 250.

Institute for Economics and Peace. *Global Terrorism Index 2014: Measuring and Understanding the Impact of Terrorism.* www.economicsandpeace.org. Accessed 24 November 2014.

Isichei, Elizabeth. *A History of Christianity in Africa: From Antiquity to the Present.* Grand Rapids: Eerdmans, 1995.

Jenkins, Philip. *The Lost History of Christianity: The Thousand-Year Golden Age of the Church in the Middle East, Africa, and Asia—and How It Died.* New York: HarperOne, 2008.

———. *The Next Christendom: The Coming of Global Christianity.* Oxford: Oxford University Press, 2002.

Juergensmeyer, Mark. *Terror in the Mind of God: The Global Rise of Religious Violence.* 3rd ed. Berkeley and Los Angeles: University of California Press, 2003.

Kenya National Bureau of Statistics. "Population and Housing Census 2009." http://www.knbs.or.ke/index.php?option=com_phocadownload&view=category&id=109:population-and-housing-census-2009&Itemid=599. Accessed 6 November 2015.

Kilonzo, Susan M. "Silent Religiosity in a Snivelling Nation: The Role of Religious Institutions in Promoting Post-Conflict Reconciliation in Kenya." *Africa Media Review* 17 (2009) 95–107.

Kim, Sebastian C. H., and Kirsteen Kim. *Christianity as a World Religion.* London: Continuum, 2008.

Kipkoros, William C. "Towards a Christian Response to Al-Shabaab's Terror Attacks on Kenyans." *Journal of Philosophy, Culture and Religion* 11 (2015) 25–33. http://www.google.ca/url?sa=t&rct=j&q=&esrc=s&source=web&cd=2&ved=0ahUKEwignIKTi8LSAhUH1oMKHYKNBXUQFggfMAE&url=http%3A%2F%2Fwww.iiste.org%2FJournals%2Findex.php%2FJPCR%2Farticle%2Fdownload%2F25963%2F26136&usg=AFQjCNHd8tEuhRMgsl7aYqdZs9SUrAAilQ&sig2=sB8-mcU3YaHoZJLxZ5pobw. Accessed 6 March 2017.

Laqueur, Walter. *The New Terrorism: Fanaticism and the Arms of Mass Destruction.* Oxford: Oxford University Press, 1999.

Marty, Martin E. *The Christian World: A Global History.* New York: Modern Library, 2007.

Milton-Edwards, Beverley. *Islamic Fundamentalism since 1945.* New York: Routledge, 2005.

Murphy, John F., Jr. *Sword of Islam: Muslim Extremism from the Arab Conquests to the Attack on America.* Amherst, NY: Prometheus, 2002.

Ndzovu, Hassan J. *Muslims in Kenyan Politics: Political Involvement, Marginalization, and Minority Status.* Evanston: Northwestern University Press, 2014.

Noll, Mark A. *The New Shape of World Christianity: How American Experience Reflects Global Faith.* Downers Grove: IVP Academic, 2009.

Odhiambo, Elijah O. S., et al. "The Reprisal Attacks by Al-Shabaab against Kenya." *Journal of Defense Resources Management* 4 (2013) 53.

Okeyo, Vera. "How Geo-Politics Made Kenya an Easy Target for Major Terror Networks." *Daily Nation.* Nairobi, 2014.

Omayio, Paul Atina. "Keeping Religion out of a Conflict: Learning from the Kenyan Church." *International Journal of Sociology and Anthropology* 7 (February 2015) 38–45.

———. "The Response of the Church in Nairobi to the Al-Shabaab Terror Attacks: A Case Study of St. Polycarp Anglican Church Jura Road Pangani and God's House of Miracles International Nairobi." MA Thesis, Norwegian School of Theology, 2014.

Rah, Soong-Chan. *The Next Evangelicalism: Freeing the Church from Western Cultural Captivity*. Downers Grove: Intervarsity, 2009.

Sanneh, Lamin O. *Whose Religion Is Christianity? The Gospel beyond the West*. Grand Rapids: Eerdmans, 2003.

Siler, Michael. "Kenya and Tanzania: Embassy Bombings, 1998." In *World Terrorism: An Encyclopedia of Political Violence from Ancient Times to the Post-9/11 Era*, 2:324–26. Armonk, NY: M.E. Sharpe, 2011.

Thackrah, John Richard. *Encyclopedia of Terrorism and Political Violence*. London: Routledge & Kegan Paul, 1987.

Watts, Clint, et al. *Al-Qaida's (Mis)Adventures in the Horn of Africa*. West Point, NY: Harmony Project, 2007. https://www.files.ethz.ch/isn/31690/al-quaida_misadv_africa.pdf. Accessed 6 March 2017.

2

A History of Christian–Muslim Relations in Kenya, 1963–2015

Newton Kahumbi Maina

Both Christianity and Islam are missionary religions eager to propagate themselves through conversion and to gain advantage over each other and other religions. Therefore, tensions, hostility, conflicts, and suspicions between the followers of the two monotheistic religions are inevitable. Generally, this scenario captures the history of Christian–Muslim relations in Kenya.

This chapter discusses Christian–Muslim relations in Kenya from 1963, the year Kenya became independent from Britain, to the present. Within this period, there are two epochs in the history of Christian–Muslim relations: 1963 to 1998, and 1998 to 2016. An atmosphere of tolerance, coexistence, and uneasiness between Christians and Muslims characterized 1963 to 1998. The period 1998 to 2015 epitomizes the rise and manifestations of Muslim radicalism and extremism on Kenyan soil, exemplified in the 1998 bombing of the American embassy in Nairobi and other terror attacks, which have had implications for Christian–Muslim relations in the country. However, before detailing the two epochs, it is important to highlight the relations between Christians and Muslims in the colonial period because of their ramifications for postcolonial relations.

THE COLONIAL PERIOD

The introduction of Islam along the East African coast predates the arrival of Christianity, which was introduced by the Portuguese in the fifteenth and sixteenth centuries and later by European missionaries in the mid nineteenth century.[1] Christianity was introduced into an environment that was predominantly Muslim and this set the pace for competition between Islam and Christianity, a situation that has continued into the contemporary period.[2] Despite Christianity's late entry, a combination of factors in the past, such as imperial and colonial advantage and seeming state patronage, conspired to ensure rapid spread and expansion of Christianity at the expense of Islam.

The colonial discourses that governed Christian–Muslim relations generally revolved around, first, missionaries' perception of Islam as a competitor and threat to the Christian work of evangelization and conversion of Africans, and second, the Muslim opposition to Christian missionary activities such as provision of education and medical services. Muslims perceived these activities, because of their evangelical nature, as "bait" luring people into conversion. The third factor was Christianity's position of power and advantage vis-à-vis Islam. These issues created an atmosphere of competition, acrimony, and antagonism that characterized the relations between Christians and Muslims in the colonial period and that sowed the seeds of contemporary hostility between Christians and Muslims.

POST-COLONIAL RELATIONS BETWEEN CHRISTIANS AND MUSLIMS

Post-colonial relations between Christians and Muslims in Kenya are rooted in the colonial discourse highlighted above. This means that the post-colonial narrative of Christian–Muslim relations is largely a mirror image of the colonial period. At independence in 1963, the spatial competition between Christians and Muslims became evident in three main areas: (1) religious practice in educational institutions, (2) evangelization, and (3) Christian perception of Islam and Muslims, terrorism, and Muslim–state relations.

---

1. See Davidson, *African Past*, 117.
2. Oded, *Islam and Politics*, 101.

The Influence of Religious Practice in Education Institutions on Christian–Muslim Relations

Religious practice in education institutions has been a source of tension in the post-colonial discourse on Christian–Muslim relations. Although the education system in the country is not supposed to champion the cause of one religion against the other(s), matters of education have influenced relations between Christians and Muslims. The *hijab* (veil) as a dress code for Muslim girls in public schools that are church sponsored is a cause of tension, and strains the relations between Christians and Muslims.

In the early 1990s, several heads of public schools were sued by Muslim parents for expelling their daughters from schools because of wearing the *hijab* in school. Most of the schools where the issue came to the fore were in Mombasa—a predominantly Muslim area; for example, Star of the Sea and Changamwe high schools where this problem occurred are both sponsored by the Catholic Church. The issue centered on the need for Muslim girls to have their religious rights on dress code respected in non-Muslim schools. Since Christian groups and organizations sponsor the majority of the schools in the country, Muslims perceived harassment in the schools where the heads insisted that the *hijab* should not be worn as part of the school uniform. This issue strained the relations between Christians and Muslims. It became recurrent, and attracted presidential intervention; a directive was issued that Muslim girls should not be forced to dress in a manner that conflicts with their religion.[3]

Related to the above was the construction of a mosque in a church-sponsored school in Isiolo in 1993. Isiolo is a predominantly Muslim county in the Eastern Province of Kenya. The construction of the mosque conflicted with the Education Act, because the Catholic Church, which sponsors the school, is the one mandated by the Education Act to promote its religion in that school. Although, according to the Act, "parents have a right to require a school to provide a place of worship and instruction for their children within the institution of learning,"[4] this does not give an outsider permission to construct a place of worship without consulting the sponsor. This was the situation at the school in Isiolo.

---

3. See Maina, "Christian–Muslim Relations: An Examination," 6.
4. Ibid., 7.

Christians could not comprehend why Muslims could put up a mosque in a church-sponsored school without consulting them, and interpreted this action as tantamount to promoting Islam in a church-sponsored school to undermine Christianity.[5] This issue raised tensions between Christians and Muslims.

The 1993 suspension of seven Muslim girls from a church-sponsored school in Meru District, Eastern Province, also affected Christian–Muslim relations. The girls had gone for prayers in a mosque in town during *Ramadhan* and were late for evening studies, thus earning the suspension. The local Muslim leaders intervened, accusing Christians of "undermining the progress of Islam." They also stormed the school demanding unconditional re-admission of the girls. The leaders also demanded that fasting—which was banned in the school for Christians and Muslims—be allowed. Since the school's administration refused to budge, the aggrieved parties were forced to seek court redress. The court ordered the unconditional re-admission of the Muslim girls, and equally gave them latitude to practice their faith without interference.[6]

Christian–Muslim relations have also been affected by other cases, including perceived discrimination in church-sponsored schools such as denying Muslims admission or refusing to allow them to practice their religion or attend Muslim festivals such as *Idd ul-fitr*.[7] For example, Muslims accused an administrator and principal of a church-sponsored school in Meru of adamantly refusing to admit Muslim girls. While Muslim students at two major boys' schools in Nairobi and Nakuru protested over lack of a place for prayer and permission to pray, other cases bordered on non-recognition of the dietary habits. Examples of the latter were in Kiambu and Murang'a districts, where students boycotted meals claiming that the meat had not been ritually slaughtered according to Islamic principles. There was also a perception that pork was to be introduced into the menu of Limuru Girls High School.[8] All these cases exacerbated hostility in Christian–Muslim relations.

The teaching of Christian Religious Education (CRE) to Muslim students has been a cause of conflicts between Christians and Muslims in Kenya. This is owing to a shortage of Islamic Religious Education (IRE)

---

5. Ibid.
6. Ibid., 8.
7. Maina, "Historical Roots," 77–89.
8. Ibid., 89.

teachers; many schools with Muslim students do not offer IRE, which is a preference of Muslims, in their curriculum. In the past, many Muslim students in church-sponsored schools were forced by circumstances to study CRE or Social Education and Ethics as alternative examinable subjects to IRE. This situation is worse at the primary school level, where Muslims have to fulfill the requirements of the Kenya Certificate of Primary Education (KCPE) by including a religion credit.[9]

The shortage of IRE teachers has an impact on Christian–Muslim relations because Christians who have studied Islamic courses at university are posted to teach IRE in secondary schools and colleges to the chagrin of, and great opposition from, Muslims.[10] Muslim leaders perceive the teaching of IRE by Christians as a way of undermining Islam. Their opinion is that a Christian could only teach IRE with an insidious motive of denigrating Islam, since "one should not teach what he or she does not believe in or practice."[11] We cannot here delve into the debate about whether a Christian should or should not teach IRE,[12] but suffice it to say that Muslims are wary of Christians who seem to be interested in studying Islam and Arabic language, arguing that the motive is to evangelize Muslims. This issue is discussed below.

Evangelization and Competition for Converts

Christianity and Islam are the two leading religions in the country. Christians are in the majority and Muslims form a significant minority.[13] Other marginal religions include Hinduism, Sikhism, and African Religion. Muslims are predominant in Coast and North Eastern

---

9. Maina, *Islamic Influence*, 233–36.

10. Various courses of Islamic studies are offered as academic subjects in many public and private universities and colleges, e.g., Kenyatta University, St. Paul's University, and Tangaza College.

11. Maina, *Islamic Influence*, 234; Maina, "Challenges of Teaching," 62–63.

12. Maina, "Challenges of Teaching."

13. Population data of Christians and Muslims depends on the sources. Christian sources portray a large number of Christians vis-à-vis Muslims, and the converse is true. Oliana (a Christian), "Theological Challenges," says that Muslims constitute 6 to 10 percent, while Christians constitute 70 percent. Oded, *Islam and Politics*, 11, citing Muslim sources, gives a Muslim population of 35 percent. The latest population census of 2009 put Christians at 80 percent to Muslims 10 percent (see http:www.softkenya.com/Kenya/Kenya-population. Accessed 15 August 2016).

Provinces but there are also pockets of Muslims in the main urban areas such as Nairobi, Nakuru, and Kisumu.

Spatial competition through evangelization is a factor in Christian–Muslim relations in Kenya. This competition involves expending huge financial and material resources in missionary work. I do not have empirical data to support this claim, but in the contemporary period a considerable amount of resources find their way into Africa from the oil-rich Arab and Muslim countries.[14] Those resources have enabled Islam to compete economically with Christianity.[15] This means, despite its numerical superiority, that Christianity must not underestimate Islam, for it is a strong competitor. The competition between the two religions has provided fodder for propaganda purposes, with accusations and counter-accusations. While Muslims accuse Christians of crusading against Islam, Christians accuse Muslims of undermining Christianity. This is demonstrated in the following examples from both sides of the religious divide.

A report appearing in *The Islamic Future*,[16] a journal published by the World Assembly of Muslim Youth of Saudi Arabia, alleged that various efforts of Christian organizations to undermine Islam were being carried out. Those included organizing religious study courses, building dispensaries near mosques to provide free medical services, and constructing houses for poor Muslims in order to convert them to Christianity. Other methods of wooing Muslims to Christianity, according to the report, were the publication of Christian books in Arabic and teaching Arabic to Christians to enable them to preach to Muslims in Arabic. In the same vein, in the 1990s, Muslims accused Daystar University—a Christian private institution in Nairobi—of using money to "buy Muslims into the Christian faith." The College principal promptly denied the allegation in a formal press statement.[17]

Conversely, Christians have accused Muslim groups of using unorthodox means to spread Islam in Christian areas. For example, in 1998, leaders of the Methodist and Presbyterian Church of East Africa (PCEA) churches reportedly accused a Muslim group of using external funding to lure Christians to Islam. The group was reportedly planning

14. See Maina, "Christian–Muslim Dialogue," 172.
15. Ibid.
16. Ibid., 173.
17. Maina, "Historical Roots," 91.

to burn a mosque in Nakuru and then have it blamed on Christians.[18] These claims were dismissed by the Supreme Council of Kenya Muslims (SUPKEM) as a "plot to perpetuate religious animosity in the country."[19] There is no empirical evidence from either side of the religious divide to suggest that either group employs the various methods mentioned above to target each other in their evangelical work. The claims and accusations do, however, illustrate propaganda and demonstrate an atmosphere of competition that ultimately heightens tensions and engenders conflicts between Christians and Muslims in Kenya.

There are other examples to demonstrate the competition between Christians and Muslims in the country. These include the various calls by clergy of the mainstream churches to intensify evangelization in order to stem the tide of the spread of Islam in Africa. In the past, this created conflict between Christians and Muslims. For that reason the Muslim community leadership heavily censured the call by the head of the Catholic Church in Kenya, the late Cardinal Maurice Otunga (1923–2003). In an opening ceremony of the Secretaries of the Episcopal Conference of Africa and Madagascar (SECAM) in Nairobi, 12–16 January 1993, the Cardinal called on "Christians to stand up and fight the spread of Islam in Africa."[20] He was critical of the Islamic teaching about Muhammad being the last prophet, arguing that "it is clearly stated it is Jesus Christ."[21] The cardinal further reportedly said that Muslims had joined all spheres of activity in order to fight Christianity.[22] The speech was very critical of Islam and reflected the Christians' anxiety about Muslims.[23] This seems to have opened a Pandora's box in Christian–Muslim relations in the country. It sparked country-wide outrage and protests among Muslims, probably because, since the Cardinal was the head of the Kenyan Catholic Church then, his sentiments may have been perceived by Muslims as the official stance of the Catholic Church. Indeed, some Muslim leaders

---

18. Ibid.

19. Maina, "Christian–Muslim Dialogue," 175.

20. Maina, "Historical Roots, 91; Maina, "Christian–Muslim Relations: An Examination," 11.

21. Maina, "Christian–Muslim Dialogue," 174.

22. Ibid.

23. Oded, *Islam and Politics*, 107.

perceived the call to be a prelude to religious wars between Christians and Muslims in the country.[24]

Another example that illustrates the competition between Christians and Muslims is the call by a former head of the Anglican Church in Kenya (ACK) in February 1994. While delivering a sermon in a church in Nairobi, the late Archbishop Manasses Kuria (1929–2005) hinted that Islam and Christianity are similar and that Muhammad was a Christian before he defected to found Islam.[25] Those assertions stoked the embers of the fire that was lit by Cardinal Otunga a year prior. Consequently, there were fierce outbursts from the Muslim community. Later in the same year, a call reminiscent of the one by Otunga was made by the prelate of the ACK, Bishop Stephen Kewasis of Eldoret. He called on Christians to intensify evangelization in North Eastern and Coast Provinces of Kenya through building churches as a method of challenging Islam, since Muslims were reportedly building mosques in all parts of the country.[26] This call aroused the anger of Muslims who perceived it as a threat and an incitement of Christians against Muslims.[27]

Christians and Muslims in Kenya engage in outreach as a method of evangelizing others. This constitutes what is commonly known in local lingo as *mihadhara*, loosely translated as "street preaching" or "public religious rallies" or "open air preaching." *Mihadhara* is one of the latest modi operandi of Muslim outreach to Christians. It is a common feature in virtually all the major towns in Kenya and other East African countries especially Tanzania. The late South African preacher and author, Ahmed Deedat (1918–2005), perfected the art of *mihadhara* in East Africa. Owing to the largely polemical nature of *mihadhara*, conflicts and physical confrontation occur between Christians and Muslims resulting in injuries and destruction of life and property.[28] There are some incidents showing how *mihadhara* causes fights between Christians and Muslims in Kenya. For example, a fight broke out between Muslims and Christians of the Seventh Day Adventist (SDA) Church in Mumias town, Kakamega County, resulting from remarks of a Christian pastor

24. Maina, "Christian–Muslim Dialogue," 174; Maina, "Christian–Muslim Relations: An Examination," 11.
25. Maina, "Historical Roots," 92.
26. Maina, "Christian–Muslim Dialogue," 174.
27. Maina, "Historical Roots," 91–92.
28. Wandera, "Christian–Muslim Co-existence," 94–107.

during a public open-air crusade.[29] In Bura, Tana River County, arrest of a Muslim street preacher who aggressively preached against Christianity and Christians led to riots by Muslim youth who stoned a police station, and torched and looted churches. The preacher, a former Christian pastor who had converted to Islam, preached offensive messages bordering on inciting Muslims against Christians. This incident took place on 13 June 2003, and the churches that were razed belonged to the ACK, Pentecostal Evangelism, Full Gospel Church of Kenya, East African Pentecostal Church, and Bethel Church.[30]

Evangelization leads to conversions but the number of Christians who have converted to Islam and vice versa may be hard to quantify. Wherever conversions occur, they cause conflicts between Christians and Muslims. For example, in Merti trading center, north of Isiolo town, Christian evangelization brought about the conversion of some Waso Borana families to Christianity, and that strained the relations between Christians and Muslims in that area.[31] In addition, although cases of physical confrontations and fights resulting from *mihadhara* may be isolated, wherever and whenever they occur, they paint a gloomy picture of Christian–Muslim relations in Kenya.

Christian Perception of Islam as an Intolerant Religion

In an environment of religious pluralism, Christians perceive Islam as an intolerant religion. This perception creates animosity that has strained the relations between Christians and Muslims. The death sentence (*fatwa*) on Salman Rushdie, the author of *The Satanic Verses*, by Ayatollah Khomeini in 1989 was considered by some Christians in Kenya to be an example of Muslim intolerance toward freedom of expression. Muslims considered this book blasphemous to Prophet Muhammad and the Qur'an. It was banned in Kenya after Muslims staged demonstrations in solidarity with Muslim communities in Pakistan, Saudi Arabia, Egypt, Iran, India, and Malaysia.[32] Following on the heels of Rushdie affair, the Muslim leaders in Kenya declared a death sentence on an identified author of a letter that was critical of Islam published in *The Standard* news-

---

29. Maina, "Historical Roots," 92.
30. Ibid.
31. Ibid., 93.
32. Maina, "Christian–Muslim Relations," 132–33.

paper of 22 July 1994. Some Christians considered the death sentence to be a further indictment of Islam as an intolerant religion.[33] In the 1990s, more examples of Islam's intolerance in the eyes of the Christians were seen in the activities of the unregistered Islamic Party of Kenya (IPK), which was extremely anti-government and behind the riots that engulfed the coastal town of Mombasa.[34]

THE INFLUENCE OF TERRORISM ON CHRISTIAN–MUSLIM RELATIONS SINCE 1998

The year 1998 marked the first act of terrorism in Kenya attributed to religious radicalism and extremism. On 7 August 1998, the American embassy in Nairobi was bombed by alleged al-Qaeda terrorists, killing 216 people and injuring many others. After that, terror attacks intensified when the Kenya Defence Forces (KDF) entered Somalia in 2011 to flush out al-Shabaab.[35] According to media reports, there have been more than forty-five terror attacks in Kenya since the year 2011, which have left more than 400 people dead, the latest being the killing of 147 students of Garissa University College on 2 April 2015.

Terror attacks have targeted churches, public areas such as restaurants and shopping malls, public transportation such as buses and *matatus* (commercial passenger vans), and bus parks/stations among others. Although Muslims have died in these terror attacks,[36] Christians largely view themselves as the targets because a number of attacks have targeted

33. See Maina, "Christian–Muslim Dialogue," 175.

34. Ibid., 175.

35. Al-Shabaab, a Somali-based militia and terrorist group, has claimed responsibility for many of the terrorist attacks in Kenya since KDF invaded Somalia. These include: the attack on two churches in Garissa on 1 July 2012 that killed 17 people; the Westgate Mall attack in Nairobi on 21 September 2013 that killed 70 people; an attach on a church in Likoni, Mombasa, on 23 March 2014 that killed 6 people; the attack on a food kiosk in Eastleigh, Nairobi, on 31 March 2014 that killed 6 people; the Mpeketoni attack that killed more than 60 people between 15 and 17 June 2014; the two attacks in Mandera: one in which 28 Nairobi-bound passengers were killed on 23 November 2014, and the other when 36 quarry workers were killed on 2 December 2014; and the Garisssa University College attack in which 147 students lost their lives on 2 April 2015.

36. The grenade attack in a mosque in Eastleigh, Nairobi—an area inhabited predominately by members of the Somali community—led to the deaths of two people and injury to the local Member of Parliament. The other attack in a bus in the city of Mombasa killed four people. See "Four Killed and Several Injured as Twin Explosions Rock Mombasa," *Sunday Nation*, 3 May 2014.

them and their churches. The bombing of two churches in Garissa and the gun attacks in a church in Likoni are just two examples. There is more evidence of the claim that terrorists target Christians. Since the Westgate attack in September 2013, one of the characteristic features of all the terror attacks is the terrorists' deliberate isolation of Muslims from Christians with the former spared while the latter are mercilessly massacred.[37] This has left no doubt in the minds of Christians that they are the targets. This was evident in the Westgate,[38] Mpeketoni, Mandera, and the Garissa University College attacks. After the Likoni church attack, the Christian clergy warned Muslim leaders to tame their youth and moderate their religious teaching. Some pastors even appealed to the government to supply them with guns for self-defense against Muslim militants.[39]

Terrorism has great impact on Christian–Muslim relations. It has exacerbated the polarization of Christians and Muslims. The terrorists use verses from the Qur'an to justify attacks on Christians.[40] Indeed, the killings of the seventeen people in the two churches in Garissa were religiously motivated, as evidenced by the report from al-Shabaab spokesman, Hassan Takar, who said: "The *Mujahedeen* (holy warriors) punished with their hands those believing and worshipping other than Allah. The militants will continue until such practice is eliminated."[41] The fact that terror groups invoke and quote the Qur'an has further confirmed the Christian view that Islam is a brutal religion that promotes terrorism. Indeed, some Christians have posed serious questions about Islam, one example being: "If the Prophet Muhammad was sent to man-

---

37. Abu Ayman, "Why Al-Shabaab Is the Number One Enemy for Kenyan Muslims," *The Star*, 11 April 2015, 1. http://www.the-star.co.ke/news/2015/04/11/why-al-shabaab-is-the-number-one-enemy-for-kenyan-muslims_c1115411. Accessed 15 August 2016.

38. In the Westgate Mall attack, the gunmen were asking the victims questions on basic Islamic concepts such as "the name of the mother of Muhammad" or the "Islamic confession of faith" as a way of distinguishing Muslims from non-Muslims, and the latter were summarily gunned down when they failed to answer those basic questions on Islam.

39. Billow Kellow, "Leave Religion Out of the Anti-terror War," *Standard on Sunday*, 6 April 2014, 17. http://www.standardmedia.co.ke/article/2000108692/leave-religion-out-of-the-anti-terror-war. Accessed 15 August 2016.

40. Some Qur'an texts used to legitimize violence and aggression towards Christians are: Sura 22:39; Sura 66:9; Sura 2:190.

41. Maina, "Historical Contextualization," 21.

kind to preach mercy as Muslims claim, why is there so much violence associated with Muslims and Islam?"[42]

Terrorism has led to a rising anti-Islamic rhetoric among Christians and has "raised the tempo for the hostile climate towards Muslims" in Kenya.[43] Consequently, the fault line between Christians and Muslims has widened.[44] Arguments by Muslims that "terrorists are not Muslims"[45] or "terrorism is the work of the devil"[46] have done little to absolve Muslims and Islam from blame as the attacks are committed by members who allegedly bear Muslim names and invoke the name of Allah. Hence the cliché "not every Muslim is a terrorist, but every terrorist is a Muslim" has gained currency as a blanket condemnation of Islam and Muslims. This has brought much tension between Christians and Muslims in Kenya, since many Christians may not distinguish the acts of an individual from those of a community and a religion.

Muslims feel that the notion of associating Islam and Muslims with terrorism should be corrected, arguing that Islam is a peaceful religion that should not be used to justify partisan political ambitions and interests and unjust acts of terrorism. It can be argued that Islam does not condone killings of innocent people and wanton destruction of property.[47] However, the activities of terrorist groups such as al-Shabaab,

42. Kariuki Ngare and Dennis Lubanga, "War against Radical Muslims 'Frustrated,'" *Daily Nation*, 28 April 2014, 6.

43. Abu Ayman, "Why Al-Shabaab Is the Number One Enemy for Kenyan Muslims," *The Star*, 11 April 2015, 1. http://www.the-star.co.ke/news/2015/04/11/why-al-shabaab-is-the-number-one-enemy-for-kenyan-muslims_c1115411. Accessed 15 August 2016.

44. Peter Kagwanja, "How Kenya Fiddled as Jihad Came to Our Country," *Sunday Nation*, 13 April 2014, 21. http://www.nation.co.ke/oped/Opinion/Kenya-Jihad-Terrorism-Extremism-Security/-/440808/2276598/-/3000uy/-/index.html. Accessed 15 August 2016.

45. This has become a mantra in any forum where there is a discourse on radicalism and extremism, touching on Muslims and Islam. For example, during the "Scientific Conference on Radicalism, Islam and World Peace" held at the University of Nairobi, 15 March 2015, the statement was repeated by various Muslim speakers.

46. This was a response by SUPKEM condemning the Westgate Mall terror attack; see Peter Obuya and Timothy Kemei, "Group Distances Islam from Raid," *Daily Nation*, 21 September 2013, 11. http://www.nation.co.ke/news/Group-distances-Islam-from-raid/-/1056/2003328/-/9whu26z/-/index.html. Accessed 15 August 2016.

47. Peace is underlined in many verses of the Qur'an (14:23; 13:24; 24:61; 39:73), and verses teach respect for human diversity and pluralism (49:13 and 30:22) and religious tolerance (2:256; 11:118); forbidden are the killing of innocent people and suicide

who use religion to pursue their vested interests, have given Muslims a reputation that is associated with violence. And this is a concern of Muslims too, as captured in the following remarks: "As a Muslim, I am deeply ashamed that the identity of my faith has been hijacked by this group who are using it as a justification to perpetrate violent acts which have only served to harm the reputation of Islam as a religion which advocates for peace, tolerance and coexistence."[48]

While the Muslim community has been blamed for terrorism, its members have been victims of discrimination. Muslims residing in areas where they are a minority are looked upon with suspicion and sometimes subjected to prejudice and profiling by Christians. For example, in the wake of the Westgate attack, members of the Somali community had to bear all sorts of harassment and discrimination, such as verbal insults and being forcibly removed from public transportation vehicles.[49]

Another impact of terrorism on Christian–Muslim relations in Kenya is the irrational or perceived fear of Islam and Muslims. The social perception of all Muslims as people who thrive on violence has led to Islamophobia.[50] Islamophobia is a socio-religious discourse that some Christian leaders of the evangelical and pentecostal churches employ to warn their followers about the Muslim menace.[51] They use sermons to spread more Islamophobia. The warning about the danger of Islam derives from a perception that Islam is competing with Christianity, as evidenced by statements and sermons from religious leaders discussed elsewhere in this chapter. The competition has provided fodder for propaganda purposes, hence more Islamophobia.[52] This does not augur well for harmonious Christian–Muslim coexistence in Kenya.

Islamophobia influenced the Christian position on the Islamic Kadhi courts debate during the 2005 constitutional review process.[53]

---

bombing (cf. 4:93; 25:68; 6:151).

48. Abu Ayman, "Why Al-Shabaab Is the Number One Enemy for Kenyan Muslims," *The Star*, 11 April 2015, 2. http://www.the-star.co.ke/news/2015/04/11/why-al-shabaab-is-the-number-one-enemy-for-kenyan-muslims_c1115411. Accessed 15 August 2016.

49. Ibid.

50. Maina, "Islamophobia," 53.

51. Ibid.

52. Ibid.

53. Ibid., 54.

The bone of contention was whether these courts could be entrenched into a new constitution. The debate rekindled conflict and brought about the greatest religious divide between Christians and Muslims in Kenya in recent memory. The debate provided a theatre of contest between Christians and Muslims. Muslims wanted the Kadhi courts enhanced by upgrading them to exist up to the national level and to allow them to preside over commercial, civil, and criminal cases. This brought hostility from Christians, who argued that inclusion of the courts into the constitution gave privilege to Islam and Muslims over other faiths and religious groups. This, it was argued, conflicted with Article 8 of the constitution, which stipulates the separation of state and religion.[54] Christians saw the entrenchment of the Kadhi courts as an attempt to introduce Sharia law in Kenya. This caused resentment against Muslims and Islam, with some Christian leaders fearing that the courts could propagate Islamic extremism.[55] Eventually the Kadhi courts were retained in the new constitution that was promulgated in 2010.

The threat of terrorism has contributed to heightened levels of Islamophobia among Christians.[56] This is due to the high level of security precautions and terror alerts that have become part and parcel of life. Kenyans are nowadays subjected to frisking and other security checks when they visit churches, shopping malls, supermarkets, high rise buildings, and when boarding public transportation vehicles. Terror attacks have prompted many churches to invest heavily in security by hiring guards and buying security gadgets and closed-circuit surveillance cameras. When Christians troop to their churches, they are thoroughly subjected to the security checks! This constantly reminds them about the threat of terrorism, and that security cannot be taken for granted even in the church, hitherto a place of refuge and safety.

ISSUES RELATED TO THE STATE

Kenya is a secular state where all religions ideally possess the same status under the country's constitution. But the presence of a heavily Christian bureaucratic and political elite at the top of the leadership ladder makes the otherwise secular government to appear "Christian."

---

54. Ibid., 50.
55. Ibid., 54.
56. Ibid., 53.

For a long time, Muslims have expressed their lack of faith in a government headed by Christians due to alleged discrimination by successive Christian-dominated governments.[57] They have complained over many issues, including socio-economic and political marginalization and disempowerment of the Muslim-predominant areas of Coast and North Eastern Provinces. Mwakimako succinctly captures this issue in the following words:

> Kenyan Muslims are a marginalized minority group deprived of educational and other social facilities. Areas with high concentration of Muslims fail [more compared to] other areas in national examination performance. Most Muslim areas are underdeveloped and characterized by poor infrastructure, inadequate social facilities, high levels of unemployment, high child mortality rates and drug addiction.[58]

These remarks underline serious concerns from a significant segment of the population. And that does not augur well for harmonious coexistence between Christians and Muslims because the Kenyan state has always been considered by Muslims as synonymous with Christians.[59]

The August 1998 bombing of the American embassy in Nairobi raised the issue of Muslim–state relations. Following these attacks, the government banned five NGOs that operated in North Eastern Province but were headquartered in Nairobi. They were: Mercy Relief International Agency, Al-Haramain Foundation, Help African People, the International Relief Organization, and Ibrahim Abd al-Aziz al-Ibrahim Foundation.[60] The government alleged that those NGOs were involved in clandestine activities, with some of their officials accused of aiding the terrorists. Most importantly, Christians feared that some of the NGOs "had as their main goal making Kenya an Islamic country within the next two or three decades."[61] Thus Christians and the government were concerned about the growth of Islamic radicalism in the country. The ban provoked the wrath of the Muslim community

---

57. Oded, *Islam and Politics*, 101.
58. Mwakimako, "Muslim NGOs," 229.
59. Billow Kellow, "Leave Religion Out of Anti-Terror War," *Standard on Sunday*, 6 April 2014, 17. http://www.standardmedia.co.ke/article/2000108692/leave-religion-out-of-the-anti-terror-war. Accessed 15 August 2016.
60. Oded, *Islam and Politics*, 84.
61. Ibid.

and some demonstrations were staged against the government on 2 October 1998.[62]

Terrorism has raised anti-Islamic rhetoric among Christians and the government. But in its war on terror, the government has attempted to downplay the role of Islam to avoid portraying Muslims as terrorists. Probably the objective is to avoid a backlash on the Muslim community and to avoid Christian–Muslim conflict. However, the response of Muslims to terrorism has been more varied and complex, with the emergence of two groups: moderate Muslims and radical Muslims.

The moderates blame terrorism on the rise of radical Muslim clerics, such as Sheikh Aboud Rogo, Ibrahim Omar, and Sheikh Abubakar Shariff (alias Makaburi), through whom radical Muslim youths took over the running of mosques in Mombasa and Nairobi. This raised concern from the moderate Muslims and also heightening the fears of terror attacks against Christians. The killing of the three radical clerics by unknown assailants on different dates brought into focus the deteriorating state of Muslim–state relations and Christian–Muslim relations in Kenya. The three openly preached hatred towards Christians.[63] Rogo was accused of spreading hatred for Christians in the name of Islam and aiding in the recruitment of youths to the al-Shabaab terror group. His assassination in 2012 set off days of violent protests in Mombasa, with several deaths and attacks on churches. Riots also broke out when Makaburi was gunned down on 4 April 2014.[64]

The radical Muslims are represented by clerics who argue that Islam is under siege by an international conspiracy, led by the United States. Makaburi saw the government crackdown on radicalism as part of the "American conspiracy" against Islam and once posed: "The Americans are attacking us because we are Muslims and we believe in the Qur'an. Would they do this to us if we were Christians?"[65] He argued that the Kenyan government intervention in Somalia was part of the American design against Islam and therefore there was need for Muslims to rise

62. Ibid., 85.

63. "Cleric Courted Controversy in Life and Death," *Sunday Nation*, 3 April 2014, 6.

64. Peter Kagwanja, "How Kenya Fiddled as Jihad Came to Our Country," *Sunday Nation*, 13 April 2014, 21. http://www.nation.co.ke/oped/Opinion/Kenya-Jihad-Terrorism-Extremism-Security/-/440808/2276598/-/3000uy/-/index.html. Accessed 15 August 2016.

65. "Are Christian–Muslim Relations under Attack across East Africa?" *East African*, 8 September 2012.

up against the Kenya government to avenge the atrocities committed on Muslims in Somalia. In this connection, he justified the killings of Westgate by alleged al-Shabaab terrorists.[66]

The government's war on terrorism has had serious impact on Christian–Muslim relations, as scores of Muslims are being arrested as terror suspects by the anti-terror police unit. This provokes uproar from the Muslim communities against the government, and has impaired the relations between Christians and Muslims. While Christians feel that Muslims are targeting their churches, Muslims resent the "Christian government" for harassment and allegedly killing Muslims. The storming of the Masjid Musa mosque by security agents on 2 February 2014, on the pretext of preempting a jihadist convention that was underway, was perceived by the Muslims as a desecration of their holy place by a "Christian government" that led to the death of seven Muslim youths.

On the whole, Muslim leaders have bitterly criticized and accused the government of polarization, and profiling the Muslim community, especially the Somali community, as terrorists.[67] The mass arrests and screening of Somalis in the first two weeks of April 2014 following a crackdown on illegal immigrants, dubbed "Usalama Watch,"[68] did not go down well with ethnic Somalis, who accused the government of discrimination.[69] The stringent vetting process for Muslims, especially Somalis, in need of identity cards and passports has been seen as a policy of collective punishment on the Muslim community by the government.[70] The same applied to the closure of 80 businesses dealing with informal money transfers (*hawala*) and foreign exchange bureaus after the Mandera bus attacks, and dusk-to-dawn curfew imposed by the government in

66. "Cleric Courted Controversy in Life and Death," *Sunday Nation*, 3 April 2014, 6.

67. "Are Christian–Muslim Relations under Attack across East Africa?," *East African*, 8 September 2012.

68. This was a security operation in response to the terror attacks in Mombasa and Nairobi Eastleigh Estate that left twelve people dead on 30 and 31 April 2014. See "Muslim Leaders Oppose Security Operation as CORD Demands Sackings," *Sunday Nation*, 6 April 2014, 15.

69. Ahmednasir Abdullahi, "Kenyan Somalis Treated like Second-Class Citizens," *Sunday Nation*, 13 April 2014, 20.

70. Abu Ayman, "Why Al-Shabaab Is the Number One Enemy for Kenyan Muslims," *The Star*, 11 April 2015, 2. http://www.the-star.co.ke/news/2015/04/11/why-al-shabaab-is-the-number-one-enemy-for-kenyan-muslims_c1115411. Accessed 15 August 2016.

the counties of Garissa, Wajir, Mandera, and Tana River following the Garissa University College attack in April 2015. Muslims considered all these acts as attempts to strangle the economy of the Somalis on the pretext of fighting terrorism by a "Christian" government.

JOINT CHRISTIAN–MUSLIM EFFORTS

There are instances of cooperation when Christians and Muslims have joined forces for a common cause. In Kenya, this was evident in 1994, when in solidarity Christians and Muslims came together to oppose the legalization of abortion and contraceptives that were advocated by the 1994 United Nations Population Development Conference in Cairo, Egypt. Related to that, in August 1995 Muslims and Christians jointly opposed the introduction of Family Life Education in schools.[71] In a joint ceremony, Cardinal Otunga and Sheikh Ali Shee led Christians and Muslim youths in burning books on sex education, condoms, and other contraceptive devices at Uhuru Park, Nairobi. The two cases were unprecedented in the history of Christian–Muslim relations in Kenya, especially in the late 1980s and early 1990s when belligerency and warmongering were prevalent. During Christian and Muslim festivals such as Christmas and Iddul al-Fitr, leaders sometimes publish and send mutual greetings. For example, on Iddul al-Fitr in 1983, Manasses Kuria of the ACK sent greetings to Muslims.[72]

The other example was the *Ufungamano* initiative of the constitutional review process when the Muslim Consultative Forum joined various churches, church organizations, and other stakeholders to form the People's Commission of Kenya, which eventually became part of the constitutional review team.[73] Another case of cooperation is shown in a letter of Al-Haj Seif Mohamed Seif, which congratulated the Little Sisters Catholic nuns for running a home for the poor, including Muslims, without discrimination. Added to that was the initiative of Muslim imams of Coast Province who intended to form a "joint Muslim–Christian alliance to fight for the dignity and rights of all Kenyans."[74]

71. Oded, *Islam and Politics*, 98.
72. Ibid., 110.
73. Maina, "Historical Roots," 99.
74. Ibid.

After Westgate, Muslim and Christian leaders in Mombasa issued a joint statement denouncing al-Shabaab's ideology and tactics as heretical teachings not based on Islam or Christianity. They denounced the Islamist group, saying the wanton killing of civilians cannot be justified under Islam or any other religion.[75] The leaders, who represented the Council of Islamic Preachers of Kenya (CIPK), SUPKEM, and the Kenya National Inter-religious Network, spoke on 22 September 2013, a day after the Westgate attack.[76] This act of condemnation from both Christian and Muslim leadership eased the rising tensions between Christians and Muslims.

Pope Francis's visit to Kenya 25–27 November 2015 demonstrated a rare occasion of cooperation between Christians and Muslims. This was evident from pilgrim caravans organized by Christians and Muslims from Mombasa and Western Kenya to attend the Papal Eucharistic mass in Nairobi.[77] During the Pontiff's visit, leaders from other denominations and religions, especially Muslims, had a meeting with Pope Francis where issues of religious dialogue and peaceful coexistence among religions were emphasized.[78]

Those examples demonstrate that, in spite of their differences, Christians and Muslims can work together for the common good of the society. They also demonstrate that the two religious groups can coexist in harmony and, if need be, could forge a common front to safeguard their interests even though the cooperation may not succeed in totally removing suspicions.

CONCLUSION

A long tradition of tolerance, mutual respect, and peaceful coexistence and harmony characterize the history of Christian–Muslim relations in Kenya from 1963 to the present. However, conflicts have occurred in equal measure. Spatial competition engendered by issues of religion and education, evangelization, terrorism, and Muslim–state relations have

---

75. "Are Christian–Muslim Relations under Attack across East Africa?," *East African*, 8 September 2012.

76. Maina, "Christian–Muslim Relations: An Examination," 1.

77. Gloria Kagonya, "40 Buses Ferried 2,000 to Nairobi," *Daily Nation*, 27 July 2015, 6.

78. Samuel Karanja, "Pope Calls for Harmony among Different Religions," *Daily Nation*, 27 November 2015, 10.

caused the conflicts between the two religions. Despite all these tensions, there have been efforts towards cooperation between Christians and Muslims. However, the threat of terrorism poses the greatest challenge to Christian–Muslim coexistence in Kenya. The future of this coexistence will be determined by the way the two communities can forge a working relationship to handle terrorism. More than ever before, there is a need for Christians to separate religious extremists from the majority of Muslims who are peace-loving. But the Muslim community leadership has an enormous responsibility of discouraging violence and correcting the negative image of Islam that has been painted through terrorism. This could be done through dialogue, which could serve as a meeting point and a vital component to mitigate the threats to harmonious coexistence between Christians and Muslims.

REFERENCES

Kenyan Newspapers

Daily Nation
East African
Standard
Standard on Sunday
The Star (Kenya)
Sunday Nation

Other

Davidson, Basil. *The African Past*. London: Longman, 1964.
Maina, Newton Kahumbi. "Challenges of Teaching Islamic Studies by Non-Muslims in Kenyan Tertiary Institutions." *Tangaza Journal of Theology and Mission* 1 (2013) 54–67.
———. "Christian–Muslim Dialogue in Kenya." In *Quests for Integrity in Africa*, edited by G. Wamue and M. Theuri, 171–84. Nairobi: Acton, 2003.
———. "Christian–Muslim Relations in Kenya." In *Islam in Kenya: Proceedings of the National Seminar on Contemporary Islam in Kenya*, edited by M. Bakari and Saad Yahya, 116–41. Nairobi: Mewa, 1995.
———. "Christian–Muslim Relations in Kenya: An Examination of Issues of Conflict." *CSIC Papers Africa*, 17 (1995) 1–21. Birmingham: Center for the Study of Islam and Christian–Muslim Relations.
———. "Historical Contextualization of Muslim–Christian Relations in East Africa." Paper presented at the Islamic Symposium, Tangaza University College, 10 May 2014.
———. "The Historical Roots of Conflicts between Christians and Muslims in Kenya." In *Interfaith Dialogue: Towards a Culture of Working Together*, edited by F. N. Mvumbi, 77–89. Nairobi: Catholic University of Eastern Africa, 2009.

———. *Islamic Influence on Education in Africa*. Dudweiler Landstr, Germany: Lap Lambert, 2011.

———. "Islamophobia among Christians and Its Challenge in Entrenchment of Kadhi Courts in Kenya." In *Constitutional Review in Kenya and Kadhi Courts*, edited by A. Tayob and J. Wandera, 45–55. Cape Town: University of Cape Town Centre for Contemporary Islam, 2011.

Mwakimako, Hassan. "Muslim NGOs." In *Islam in Kenya: Proceedings of the National Seminar on Contemporary Islam in Kenya*, edited by M. Bakari and Saad Yahya, 222–33. Nairobi: Mewa, 1995.

Oded, Arye. *Islam and Politics in Kenya*. Boulder, CO: Lynne Rienner, 2000.

Oliana, G. "The Theological Challenges of Religious Pluralism: Towards a Christian Theology of Other Faiths." *Tangaza Journal of Theology and Mission* 1 (2010) 9–30.

Wandera, Joseph. "Christian–Muslim Co-existence." In *Christian–Muslim Co-existence in Eastern Africa*, edited by F. Stenger et al., 94–107. Tangaza Occasional Papers 22. Nairobi: Paulines, 2008.

3

Christian Responses to Terror in Kenya

JOSEPH D. GALGALO

KENYA HAS EXPERIENCED MORE terrorism than any other country in the East African region. In each decade of its fifty-year history as an independent state, Kenya has faced repeated terror attacks. The lasting effect is mainly a political rift and a visibly continued precarious relationship between the people of the affected region and the successive national governments. Mistrust abounds and years of systemic marginalization and occasional high-handedness by the authorities in dealing with the locals have done little to promote meaningful integration. Security in threatened regions is typically shaky at best. Also, the fact of limited or nonexistent public services often fuels resentment and continually undermines efforts towards influencing a common embrace of national values. The background to this tragic state of affairs is complex and intricately linked with the region's colonial history. This chapter examines the difficult question of how Kenyan Christians may best respond to the threat of terrorism or actual terror attacks. The approach is interrogative and analytical, and includes an examination of historical precedents and possible reasons why various terrorists have frequently targeted Kenya. It explores various sources to find answers to this concern, and how best to respond to it.

TERROR ATTACKS IN KENYA: A PRECEDENT

The north-eastern region of present-day Kenya was called Northern Frontier District during the colonial era. It was renamed North Eastern Province after the country's independence from Britain in 1963. The region is home to a predominantly Muslim population of ethnic Somalis and was carved out of the larger Juba land of Southern Somalia and annexed to colonial Kenya in 1925. The colonial government did not appreciate the economic value of this largely arid and semi-arid land but saw its usefulness as an effective buffer zone to protect any encroachment on the fertile regions of Kenya then appropriated by white settlers. The colonial government evolved a policy of isolationism and the region was largely a closed district. Movement in and out of the frontier district was tightly controlled under the pretext of security. The colonial policy of isolation continued even after Kenya became an independent state and the Province continued to experience years of marginalization and underdevelopment. Consequently, the people in this part of the country live with a great sense of alienation from the rest of Kenya.

At Kenya's independence in 1963, the Kenyan Somali had little to celebrate in a country they saw as a land of their captivity. They were eagerly looking east to join the people of the Republic of Somalia with whom they shared closer ethnic and religious affinity. The British had promised that the vast Northern Frontier District would be given back to Somalia once Kenya gained independence. This never happened, as the independence government refused to cede any part of the country and sternly warned the secessionists that their claim to any part of Kenya would be treated as an act of aggression. With the hope of a negotiated settlement dashed, armed conflict seemed inevitable. This is the genesis of a conflict infamously baptized the Shifta War (1963–67).[1] Driven by the desire for self-determination and wanting to correct perceived historical injustices, the Somali people resorted to armed struggle to try to force the government to allow them to secede.

The war dragged on for years. Although the initial fallout was politically motivated, over time cultural and religious differences have continued to be the most visible and definitive marks of the existing fault lines. The government of Kenya saw the Shifta War as a security

---

1. Ringquist, "Bandit or Patriot: The Kenyan Shifta War 1963–1968"; Laitin, *Politics, Language, and Thought*; Mburu, *Bandits on the Border*; Hornsby, *Kenya: A History since Independence*.

menace perpetrated by lawless bandits (or *Shifta*, in the local language). The Somalis who took up arms and were thus so labeled believed in the legitimacy of their cause to fight for the right to self-determination. They demanded a reversal of the 1925 annexation of their region so that they could join the Somali nation with which they shared cultural and religious affinity. The result of the war was devastating. The human cost in terms of lost lives was immeasurable.[2] The inhabitants of the vast province were reduced to destitution as their nomadic way of life was largely curtailed, their freedom of movement limited, and their everyday lives controlled through all sorts of repressive measures including detention or imprisonment of their leaders and forceful settlement of entire populations into detention-like camps of strictly controlled villages. To date, the feeling of being trapped in their own land, and the sense of powerlessness to determine their own cause, is a reality for many a Kenyan Somali. In many ways, the Shifta War could be seen as the first of the three distinct phases of Kenya's unfolding experience of terrorism.

The relationship between the successive governments and the Somali populations has been full of stress ever since the Shifta War.[3] It is sad to note that nearly fifty years after the end of the war, the region still largely bears an unfortunate reputation for "banditry." The region has also continued to suffer neglect. The government seems to invest only minimally in education, health care, security, and other areas of important infrastructure. To make matters worse, the population has continued to suffer gross human rights violations long after the end of the war. The worst of such incidents are perhaps the Wagalla and the Garissa massacres suffered by the people at the hands of the government security forces.[4]

---

2. The Truth, Justice, and Reconciliation Commission describes the many atrocities suffered by the general populace at the hands of the government forces. Indiscriminate shootings, rapes, mass murders and forced displacements were generally committed. The report, which states, "The issue of mass killings during the Shifta War presented . . . familiar but daunting problem of limited and sketchy data" (131) estimates up to 7000 deaths (142). See *Report of the Truth, Justice and Reconciliation Commission*, 2A:131–43.

3. A case in point of repeated major government operations includes the Garissa Massacre of 1980. See, for example, Hassan, "Legal Impediments to Development in Northern Kenya." Elsewhere in this chapter, I also discuss the example of the Wagalla Massacre of 1984 (see the following note).

4. These massacres, especially the Wagalla massacre of 1984 where over 5000 (note: the Kenya government disputes this figure and asserts that only fifty-seven people died for resisting disarmament and endangering lives of security forces) Somalis

The Shifta War may not be classified by many as terrorism in the classic sense of the word, but it effectively instilled terror in all of Kenya's populations. The pain of the war was felt far and wide. Many Kenyans who had never set foot in Northern Kenya shared this pain through the loss of loved ones who served in the region as either security personnel or civil servants. Kenyans from other parts of the country have always found it perilous to conduct business ventures in this part of the country or to freely conduct religious events such as Christian rallies or public prayers. The conduct of the Kenyan government with regard to the Shifta War set some precedents hard to ignore. The high-handedness with which affairs were conducted fostered hatred and killed trust. The continued sense of alienation, frequent security crackdowns in the area, and profiling of the people have not helped the matter. Considering the circumstances, it is not surprising if terrorists find a foothold in this region or are able to win over sympathizers.

It is against this backdrop that it seems fair to say that Kenya has unique regional and historical factors that probably explain why it has borne the brunt of terrorism much more than its neighbors. This notwithstanding, Kenyan Somalis do fully embrace Kenyan citizenship as a matter of fact, and are not necessarily any less patriotic than Kenyans from any other part of the country. This has not stopped frequent profiling, a source of bitter resentment that a people who have no other country are often derogatorily and collectively labeled "bandits," or whole communities profiled as suspects in matters of terrorism. That most terrorists in the recent past have associated with Islam and that almost all Kenyan Somalis are Muslims has not helped matters. Unfortunately, common perceptions often lead to such naive conclusions that uncritically and simplistically associate Somalis and Islam. To make matters worse, the most significant terror threat to Kenya in the most recent past has been from al-Shabaab, a group largely composed of Somali Muslims. This lends further support to the assumption that the three—

---

were rounded up, tortured, and murdered has become the subject of many films, documentaries, and debates. See, for example, Boniface Ongeri and Victor Obure, "Fading Images: How Province Is Fighting One-eyed Bandit's Legacy," *Standard*, 9 December 2004. See also "Kenya Admits Mistakes over 'Massacre,'" *BBC News Online*, 18 October 2000; http://news.bbc.co.uk/2/hi/africa/978922.stm; Abdi Latif Dahir, "In New Documentary, Wagalla Massacre: Victims Recount Horror of Dark Days," *Sahan Journal*, 16 February 2015. See also "Wagalla Massacre," in *Report of the Truth, Justice and Reconciliation Commission*, 2A:221–28.

Islam, Somalis, and terrorists—are one. The assumption is fueled by fear, and not least, ignorance. This often leads to one absurd conclusion: that since Islam seems to sanction "divine terror," and given that all Somalis are Muslims, then any Somali fits the profile of a typical terrorist. Such erroneous perception has only served to victimize innocent citizens and has grossly undermined effective response to prevention of terror.

THE CONTEMPORARY KENYAN EXPERIENCE OF TERROR

Analysis of the Kenyan experience shows that terror threats are from multiple sources. The first of Kenya's terror experiences was a bomb blast in 1975 when twin explosions hit the Nairobi Starlight night club and a travel bureau in the new Hilton Hotel, also in Nairobi. A few days later, another bomb blast in a Nairobi commuter bus killed thirty passengers. The identity of the perpetrators of the 1975 bombings has to date remained a mystery. The next major incident happened in 1980 when a bomb went off in Norfolk Hotel in downtown Nairobi, killing twenty people and injuring dozens of others. The worst was yet to come when, after a long lull, the American embassy in Nairobi was bombed in 1998. Over 200 Kenyans lost their lives alongside a dozen American staff at the embassy. Indiscriminate terror attacks directly targeting ordinary Kenyans began to be experienced only after 2010. This marked a shift, at least in terms of intended targets, ushering in a third phase of Kenya's experience of terrorism. This development is largely associated with the rise of the al-Shabaab militant group.[5] This group is believed to be comprised mainly of Somali Islamists.[6] The attacks particularly escalated after Kenya sent troops into Somalia with the intention of eliminating the terror threat at the source. This conflict is reminiscent of the Shifta War, and, if motives may have changed, the old sentiments and biases are very much alive and make it look like the Shifta War has come full circle.

---

5. According to Thomas, "Exposing and Exploiting," al-Shabaab was part of the Islamic Court Union of Somalia until 2006, when it became a distinct militant group before its affiliation with al-Qaeda in 2012.

6. Stig Jarle Hansen estimates that by 2012, Al-Shabaab drew about 10 percent of its membership from Kenya, mainly from the Islamic communities of the Coastal and the Northern Region but also a few converts from other parts of the country. See Hansen, *Al-Shabaab in Somalia*, 128–32.

Government Response

Kenya's official response to terrorism has been two-pronged: legislative and military. The most comprehensive legislative piece was the *Prevention of Terrorism Act* 2012. It gave the police powers for the purpose of investigation or prevention of a terrorist act to "intercept, interrupt or tap communication, seize property and limit certain constitutional rights of an individual," including such rights as the right to privacy and the rights of an arrested person as specified in Article 49(1)(f) of the Constitution of Kenya.[7] The military response was named Operation Linda Nchi (protect the country) and was launched in 2011 when Kenya sent troops into Southern Somalia. The military set out primarily to disrupt the terrorists' economic network and to degrade their capacity to carry out attacks in Kenya.

Both the legal and military responses have continued to receive criticism and praise in almost equal measure. The anti-terror bill was strongly opposed by some politicians, especially some from the northeastern parts of the country, as well as by a section of Muslim leaders. One of the country's leading newspapers, *The Standard*, noted that before its final enactment, the bill became a "subject of heated debate and controversy."[8] The sending of the military into Somalia was also seen by many critics as ill-advised. If the decision was a bold proactive move to eliminate the al-Shabaab threat, the objective has not been even half achieved. The effort has not deterred or curtailed the terrorists' ability to hit Kenya at will. Indeed, some of the worst terror attacks in the country happened after Kenya sent the military into Somalia.

The second phase of Kenya's experience is in a category of its own. Terror attacks were carried out by foreign elements and almost always targeted foreign interests in the country—like Israeli or American installations or businesses. The majority of casualties were, however, always Kenyans. If this phase has any connection with the present and the third phase of terror experiences in Kenya, it is perhaps the inspiration that al-Shabaab may draw from these earlier incidents. The perpetrators firmly believe in the legitimacy of their cause and are determined to achieve

---

7. See "Prevention of Terrorism," Act No. 30 of 2012, cf. Act No. 38 of 2013, Act No. 19 of 2014, Act No. 25 of 2015, referenced online at www.kenyalaw.org.

8. See "Kibaki Signs Historic Anti-terrorism Bill," *Standard Digital*, 14 October 2012: http://www.standardmedia.co.ke/article/2000068354/kibaki-signs-historic-anti-terrorism-bill.

their goals regardless of the cost or the means by which their aims may be realized. One common thread that runs through their cause of action is the insistent search for justice, however this is understood. They also seem unrelenting in random attacks with the intention to inflict maximum pain, instill terror, and indiscriminately terrorize the whole country.

The Variety of Christian Responses to War

The atrocities of war and the violent nature of terrorism affect everybody. A staunch pacifist, a silent bystander, an innocent child, and a decidedly neutral citizen are all equally exposed to the dangers of terrorism. What should be the appropriate Christian response? There is no easy answer to this question. Terrorism is evil and the question of what purpose evil may serve in human life, and an adequate response to it, is one of those theological grey areas. The following discussion outlines three possible responses, with a particular focus on how justice should be the guiding principle in whichever choice one may make when faced with the question, "How best should a Christian respond to the challenge of terrorism?"

The three possible responses could be outlined as follows: pacifism, resistance, and prevention. The last two are concerned with how war may be prevented or waged justly and differ only in fine details. Both are about either resisting or preventing evil by use of just means, which may mean resorting to war or the use of necessary force either to uphold the right to self-defense or to prevent injustice. Pacifism and just war are markedly different but not necessarily irreconcilable. If the possible means to bring about the desired goal of peace and justice are markedly different, then genuine concern for the right moral and ethical choices is to find the ones that bring about greater good.

Pacifism is opposed to war or any form of violence as a matter of principle. Pacifists hold that any form of violence, including in self-defense or even defending another person, is incompatible with Christian ethics and theology. As Peter Brock and Thomas Socknat define it, pacifism is "an unconditional rejection of all forms of warfare."[9] Within this broad definition, forms of Christian pacifism differ in positions, casting a wide spectrum of views ranging from non-violent resistance on one

---

9. Brock and Socknat, *Challenge to Mars*, ix.

end to absolute pacifism on the other.[10] The theological rationale for Christian pacifism is generally built on the life, teaching, and ministry of Jesus. The Sermon on the Mount, Jesus' refusal to resist arrest and torture, and the cross are the three core sources that reference the pacifist's argument.

Whereas pacifists generally agree that there can never be any moral ground to support resorting to war,[11] not all agree on the best way violence may be resisted or possible ways in which a genuine search for justice may be supported. The differences are influenced by the varied interpretations arising from the biblical sources. Absolute pacifism, for example, sees Jesus as the model pacifist. He taught non-resistance and non-retaliation, to love the enemy, and endure abuse and injustice when oppressed. The classic text often quoted and interpreted literally is drawn from the Matthean version of the Sermon on the Mount (Matt 5:38–48).[12] Some pacifists who differ with this interpretation read the Matthean text in light of the Gospel of Luke.[13] Two references with regard to this interpretation are particularly important. The instances where Jesus drove out the unscrupulous temple traders (Luke 19:45–48) and where Jesus directed his disciples to sell their cloak and buy a sword (Luke 22:36) allow some pacifists to consider active resistance, especially in defense of the other. Of particular interest to note is that Jesus' action was aimed towards the correction of malpractices such as corruption and theft, and not, strictly speaking, towards the traders per se. Pacifists are not oblivious to the Old Testament texts where God himself seems to sanction wars to achieve divine purposes. The Old Testament wars, however, are treated with great exception and the commandment forbidding murder (Exod 20:13) is believed to be the absolute normative position. God's ideal is perfect peace, as it will be in the messianic age (Isa 2:4; 11:6–9). This explains, for instance, why God stopped David from building the temple, telling him: "You have shed much blood and have fought many

---

10. For example, Grimsrud and Early, "Prologue," 1, reckon that John Howard Yoder, in his *Nevertheless: Varieties and Shortcomings of Religious Pacifism*, "describes no less than twenty-nine different types of religious pacifism."

11. Orend, *War and International Justice*, 145–67.

12. Another important passage drawn from Matthew is Matt 26:52: "put your sword back in its place . . . for all who draw the sword will die by the sword."

13. See, for example Geddes, *Christianity: Behaviour*, 75.

wars. You are not to build a house for my Name" (1 Chron 22:8). War are, therefore, far from God's intended ideal.

The differing views among varied shades of pacifism notwithstanding, its varied forms have been integral to Christian thought, beginning with the writings of the church Fathers. The Early church pursued the philosophy of "love of the enemy" and "turning the other cheek," embracing suffering as a means of winning the enemy over. It did not mount organized resistance or see it right for a Christian to serve in the army, counting the allegiance required of soldiers as contrary to loyalty to one true Lord, Jesus Christ. Hippolytus of Rome (AD 170–235), for example, wrote, "A soldier of the civil authority must be taught not to kill men and to refuse to do so if he is commanded. . . . If a believer seeks to become a soldier, he must be rejected, for he has despised God."[14] Tertullian (AD 160–220) endorsed a similar view, explaining, "One soul cannot be due to two masters—God and Caesar."[15] Arnobius (d. 330) made it clear that Jesus' position—which should be the same for his followers—was to lay down one's life rather than to take that of another. He contends, "We [Christians] have learned from His [Jesus'] teaching and His laws that evil ought not to be requited with evil, that it is better to suffer wrong than to inflict it, that we should rather shed our own blood than stain our hands and our conscience with that of another."[16]

The christianization of the Roman Empire led to a shift in the view of the church from absolute pacifism to the need for use of just force for the purpose of maintaining public order. Augustine (AD 354–430) and Aquinas (AD 1225–74) are the classic reference points in this regard. The Reformers' approaches were varied, with leading Reformers including Luther and Calvin endorsing the need for the civil authority to use legitimate power for public good. Also to note are leading Anabaptists, prominent among them Menno Simons, overwhelmingly in support of absolute pacifism. In more recent times, the teachings of Pope John XXIII[17] and some prominent Roman Catholics like Dorothy Day and Henri Nouwen have proved influential reference points for the pacifists.

---

14. *The Apostolic Tradition of Hippolytus of Rome* 16.9.
15. Tertullian, *On Idolatry* 19.
16. Arnobius, *Adversus gentes* 1.6.
17. His basic ideas are found in his *Pacem in Terris*, a Papal Encyclical published on 11 April 1963. See Hebblethwaite, *John XXIII*, 467–88. Also for varied views on the Pope's exact theological position, and the arguments that his views on pacifism

Would pacifism be an effective and appropriate response for Kenyan Christians to the challenge of terrorism? Before attempting to answer this question, what follows is a consideration of the arguments for just war. Once that is accomplished, there will be a recasting of the question in light of which of the two positions should be preferred.

Is war or violence of any kind ever justified? In response to this question, just war theorists build their case on three pillars: tradition, Scripture, and the analysis of social-political realities. Just war theory presupposes the real possibility that in some situations war could be the only viable option if it could avert atrocities, eliminate or correct injustice, contain certain violence, or remove oppression. According to Augustine, for example, war is justified if the purpose is to "defend against an unjust oppressor, protecting or rescuing innocent victims in hostile territory, defending an ally, and repelling an assault while traveling."[18] Murray Rothbard succinctly describes the purpose of a just war as the effort of a person or a people "to ward off the threat of coercive domination by another people, or to overthrow an already-existing domination."[19] In such circumstances, it is justified to go to war but only if certain criteria are met. The first of these criteria is the concern that the cause for which one may go to war must be just, and the second criterion is concerned with the morality that guides the conduct of war. In both cases, the principle of justice is central and to guarantee objective interpretation and application of justice, the decision to use force must always lie with legitimate authority, with whom also rests the responsibility to judge the legality, proportionality, intentionality, and possibility of success.[20]

The best of the arguments for just war theory and just war tradition build on Augustine and Thomas Aquinas. Aquinas, for example, systematically deals with objections raised on the basis of Scripture, and

---

are only implicit, see Douglas, *Non-violent Cross*, 81–136; Peter J. Riga, "Beyond Anti-Communism," *Catholic Worker*, January 1966, 2.

18. Cited in, Charles, "Just War Moral Reflection," 596. See also Augustine, *City of God*, 19.5.

19. Rothbard, "America's Two Just Wars," 119.

20. Thomas Aquinas, *Summa Theologica*, see *Secunda Secundae* (2.2) Q. 40, 1353–57; Also, for detailed treatment of these views, see Walzer, *Just and Unjust Wars*, 196–98; Charles, *Between Pacifism and Jihad*, 149–68, and his article, "Just War Moral Reflection," 605; Clouse, *War: Four Christian Views*; Orend, *Morality of War*; O'Brien, *Conduct of Just and Limited War*; Coates, *Ethics of War*.

building also on Augustine's thoughts concludes that just war is borne out of the necessity to resist evil. In his treatment of the subject, he contrasts possible objections to the morality of any war and responds to each. One of the objections he anticipates, for example, is the argument that war is sinful, as it is contrary to the will of God, and also contrary to such biblical injunctions as "do not resist an evil person" (Matt 5:39), or "do not repay anyone evil for evil . . . do not take revenge . . . but leave room for God's wrath" (Rom 12:17, 19). In response to this objection, Aquinas distinguishes personal and public good. In the interest of the latter, legitimate authority can, with good intent, justly wage war or use force purposely to bring about peace, restore order, and punish sinners in exercise of its God-given authority. Whereas an individual in obedience to the scriptural injunctions should not resist evil, even for such reason as self-defense, it is a moral duty for the civil authority to do so.[21]

In response to whether a Christian should bear arms in the service of the civil authority, Aquinas again appealed to Scripture: "If the Christian Religion forbade war altogether, those who sought salutary advice in the Gospel would rather have been counselled to cast aside their arms, and to give up soldiering altogether. On the contrary, they were told: 'Do violence to no man . . . and be content with your pay.' If he commanded them to be content with their pay, he did not forbid soldiering."[22] In sum, the proponents of just war theory contend that it is immoral to do nothing about abhorrent evil, and doing nothing is more sinful than resorting to use of just force in order to achieve peace.[23]

On the contrary, the opponents of just war theory often argue that it does not have sufficient biblical basis. It is considered absurd that the life of one can be taken, at least in principle, to preserve or protect that of another. There is also no guarantee that violence will not beget more violence, and war only multiplies the suffering of all and sundry, especially given the availability of extremely deadly firepower capable of destroying the world over. As Pope John Paul II once said, "Today, the scale and the horror of modern warfare . . . whether nuclear or not—makes it

21. Thomas Aquinas, *Summa Theologica* (excerpt, part 6), 2.2, Q. 40, Article I.
22. Ibid.
23. See, for example, Thomas Aquinas, who quoting Augustine (*Ep. ad Bonif.* 189) says, "We do not seek peace in order to be at war, but we go to war that we may have peace." Aquinas also says, "Those who wage war justly aim at peace, and so they are not opposed to peace, except to the evil peace, which Our Lord 'came not to send upon earth'" (Matt 10:34). *Summa Theologica* (excerpt, Part 6), 2.2, Q. 40, Article I.

totally unacceptable as a means of settling differences between nations."[24] Against just war theory is also the argument that there can never be a moral reason to meet terror with terror because any form of violence, whether in self-defense or intended to eliminate a violent threat, is, regardless of this good intention, inherently immoral.

The Kenyan Church

The Kenyan church has not shown a systematic and sustained theological response to the threat of terrorism. Statements often issued in response to specific attacks have always condemned terrorism as evil, called upon the government to improve security, and often sought to distance terror acts from the religion of Islam, even where individual Muslims are implicated in the commission of terror. With time, the mainline churches seem to have taken the view that Christians are targeted and that the government must contain the threat; the fear is that some Christians—often unduly influenced by an uncritical association of terrorism and Islam—may be tempted to take the law into their own hands to assert the right to self-defense. For example, the leaders of the mainline churches including the Roman Catholic Cardinal, the Archbishop of the Anglican Church, and the chairperson of the National Council of Churches, among others, in response to the Garissa University College massacre carried out by the al-Shabaab terror group, issued a joint statement, which in part read:

> Dear Christians, fellow Kenyans and people of goodwill, we the shepherds of the flock of Christ are pained to admit that this was another case of Kenyans targeted because of their religion. We regret to note that most of those killed were young Christians in a prayer session. The systematic profiling, isolation and massacre of Christians in different parts of Kenya must stop. While urging our Christians to be peace makers, we will not remain silent as they continue to be massacred.[25]

While the statement categorically condemns targeting of Christians and urges Christians to be "peace makers," it does not give any pastoral, biblical, or theological guidance on how best to proceed. It can only be

---

24. Quoted by the US Catholic bishops in *The Challenge of Peace*.

25. Tom Mboya, "Kenya's Top Church Leaders Declare after Al-Shabaab Garissa Attack: Systematic Profiling, Isolation and Massacre of Christians Must Stop," *The Christian Post*, 13 April 2015.

assumed that Christians should actively ("be peace makers") seek to reach out to their Muslim neighbors and peacefully work together in identifying and reining in dangerous elements who may arise from or take cover within their communities. This will presumably involve seeking to actively dissuade those who radicalize youth with ill intentions to get them to join the ranks of the terror groups. Whereas, reading between the lines, pacifism seems to be the desired ideal, the need for the government to employ necessary force is silently endorsed and seen as the most practical option in response to the threat of terrorism.[26] From experience it can be said that self-defense is commonly embraced by Christians who are faced by danger. A common view is that the death of an aggressor is not contrary to God's will, and one who sows violence will reap the wrath of God and receive due dessert, as "the wages of sin is death" (Rom 6:23). This is a prevalent popular theology, which is more akin to just war arguments than outright pacifism, although the correct interpretation and application of this and other such texts is often stretched and ignores the scriptural context.

It must also be noted that segments of church-goers see attacks on the churches as God's punishment for sin, for it is believed that nothing happens without God permitting it. In the face of this, the call to repentance, forgiveness, and love of the other ("the outsider") has become a common narrative to counteract bitterness and help overcome the temptation to condemn innocent people simply on account of their religion or the unfair profiling that often wrongly associates one community or religion with violence. This approach is not without some benefit, as it can afford some psychological satisfaction.[27]

The church has done well in walking a tight rope in response to a very difficult situation. The best of pacifism encourages embracing tolerance and perseverance, while advocacy of just war beckons with the best of its principles where the government is needed to eliminate terror. The government is also tasked to do whatever is possible to build a just society, where no citizen has the reason to feel targeted, unfairly profiled, or alienated. Taking a cue from the approach of the Kenyan churches, here are a few recommendations.

The Bible is the Christian's moral and ethical guide, especially by what it reveals about the life, teaching, and redeeming death of Jesus

26. Omayio, "Keeping Religion Out."
27. Ibid., 42–43.

Christ. There is no denying that God in his perfect will desires peace and harmony for the whole of humanity. The kingdom of God espouses a progressive realization of this ideal, where all individuals and communities, without exception, are invited to submit to the fear of God, learn in wisdom, do to others as they would have them do to them, and love the enemy and the neighbor as oneself. The object of this call is to progressively build a redeemed new humanity that in seeking God can create a just society in which all can enjoy a foretaste of the eschatological perfect peace.

It is in this light that we suggest the need for Christians to form communities of peace, seek to learn the way of Christ, to love God in wisdom, and to reach out to those different from them. This will require building bridges of compassion and understanding, mutual acceptability, tolerance, and patient learning in the ways of God, seeking justice for all humanity. Surely, active pacifism on one hand and the use of just force on the other are like two sides of the same coin. Scripture espouses this ideal as well as the need for effecting interim measures including the enforcing of church discipline. This may include turning the tables on the corrupt, and binding or loosing (Matt 18:18), whichever way this may be necessary. Christians are called not only to be peacemakers but also to be the bearers of the image of the Prince of Peace, in obedience to whom they live, and whose example they follow. They are called to pay due reverence to secular authorities and render service when called upon.

In the most practical sense, some of the things the church could do in obedience to Christ should include advocacy, neighborhood watch, reconciliation, influencing policies for greater political and social justice, prayer, leading a peaceable life that serves as a testimony to one another, social and community interventions, as well as participation in works of charity. Beyond intra-community engagements, the church, through mobilization and education of the faithful, should always seek to build bridges of compassion across cultures. This can be done through facilitation of events where varied cultures meet for mutual interaction. They need to look for ways that cultures can support each other and can reduce such conflicts as are based on fear, suspicion, prejudice, a sense of cultural and religious or racial superiority, and discrimination. One way this may be done is by building creative and critically considered alliances and collaborations for the sole goal and express purpose of building a lasting peace, mutual support, and peaceful coexistence of different peoples with one another.

The government could also be encouraged and supported to pursue diplomatic engagements and build alliances with international communities in order to secure the elimination of the selling and supply of arms to terrorists. It is common knowledge that the arms in the hands of most terrorists the world over are not manufactured in the countries in which terrorist acts are committed. The government needs to rally the support of international communities and work closely with its allies in order to disrupt the terrorists' sources of funding, dismantle their networks, and stop the flow of arms.

At the national level, it is absolutely necessary for the government to address outstanding issues of historical injustices with the intention of making amends, but even more to build one strong nation and a cohesive society where no community feels foreign within its own country. Kenya's national anthem, which indeed is an earnest prayer, asking "May justice be our shield and defender," provides an excellent philosophical framework for envisioning a just society. If all are treated justly, the chance for peace is greater than the possibility of war. Strong bonds of unity and the shaping of common identity can definitely be encouraged and achieved if all are justly accommodated in order to belong. The onus is on the government to make and pursue such a commitment. This may entail, but not be limited to, strategies for strengthening patriotism among citizens through common education and social projects. It could also emphasize the promotion of unity as a paramount national value. To achieve this, the government must ensure just distribution of resources, fair and equitable political representation, promotion of national unity and social cohesion, tolerance and embrace of diversity, interfaith dialogue, and collaborations across different religious divides. Christians can play a part in aspiring to leadership roles that will afford them opportunities to work for these desired goals in pursuit of building a just and equitable society with greater prospects for peace.

CONCLUSION

In conclusion, Kenya has suffered horrific terrorist attacks and has been more frequently targeted than any other country in the region. We note that Kenya shares a lot of similarities with the East African nations—including communities of similar ethnic extraction, historical and cultural affinities, economic interests, and similar religious affiliations. It is imperative that Kenya recognize the factors that make it a target and seek to address each. It is also imperative that Kenya work with all Kenyan communities, not in ways that make them antagonized, profiled, and treated differently, but to win their trust and support, as well as work with international partners to secure support that can guarantee a speedy victory over terror groups. All citizens of goodwill must play their part by working for a just society, for where there is justice, peace prevails.

REFERENCES

Newspapers

BBC News, Online Edition (http://www.bbc.com/news)
Catholic Worker
Christian Post, World Edition
Sahan Journal, Kenya
Standard Media, Kenya (http://www.standardmedia.co.ke/)

Other

Brock, Peter, and Thomas Paul Socknat, eds. *Challenge to Mars: Essays on Pacifism from 1918 to 1945*. Toronto: University of Toronto Press, 1999.
The Challenge of Peace: God's Promise and Our Response. Washington: United States Catholic Conference, 1983. http://www.usccb.org/upload/challenge-peace-gods-promise-our-response-1983.pdf.
Charles, J. Daryl. *Between Pacifism and Jihad: Just War and Christian Tradition*. Downers Grove, IL: InterVarsity, 2005.
———. "Just-War Moral Reflection, the Christian, and Civil Society." *Journal of the Evangelical Theological Society* 48 (2005) 589–608.
Clouse, Robert G., ed. *War: Four Christian Views*. Downers Grove, IL: InterVarsity, 1991.
Coates, A. J. *The Ethics of War*. Manchester: Manchester University Press, 1997.
Douglas, James W. *The Non-violent Cross: A Theology of Revolution and Peace*. New York: Macmillan, 1968.
Geddes, Gordon, et al. *Christianity: Behaviour, Attitudes and Lifestyles*. GCSE Religious Studies for AQA. Oxford: Heinemann, 2004.
Grimsrud, Ted, with Christian E. Early. "Prologue." In *A Pacifist Way of Knowing: John Howard Yoder's Nonviolent Epistemology*, by John Howard Yoder, edited by Christian E. Early and Ted G. Grimsrud, 1–21. Eugene, OR: Cascade, 2010.
Hansen, Stig Jarle. *Al-Shabaab in Somalia: The History and Ideology of a Militant Islamist Group, 2005–2012*. London: Hurst, 2013.
Hassan, Ahmed Issack. "Legal Impediments to Development in Northern Kenya." A Paper presented at the Consultative meeting for Members of Parliament at Naivasha, Kenya, 22–23 August 2008. https://web.archive.org/web/20121023104324/http://www.scribd.com/doc/5466737.

Hebblethwaite, Peter. *John XXIII: Pope of the Council.* London: Geoffrey Chapman, 1984.
Hornsby, Charles. *Kenya: A History since Independence.* London: I. B. Tauris, 2013.
Laitin, David D. *Politics, Language, and Thought: The Somali Experience.* Chicago: University of Chicago Press, 1977.
Mburu, Nene. *Bandits on the Border: The Last Frontier in the Search for Somali Unity.* Trenton, NJ: Red Sea, 2005.
O'Brien, William V. *The Conduct of Just and Limited War.* New York: Praeger, 1981.
Omayio, Paul Atina. "Keeping Religion Out of a Conflict: Learning from the Kenya Church." *International Journal of Sociology and Anthropology* 7, no. 2 (February 2015) 38–45.
Orend, Brian. *The Morality of War.* Peterborough, ON: Broadview, 2006.
———. *War and International Justice: A Kantian Perspective.* Waterloo, ON: Wilfrid Laurier University Press, 2000.
Report of the Truth, Justice and Reconciliation Commission, vol. 2A. Nairobi: Noel Creative Media, 2013. https://blogs.qub.ac.uk/remedy/files/2014/02/TJRC_report_Volume_2A.pdf.
Ringquist, John. "Bandit or Patriot: The Kenyan Shifta War 1963–1968." *Baltic Security & Defence Review* 13, no. 1 (2011) 100–121.
Rothbard, Murray N. "America's Two Just Wars: 1775 and 1861." In *The Costs of War: America's Pyrrhic Victories*, edited by John V. Denson, 119–34. 2nd ed. New Brunswick, NJ: Transaction, 1999.
Thomas, Matthew J. "Exposing and Exploiting Weaknesses in the Merger of Al-Qaeda and Al-Shabaab." *Small War and Insurgencies* 24, no. 3 (2013) 413–35.
Walzer, Michael. *Just and Unjust Wars: A Moral Argument with Historical Illustrations.* 5th ed. New York: Basic, 2007.
Yoder, John Howard. *Nevertheless: Varieties and Shortcomings of Religious Pacifism:* Scottdale, PA: Herald, 1992.

4

A Pacifist Response to Terrorism

Joseph B. Onyango Okello

Various voices, from local Kenyan citizens to the mass media, routinely urge the Kenyan government to put strategic frameworks in place that would not only improve the security of Kenyan citizens but also forestall possible future terrorist attacks. Such frameworks, the voices urge, would involve measures such as pre-emptive strikes against possible terrorist cells operating within Kenya and inside neighboring Somalia. The measures would, perhaps, go as far as engaging those terrorists in some determinate military conflict of the sort already engaged in by the Kenya Defence Forces. However, is there an effective, alternative, and nonviolent response to terrorist attacks that could be made instead of the sort of direct violent military confrontation carried out by the Kenyan government against al-Shabaab? This chapter locates and describes the nature of just such a response. It proposes the pursuit of a specific nonviolent variety of pacifism hitherto unexplored in order to achieve the goal of forestalling possible future terrorist attacks on Kenyan soil. But first we need a definition and explanation of the nature of Christian pacifism.

THE NATURE OF PACIFISM

Pacifism Defined

Although they retain the general motif of peacemaking, different ethicists, theologians, and philosophers define pacifism differently, and their definitions range from mere synonymic one-word definitions, such as abolition,[1] nonviolence,[2] and nonresistance,[3] to more elaborate ones. The word pacifism gets its semantic derivation from "pacific" which means peace making. The Latin *paci* comes from *pax*, meaning peace, and *fictus* meaning *making*. Literally, therefore, *pacifictus* means peacemaking. The most famous use of the word pacifism, translated to Latin directly from the Greek New Testament, appears in Matt 5:9. Here, the Greek word *eironopoios* (*eirene* meaning *peace* and *poios* meaning *make*) gets translated in Latin as *pacifi*.[4] This brief word overview, as we shall see below, provides a general understanding of what pacifism entails, usually an understanding ranging from "a commitment to nonviolence" to a narrower "anti-war" position.[5]

Alexander Moseley thinks of pacifism as the theory that peaceful relations, and not violent or belligerent ones, should govern human interaction and, for that reason, arbitration, surrender, or migration should be used to resolve disputes.[6] Andrew Fiala defines pacifism as "a commitment to peace and opposition to war."[7] Fiala and Moseley come from a religiously neutral background and, for that reason, do not necessarily present their definition with religious overtones. In spite of this religious neutrality, notice Moseley's acknowledgement that conscientious objectors to war, who happen to be martyrs in much of European history, have often been specially recognized for their moral bravery in refusing to take up arms.[8]

However, consider the definitions offered by thinkers with a background in religion. Nels F. Ferre, former professor of philosophical theology at Vanderbilt University School of Religion, defines pacifism as the refusal to use all physical force.[9] Whereas Ferre does not exactly explain his understanding of the expression "physical force," his meaning seems a clear reference to violence. Ferre's definition comes from a predomi-

1. Northridge, "Peace," 67.
2. Ibid.
3. McQuilkin and Copan, *Introduction to Biblical Ethics*, 407.
4. Fiala, "Pacifism," *para*. 2.
5. Ibid.
6. Moseley, "Pacifism," para. 1.
7. Fiala, "Pacifism," para. 1.
8. Moseley, "Pacifism," para. 1.
9. Ferre, "Christian Perspective," 49.

nantly Christian context. Dennis P. Hollinger, a Christian ethicist, defines pacifism as a rejection of participation in violence.[10] Christian philosopher and ethicist Norman Geisler agrees with Hollinger's idea when he presents pacifism as the view that finds all forms of participation in war morally repugnant.[11] Thomas D. Kennedy, also a Christian philosopher and ethicist, offers another understanding of pacifism by suggesting how the way of Christ must be seen as the way of nonviolent, suffering love.[12] A. James Reimer characterizes pacifism as the opposition to and refusal to participate in warfare or armed conflicts of all kinds. He observes how, in spite of the varieties of limited forms of pacifism in existence today, most pacifists remain committed to resolving conflict assertively by nonviolent peacemaking, negotiation, or mediation. Moreover, they view reconciliation as a way of life.[13] Consider one more definition of pacifism, from David Kinsella and Craig L. Carr. According to Kinsella and Carr, pacifism, in its purest and perhaps most coherent form, holds that war is never justified from a moral point of view.[14]

From these various definitions, a Christian definition of pacifism might be cumulatively and broadly given as follows: Christian pacifism is a commitment to Christ's way of nonviolent suffering love, entailing a rejection of, and a refusal to participate in, war owing to the moral repugnance of the violence it represents. This definition, of course, finds its basis in Christian teaching. If these definitions are applied to the Kenyan context, Kenyan pacifists would find all forms of violence, including the terrorist attacks on Kenyan soil, morally repugnant, and the pacifists, presumably, hope just war theorists share similar convictions. The pacifists part ways with just war theorists when they try to suggest or locate workable means of preventing the occurrence of future forms of violence, including terrorist attacks. The just war theorists would, of course, leave open the option of physical and forceful aggression against would-be attackers. The Kenyan pacifist sympathetic to the definition of pacifism hitherto adumbrated would seek more peaceful means of resolving this aggression

10. Hollinger, *Choosing the Good*, 175.
11. Geisler, *Christian Ethics*, 221.
12. Kennedy, "Can War Be Just?"
13. Reimer, *Christians and War*, 4.
14. Kinsella and Carr, *Morality of War*, 33.

The broad definition already presented, however, may not cover all the varieties of pacifism in existence today. Recent scholarship categorizes four major types of pacifism, with at least one of them finding further subdivisions based on different realities countenanced by pacifists committed to nonviolence, on the one hand, but finding specific forms of physical aggression, on the other, completely unavoidable. The different forms of pacifism find classification among a variety of Christian and non-Christian ethicists as absolute deontological pacifism, absolute consequentialist pacifism, contingent deontological pacifism, and contingent consequentialist pacifism. I propose a fifth version alluded to by scholars though left somewhat unexplained. I will propose a possible explanation for this form of pacifism specifically because I find it most promising for the Kenyan context if applied in a manner consistent with its postulates.

Pacifism Categorized

Let me begin with the first type of pacifism, namely, absolute deontological pacifism. This type of pacifism finds its basis in deontological ethics, variously defined as rule-based ethics or duty-based ethics. In other words, pacifists find commitment to the rule of nonviolent physical aggression as their duty. The rule of commitment to nonviolence must not be compromised because it is an absolute rule. To be sure, an absolute deontological pacifist will find war and violence always wrong and the pacifist in question will remain committed to the maximal and universal rejection of violence and war.[15] Kinsela and Carr note, for example, that the pacifist could find war immoral because it involves killing or violence, or both, and these courses of action are terrible moral wrongs.[16] Also, according to Moseley, refraining from aggression, the use of force or military action against a fellow human being, remains incumbent upon the pacifist. All possible circumstances of violence countenanced by the pacifist demand this form of refraining without exception.[17] Deontological ethics, of the sort upheld by Immanuel Kant, finds all morally good actions intrinsically good.[18] Hence, the absolute

---

15. Fiala, "Pacifism," para. 24.
16. Kinsela and Carr, *Morality of War*, 34.
17. Moseley, "Pacifism," para. 21.
18. Kant, *Groundwork*, 31.

deontological pacifist will find nonviolence and its consequent rejection of violent confrontation not only moral, but also good in itself.

The Kenyan Christian committed to absolute deontological pacifism will anchor the absolutist nature of the rule in question on the words of Jesus Christ. As Fiala correctly notes, this form of pacifism finds its ideal of nonresistance to evil in Christ's requirement placed on the Christian to resist no evil person in Matt 5:39,[19] which reads: "But I tell you, do not resist an evil person. If someone strikes you on the right cheek, turn to him the other also. And if someone wants to sue you and take your tunic, let him have your cloak as well."

How, then, would a Kenyan Christian committed to absolute deontological pacifism respond to terrorist aggression of the sort perpetrated on Kenyan soil in recent months? He or she must either flee or passively face death. If such pacifists find an opportunity to flee from the aggressor, no biblical injunction bars them from fleeing. To be sure, the deontological pacifist has a biblical example in the apostle Paul. Consider that by having himself lowered through a window in a basket, the apostle Paul fled when the threat to his life was imminent (Acts 9:25). However, if escape seems impossible, then the pacifist remains at the mercy of his or her aggressor. The option to flee certainly seems logical. The option to wait for one's fate to play itself out surely seems illogical and costly.

Without necessarily registering any commitment to a possible pacifist position, many Kenyans found themselves in this very position during the terrorist attacks at the Westgate Mall in Nairobi on the weekend of 21 September 2013 and in Garissa University College on the weekend of 2 April 2015. On several occasions, the terrorists distinguished between Christians and non-Christians by asking their victims to recite portions of the Qur'an. Victims who could not recite the Qur'an were shot to death. Records that they offered any resistance seem unavailable. To be sure, all indications seem to point to the possibility that many victims left themselves at the mercy of the terrorists and accepted their fate without resistance. Christian victims who died in this way would, therefore, be considered contemporary Christian martyrs. Though the Christian victims quite possibly never made specific commitments to absolute deontological pacifism, they lived it out in their lives. Quite possibly, if the Christians possessed means of deterring such forms of aggression such as guns or their equivalents, they would have

---

19. Fiala, "Pacifism," para. 2.

tried to defend themselves with a counter-attack. The Kenyan Christian committed to absolute deontological pacifism, however, would laud their non-resistance to physical force and aggression as morally worthy. According to this kind of pacifism, the victims did the right thing by following one of two options: flee or surrender. The possibility of a counter-attack would not be a morally praiseworthy option under such circumstances from the absolutist deontological pacifist position.

The just war theorist would, of course, find objectionable the admonition to hold oneself back from self-defense against terrorist attacks, especially if one possessed the means to defend oneself. However, this objection remains abhorrent to the absolute deontological pacifist, specifically because aggression of any kind would not be part of the pacifist's moral frame of reference. The pacifist thinks nonviolence of the sort demonstrated by the victims of Garissa University College terrorist attacks morally laudable. They died heroically. Similarly, also consider that the early church demonstrated such a disposition by rejoicing for being persecuted for the sake of Christ (Acts 5:41). As we shall see later in this chapter, pacifism embraces more tenets than mere inertness in the face of violence. These considerations provide a snapshot of the entailments of absolute deontological pacifism in the Kenyan context.

The next version of pacifism to be considered is absolute consequentialist pacifism. According to this view, the evils resulting from violence, force, or war far outweigh any of the good that may arise from participation in war.[20] Absolute consequentialist pacifism finds its basis in utilitarian principles of ethics. According to a broad construal of utilitarianism, an action is deemed morally good if and only if it produces or promotes the greatest happiness (pleasure) for the greatest number of people. By inference, therefore, an action is deemed morally bad, or evil, if and only if it promotes the greatest unhappiness (or pain) for the greatest number of people. An absolute consequentialist pacifist, therefore, would find violence evil specifically because it promotes unhappiness more than it promotes happiness or pleasure.

Ethical theorists distinguish between rule-utilitarianism and act-utilitarianism. Rule-utilitarianism urges the moral agent to live his or her life according to the rule that promotes the greatest happiness for the greatest number of people. The act-utilitarian urges the moral agent

---

20. Moseley, "Pacifism," para. 26.

to follow the course of action that would have pleasurable consequences and avoid the course of action that would result in painful consequences.

How does this formulation work for the absolute consequentialist pacifist? The absolute consequentialist pacifist in the Christian tradition, if committed to rule-utilitarianism, will locate a rule in Scripture that urges him or her to follow the course of action that promotes happiness more than it promotes pain. Indeed, such a rule can be identified. Consider, for example, the following words from the apostle Paul:

> Do not be deceived: God cannot be mocked. A man reaps what he sows. The one who sows to please his sinful nature, from that nature will reap destruction. The one who sows to please the Spirit, from the Spirit will reap eternal life. Let us not become weary in doing good, for at the proper time we will reap a harvest if we do not give up. Gal 6:7–9

Seemingly, this passage of Scripture implies that actions have consequences. An action that brings destruction should be avoided because the kind of destruction alluded to here seems to entail insurmountable pain, which the rule-utilitarian wants to avoid. An action that brings eternal life should be embraced, once again, because Christian theology teaches that eternal life entails endless joy. The action that brings eternal life should be pursued tirelessly, according to the apostle Paul.

Meanwhile, the absolute consequentialist pacifist in the Christian tradition, if committed to act-utilitarianism, will follow the course of action promoting more happiness than pain. In this regard, the act-utilitarian pacifist will consider possible prior analogous examples in order to make reasonably active predictions of future outcomes. Whereas this procedure may seem quite difficult to follow in different situations, the absolute consequentialist pacifist committed to the Christian tradition could argue as follows: previous instances of war have historically produced more evil than good. Therefore, we can be sure that future instances of war will more than likely produce more evil than good. Consider Fiala's description of this position: "A utilitarian argument for pacifism could be grounded in the claim that history shows us that wars tend to produce more harm than good."[21]

How, then, would Kenyan Christians committed to absolute consequentialist pacifism respond to issues of terror in the Kenyan context?

---

21. Fiala, "Pacifism," para. 54.

Upon facing such situations, the pacifist in question will, in the absolutist sense, obey the rule of non-retaliation, or follow the act of non-retaliation, specifically because possible instances of retaliation would promote more pain than pleasure. Rather than look for means of violent confrontation, the Christian absolutist committed to consequential pacifism will look for means of promoting peace rather than perpetuating violence. Possible candidates for such means will receive due attention toward the end of this chapter.

Consider, for example, how Kenya's war with terror escalated upon Kenya's defense forces' invasion of Somalia in 2011. This invasion was an attempt by the Kenyan government to wipe out terrorist cells that previously operated sporadically in crowded areas in specific spots in Kenya. Kenya's intelligence determined that those terror cells originated from neighboring Somalia, and were linked to al-Qaeda. To stamp out the terror cells, Kenya's president at that time ordered the Kenya Defence Force to invade Somalia. Not long after the invasion, Kenya's war escalated, and the terrorists cited their reason for attacking Kenya, namely: Kenya attacked Somalia. They acted in the name of Allah whom they described as Most Gracious and Most Merciful. Ironically, what they did was anything by gracious or merciful. In light of this, though, the pacifist admits that the goal to wipe out terrorist activities was noble. However, the utilitarian pacifist in the absolutist tradition will be the first to remind anyone committed to the principle of retaliation that violence begets violence.

Meanwhile, from absolute consequentialist pacifism, the focus shifts to conditional deontological pacifism. This version of pacifism admits the use of violence or war under certain conditions. It admits that specific application of a certain variety of duties may not be possible in isolation. Moreover, the duty to maintain peace and nonviolence may be at odds with the duty to save or defend lives against aggression.[22] Thus conditional pacifists (also called contingent pacifists) may find some wars necessary or acceptable in some respects and reject war in others.[23]

One may find a variety of pacifisms under conditional pacifism. For example, one may find what may be termed profession-specific pacifism. Under this variety, pacifism remains a professional obligation of certain religious vocations, being a choice of conscience not universally

22. Moseley, "Pacifism," para. 32.
23. Fiala, "Pacifism," para. 24.

Part 1: Essays

ired. A priest or a nun, for example, would not wish to engage in war
ng to their profession. One will also find what Fiala calls prudential
cifism, which considers any war unnecessary if and only if its policy
is prudentially unwise. Support for a war, therefore, is rejected if the war
can be determined to cause more harm than good. A third variety is just
war pacifism. It finds modern war in conflict with the standards of just
war theory owing to its use of aerial bombardments and other means
that fail to discriminate between combatants and non-combatants. Most
just war pacifists object to the way modern wars are fought. They may
also reject the legitimacy of the authority behind the fighters.[24]

How would this form of pacifism apply to the Kenyan situation? It would follow the sort of pacifism presented by Lyman Abbott.[25] We could recall Abbott's willingness to surrender his purse to a highway robber should the robber demand for it. We would also recall, however, Abbott's refusal to allow forms of aggression to be directed towards his wife and child should such an occasion present itself to him. In such circumstances, failure to do anything would bring about more harm than good.[26]

Perhaps, then, an individual, in the Kenyan context, committed to conditional deontological pacifism, will pursue a specific means of deterrence sufficient to stop the advance of the aggressor but also merciful enough to give the aggressor the opportunity to retreat, repent, and be encouraged to enter into some form of dialogue that would help address the terrorists' needs. Whereas this course of action may sound theoretically appropriate, it might, admittedly, be quite difficult to uphold in real-life situations, for one major reason: in real-life situations, individuals do not seem to have the time to reflect on just how they would deter an aggressor in the way described. Ordinarily, events unfold relatively fast. For the most part, urgent immediate need for the pacifists' personal survival is what seems to remain in pacifists' minds rather than their aggressor's survival.

This observation, however, does not imply that the situation described may never present itself at all. What the observation tries to ad-

24. Ibid., para. 30–35.

25. Lyman Abbott was a nineteenth-century Congregationalist minister who championed the cause of the social gospel movement. He believed that war might be needed at times to establish peace.

26. Abbott, *Christianity and Social Problems*, 240.

dress is the possibility of demonstrating a course of action consistent with conditional deontological pacifism should the agent committed to this variety of pacifism find himself or herself facing situations that demand the use of deterring maneuvers against the aggressor. At any rate, the pacifist duly notes the reality that such states of affairs rarely obtain.

Another version of conditional pacifism is conditional consequentialist pacifism. This form of pacifism demonstrates ascription to act-utilitarianism wherein the moral nature of each instance of war is examined on the basis of its likely outcome. Conditional consequentialist pacifists would, therefore, claim that generally, war fails to produce favorable results. However, they find specific instances of war that seem acceptable, including self-defensive wars, or wars aimed at protecting individuals under the threat of genocide.[27] Consider, for example, the following commentary on a scenario that played itself out during the Westgate Mall attack in Nairobi:

> The picture that emerges is of a woefully disorganized response from authorities, where infighting and a clash of egos left a handful of Kenyan officers, an off-duty British soldier and an Israeli security agent, backed by Kenyan-Indian vigilantes, to fight heavily armed militants in a bid to rescue hundreds of shoppers.[28]

Notice the allusion to the ineffectiveness of the authorities, and the inadequacy of the individuals who volunteered to help deter the terrorists. The conditional consequentialist pacifist would find the ineffectiveness of the authorities morally reprehensible specifically because the situation demanded urgent attention. More specifically, it demanded the intervention of the security forces in order to protect the victims. Additionally, the conditional consequentialist pacifist would applaud the efforts of the handful of Kenyan officers and the off-duty British soldier as well as the Israeli security agent because they acted in a manner that met the conditions under which the pacifist committed to conditional consequentialism would find war morally acceptable.

A final type of pacifism that merits consideration is one I will call virtue-based pacifism. As the name suggests, this form of pacifism finds its basis in virtue ethics. Virtue ethics stresses the importance of a person's character and internal maturity over merely obeying rules without

---

27. Moseley, "Pacifism," para. 65.
28. Howden, "Terror," para. 5.

the requisite character formation. The importance of virtuous nurture in one's life received wide endorsement from Socrates in his dialogues with Polymarchus and Adeimantus,[29] as well as Aristotle. Aristotle, for example, accepted Socrates' contention that one's rational faculties remained crucial to the person's internal character formation.[30] Many ethicists view Socrates and Aristotle as important figures in the history of virtue ethics.

Christian virtue-based ethics, however, recognizes the major role of the Holy Spirit in a person's internal character formation. Thus, a Christian committed to virtue-based pacifism will accept that a morally virtuous person will overflow with the fruit of the Spirit—a fruit characterized by peace, among other elements, as demonstrated by Gal 5:22–23. The Christian committed to virtue-based pacifism understands, therefore, that the root of the problem of terrorism can be traced to the internal character of the terrorist. The requisite character maturity seems lacking. More exactly, the terrorist exemplifies a life woefully deficient in the requisite spiritual maturity consistent with Gal 5:22–23. Deadly attacks in malls and universities exemplify the logical outworking of an internal character malfunction, more in line with Gal 5:19–21. The virtue-based Christian pacifist will seek ways to foster peace by beginning with constructing frameworks that help to create workable opportunities for proper character formation.

Hence, when virtue-based Christian pacifists face violent situations such as those characterized by the attacks in the Westgate Mall and Garissa University College, they see such situations as an internal spiritual problem that must not be targeted aggressively or violently. Violence, the virtue-based Christian pacifist will insist, hardly creates any opportunities for character formation. Violence may indeed force one's enemy to lay down his or her arms. However, it may not create frameworks for lasting peace.

I offer this version of pacifism (virtue-based pacifism) as the one most promising in helping, on the one hand, to mitigate future instances of terrorist attacks and, on the other, to create the most reliable frameworks for fostering interpersonal, intersocietal, and international peace. How, exactly, might this reality play itself out? I outline possible suggestions in the next section.

29. Plato, *Republic*, 443a–445b.
30. Aristotle, *Nichomachean Ethics*, 1144b.15–20.

A COMPREHENSIVE PACIFIST RESPONSE TO TERROR

In light of what has been examined concerning the varieties of pacifism and their possible responses to aggressions of the sort exemplified by recent terrorist attacks in Kenya, it can be fairly contended that virtue-based pacifism remains the most promising form of pacifism in combating violence. I underscore the significance of this thesis based on the consideration that the attention given to virtue-based pacifism remains rather sketchy, perhaps because pacifism in general rarely merits much attention on the Kenyan scene. Very little literature exists devoted to a determinate treatment of pacifism in light of Kenya's frequent encounters with violent terrorists. Moreover, whatever literature there is that addresses the pacifist response to terror or any form of violence in Kenya remains confined to the library shelves, and very little application of pacifist postulates has been made.

Additionally, this thesis remains significant because pacifism is routinely rejected for what its objectors find as its un-livability and impracticality. As we shall see, and as we have already seen albeit briefly, a variety of pacifism (namely, virtue-based pacifism) seems quite livable. Moreover, the early church demonstrated the livability of pacifism in general quite forcefully owing to its refusal to go to war or engage in military service. Moreover, the Christian martyrs were pacifists, and they found it morally praiseworthy to die for their Lord Jesus Christ. Of course, in their time pacifism had not received the sort of categorization it has received in contemporary literature. Just the same, its upholders demonstrated quite sufficiently that pacifism can, indeed, be applied in real-life situations. To be sure, the believers lacked the advantage of the sort enjoyed by Kenyan Christians, that is, they did not have the advantage of civil rights that characterizes the democratic atmosphere enjoyed by Kenya's current civil society. Remarkably, however, even without the benefit of civil rights, their Christian life and their pacifism penetrated the then contra-Christian civil society well enough to bring about specific moral transformation from the ordinary citizen to the government of the day. Whether or not leaders such as Constantine experienced spiritual transformation remains unclear to this day. However, the fact that Christianity had enough impact to become the state religion, specifically because of a few faithful believers who lived out its postulates from the very beginning, should give one reason to believe analogous outcomes could be witnessed in Kenya's contemporary society.

The focus now is a defense of my argument that virtue-based pacifism remains the most promising form of pacifism for combating violence. Several reasons can be advanced for this contention. First, virtue-based pacifism is more comprehensive than other varieties in that its postulates not only remain consistent with deontological and consequential pacifism (both absolute and conditional), but also seem to surpass the limitations afflicting those varieties. Second, whereas rival theories of war—namely, just war theory and divinely sanctioned war—seem geared merely to create peace by stamping out violence, the peace they foster seems temporary. Virtue-based pacifism, by comparison, aims at creating frameworks for more permanent peace.

Let me begin with the first reason, namely, virtue-based pacifism seems comprehensive and all-embracing of deontological and consequential pacifism. Deontological and consequential pacifism, however, may not be regarded as comprehensive. In order to see this, compare virtue ethics in general with deontological ethics in general. As already noted, virtue-based ethicists emphasize nurturing one's internal being and character rather than obedience to rules, specifically because the virtue ethicists know how the cultivation of right character makes one's commitment to stipulated rules more likely. Deontological ethicists, by contrast, emphasize obedience to rules as a matter of duty irrespective of one's internal constitution in terms of character. When outcomes between the two are compared, the virtue ethicist will obey stipulated rules more consistently than the deontological ethicist.

Suppose, then, this very notion becomes applied to pacifism. Having been nurtured internally in terms of character, the virtue-based pacifist will obey the rule to reject all forms of violence and physical aggression of the sort we find among terrorists. Moreover, the virtue-based pacifist will have little difficulty obeying what pacifists consider a pacifist motif established by Christ in Matt 5:39–40. In other words, owing to the fact that the virtue-based pacifist has been nurtured into a sufficient level of maturity for moral character, the pacifist will have little difficulty in resisting an evil person and will gladly "turn the other cheek," to use Christ's words.

Admittedly, the deontological pacifist may, in fact, obey this very rule. However, the difference between the deontological pacifist's obedience and the virtue-based pacifist's obedience is the question of desiring to obey the rule. For the deontological pacifist, the temptation to disobey the rule in question will be rather strong, specifically because he or she may not have matured well enough to desire to obey this rule consistently. He or she obeys the rule merely as a matter of duty and not as a matter of desire. The virtue-based pacifist, by contrast will face little to no temptation to disobey the rule, and in fact will desire to obey it. The apostle Paul powerfully illustrated this difference when he bade farewell to the Ephesian elders. Whether or not Paul was a just war theorist is not the issue here. The important thing, the virtue-based pacifist will point out, is that obeying this rule, or one similar to it, remains a very real possibility, as we see in these words:

> After we had been there a number of days, a prophet named Agabus came down from Judea. Coming over to us, he took Paul's belt, tied his own hands and feet with it and said, "The Holy Spirit says, 'In this way the Jews of Jerusalem will bind the owner of this belt and will hand him over to the Gentiles.'" When we heard this, we and the people there pleaded with Paul not to go up to Jerusalem. Then Paul answered, "Why are you weeping and breaking my heart? I am ready not only to be bound, but also to die in Jerusalem for the name of the Lord Jesus." When he would not be dissuaded, we gave up and said, "The Lord's will be done." Acts 21:10–14

What we read in Paul's words is his willingness to submit to aggression from the Jews in Jerusalem in a manner quite consistent, not only with Christ's commandment, but also Christ's submission on his way to the cross. The virtue-based pacifist could, quite reasonably, underscore the possibility of desiring to obey Christ's rule even if such obedience should become a matter of life and death. The deontological ethicist, however, might face the temptation to retreat, just as, for example, Luke and the others, Paul's companions, demonstrated by urging Paul not to go to Jerusalem.

We obtain similar results when we compare virtue-based pacifism with consequentialist pacifism. The two major examples to be compared here would be rule-utilitarianism and act-utilitarianism. As previously noted, rule-utilitarianism is the view admonishing the moral agent to obey the rule that produces the greatest good for the greatest number of people. This "good" routinely is considered to be synonymous with happiness, which in turn is used synonymously with pleasure. Granted, what the utilitarian may call good may not necessarily be identical to what the virtue-ethicist may call good. However, both would, quite conceivably, agree on the heinousness of terrorism, such as that witnessed in the Kenyan context. The rule-utilitarian pacifist could reason as follows: one must act according to the goal of obeying the rule, which, if followed, results in promoting the greatest happiness for the greatest number. War, however, promotes the greatest pain for the greatest number of people, and for that reason war should be avoided.

The difference between the virtue-based pacifist and the rule-utilitarian pacifist rests on the question of temptation to retaliate: whereas, on the one hand, the likelihood for a consequential pacifist to fall into the temptation of retaliation against the terrorist remains high given the conditional nature of utilitarianism, on the other, the likelihood for the same to happen to a virtue-based ethicist remains relatively low in light of the virtue-based pacifist's spiritual and moral maturity.

The upshot of this discussion of the first reason is to show that virtue-based ethics remains the most promising view to adopt in undercutting the scourge of terrorism specifically because of its comprehensive all-embracing nature compared to the other versions of pacifism. If, however, we stop here, we have only dealt with the pacifist's submission to violence. If this submission represents all and only what virtue-based pacifism can do, then it lacks the potency to forestall the advance of terror. Virtue-based pacifism seeks much more than merely submitting to aggressors.

This fact leads me to the second reason I find virtue-based pacifism offering the best promise, compared to its rival theories, in forestalling the advance of terrorism in Kenya. I noted earlier how rival theories of war try to create peace by merely stamping out aggressors in war. A major flaw with this way of dealing with terrorism seems to be its tendency to perpetuate the very violence it tries to eliminate. As the common dictum goes, violence begets violence. Maryann Kusimano Love is essentially correct when she notes how combating terrorism by eliminating a terrorist leader in one area only serves to facilitate the rise of other leaders in different areas.[31] For this reason, a strategy might need to be changed in significant ways. It appears that virtue-based pacifism might have a clue to what the strategy might entail.

Virtue-based pacifism does not stop at the peace gained through submission. To be sure, peace can result in just such situations. However,

---

31. Love, "Effective Ways."

this kind of peace remains tantamount to slavery, owing to the fact that the aggressors force their victims to submit to their rule. Once the victims submit, aggression is no longer necessary. However, as Fiala notes, this state of affairs results in a master-slave relationship. The situation seems to fit the description of peace as a mere truce or mere absence of war. Absolute deontological and consequential pacifisms seem vulnerable to this kind of peace. The difficulty with this understanding of peace is its superficiality. Internally, however, those finding themselves under the servitude of their conquerors will always remain in turmoil. Such a state of affairs does not reflect the existence of justice.[32]

Whereas virtue-based pacifism applauds any kind of ceasefire, it does not stop at truce. It seeks something more than mere truce, specifically because superficial peace fails to address the grievances of the oppressed. The grievances of the oppressed and the hostilities of the oppressor need to be addressed. Martin Luther King, Jr. noted how oppressed people cannot remain oppressed very long and that the yearning for freedom eventually manifests itself.[33]

Quite understandably, the just war tradition would justify going to war as a way of addressing these kinds of conditions. For example, tyrannical leaderships that fail to listen to the grievances of the oppressed may need to be diffused. Just war theorists find their goals of addressing such grievances militarily quite just. Whereas the virtue-based pacifist sees the need to address such grievances, he or she knows how military confrontations may succeed only in forceful elimination of the state of affairs but beget more violence, the very thing we are all trying to eliminate. Such confrontations fail to achieve the framework necessary for preventing future occurrences of such situations.

This fact was powerfully illustrated by the United States' invasion of Afghanistan and Iraq. The long-term goal was to make America safe by attacking al-Qaeda's home base in Afghanistan. Another goal, by default, was to eliminate the oppression characterized by the Taliban regime, wherein women were routinely subjected to servitude and denied the empowerment they needed through avenues such as education. We know that the Taliban was driven out. Also, Saddam Hussein's so-called oppression of his people was eliminated. We also know, however, that the war continues. Iraq still remains one of the most dangerous places

32. Fiala, "Pacifism," para. 12–13.
33. King, "Letter from a Birmingham Jail."

on earth to live. The wars in Iraq and Afghanistan were both meant to be just, with the goal of eliminating oppression. The goal to eliminate the oppressions represented by these different regimes was noble. We now know, in hindsight, that the method needed serious re-thinking.

How would virtue-based pacifism handle things differently? Virtue-based ethics admits that all terrorists are shaped by the ideas they embrace. The violence meted out against innocent civilians by terrorists represents the logical outworking of the ideology adopted. This ideology, of course, stems from deviant nurture that causes serious character flaws in the life of the terrorist. It reflects what Socrates called "a sickness of the soul."[34] Maryann Cusimanno Love locates this very problem in her assessment of the terrorist's mind when she writes:

> Ultimately, terrorism is a battle of ideas more than a battle of competing militaries. Groups choose terrorism to try to compensate for their small numbers and their military inferiority by using the power of ideas and the power of fear. While terrorism is a tactic used by groups with varying ideological agendas, it is always a tactic of asymmetrical conflict used by militarily weaker parties. The reactions that terrorists seek to provoke—fear, shock, panic, and attention to their views and goals—are the real weapons, regardless of whether guns, bombs, or airplanes are employed.[35]

I think Love is right in this regard. She does not state whether or not she subscribes to the pacifist tradition. However, her writings here well illustrate the goal of virtue-based pacifism. Her next paragraph is even more telling:

> Military efforts abroad largely do not engage the terrorists on their real battlefield, the war of ideas. We must cut the flow of recruits willing to lay down their lives for al-Qaeda's ideas, the financiers willing to bankroll terrorism, and the governments willing to overlook terrorist activities so long as the terrorists are not conspiring against domestic targets. To do this, we must conquer al-Qaeda's ideas and the power of fear with more attractive and powerful ideas and norms.[36]

---

34. Plato, *Republic*, 444b–e.
35. Love, "Effective Ways," 21.
36. Ibid.

According to Love, the most powerful tool at our disposal in combating terrorism is not the gun. Rather, the tools consist of ideas, moral persuasion, moderated responses that protect innocents, and the ability to craft a message effectively and then disseminate it and persuade others of it abroad.[37] Consonant with this view is the sentiment of a former columnist for the *Washington Post*, Colman McCarthy, who affirmed the existence of alternatives to violence. In his view, if individuals and nations can organize themselves properly, they will find nonviolent force stronger, more enduring, and assuredly more moral.[38]

In what ways do these findings apply to the Kenyan individual committed to virtue-based pacifism? Mature, virtue-based pacifists will seek not just the moral and spiritual maturity of individuals around them. They will also seek to spread their principles of moral and spiritual formation beyond their immediate environment. They will seek dialogue with individuals holding dissenting views as a way of sharpening their own views. They will share values near and dear to their hearts and locate, among those values, specific ones they hold in common. One such value is the fostering of positive peace. This peace is not the kind existing as mere truce, or as the elimination of hostility and addressing of grievances. It goes beyond these stages by fostering a more positive kind of peace. A morally mature individual will agree that neither the aggressor nor the victim is helped when a member of their immediate environment lacks this kind of peace. Members of the Kenyan community will determine where, for the condition of wholeness discussed here, lies the gift of solidarity, mutual respect, and satisfaction of needs wherein genuine community and human flourishing truly exists. According to Fiala, this kind of peace reflects a just and tranquil order that points toward something similar to a condition of wholeness.[39]

How would it work in light of the recent terror attacks in Kenya? Besides the personal growth of the potential victims of terror attacks, the virtue-based pacifist can take the responsibility of reaching out to all humans to help educate all people on the importance of peace, including potential terrorists. Indeed, the fact that some of the terrorists were recruited from Kenyan youth is common knowledge. To forestall the possibility of future attacks, such youths must receive the kind of

37. Ibid., 22.
38. McCarthy, *I'd Rather Teach Peace*, §153.
39. Fiala, "Pacifism," para. 16.

nurture that helps to inculcate the desperately needed state of peace. Owing to the fact that their personal growth in character is important, the virtue-based pacifists must take it upon themselves to conduct aggressive countrywide campaigns targeting the youth of the nation. The virtue-based pacifist seeks to include moral formation as part of the curriculum. Is this goal realistic?

To answer this question, consider how certain individuals have been cultivating this idea over decades. Colman McCarthy remains widely regarded as a pioneer in this venture, and he makes a noteworthy observation:

> Yes, the young are passionately seeking alternatives to violence. Yes, our schools should be educating as much about peacemakers as peace-breakers. Yes, whether the killing and harming are done by armies, racists, corporations, polluters, domestic batterers, street thugs or boardroom thugs, terrorists, schoolyard bullies, animal exploiters or others in this graceless lot, the cycle of violence can be broken—but only if choices are laid out, starting in the nation's 78,000 elementary schools, 31,000 high schools and 3,000 colleges.[40]

What Kenya needs is the ability to put frameworks in place that would foster the growth of a movement dedicated to this end. The youths will not be the only target group. College students need similar training. The virtue-based pacifist could, for example, conduct campaigns with the ministry of education as well as various universities and colleges to include moral and character formation in the pacifist tradition as a subject in the university curriculum. The goal is to produce graduates morally established in their character in a way that forestalls possible brainwashing by would-be terrorists. The gesture to nurture the university students in this way comes from the consideration that one of the terrorists in the Garissa University College massacre happened to be a graduate of the University of Nairobi. Clearly, this student missed his proper moral formation.

Churches and para-church organizations provide another important target group. To be sure, the view of the virtue-based pacifists resonates most comfortably within the Christian setting owing to its emphasis on internal character formation. Christian organizations have the best chance of putting in place the needed moral framework that would

---

40. McCarthy, *I'd Rather Teach Peace*, §199.

forestall possible recruitment by potential terrorists. Pastors, priests, and chaplains will need to be encouraged to provide rigorous disciple-making programs that focus on the character formation of their members. If the statistic of the percentage of Christians in Kenya is reliable, then 75 percent of Kenyan citizens stand a really good chance of protecting their country by allowing themselves to be continually grounded in character.

The Christian virtue-based pacifist can also engage members of different religious groups in Kenya. Versions of virtue ethics do not remain confined to the Christian religion alone. This fact, of course, does not imply commitment to salvific universalism—the view that all religions are salvifically valid and that no religion enjoys any privileged position as the sole custodian of truth. To be sure, the idea of internal character formation of the individual should resonate quite well with all individuals committed to promoting peace. Anyone at peace with himself or herself with respect to his or her internal character formation should desire this state of affairs for others, and should desire to share possible ways in which such a state of affairs can be obtained for the individual. An inter-faith dialogue for peace, therefore, should not be seen as a compromising gesture when all that the interlocutors are seeking is a state of peace. Indeed, this state of affairs seems quite possible without having to promulgate specific postulates of our own faith to non-adherents and without having to compromise those postulates due to external influence from non-adherents. The virtue-based ethicist will, therefore, look for ways in which this state of affairs can play itself out.

The project of conducting a massive character-formation campaign should be extended to the leadership of the nation, from elected government officials to appointed administrators and law enforcement officers. The idea of virtue-based pacifism, however, would be tough to sell to the police and the military who must, of necessity, remain committed to engage in physical aggression and violence when duty calls. Still, no one would doubt the importance of having a morally mature squad of military personnel and law enforcement officers. Even if they may find themselves engaging in war, they can still appreciate the opportunity to receive specific direction on moral formation. Ideally, the goal would be to engage in an aggressive campaign for character formation that would ease the burden of law enforcement officials having to put their lives on the line protecting Kenyans from would-be terrorists.

Finally, the virtue-based pacifist will try to reach out, whenever possible, to the terrorists themselves and engage them at the level of ideas. This gesture, perhaps, might be the most ambitious and perhaps even unrealistic. How does one engage terrorists in dialogue without, on the one hand, offending one's government seeking the destruction of the terrorists, and on the other, exposing oneself to violent aggression from the terrorists themselves? A notable Kenyan politician suggested a possible solution that would have, potentially, overcome this dilemma if authorities had taken his suggestion seriously. Consistent with the goals of virtue-based pacifism, the politician noted how military aggression continued to leave the Kenyan citizen more vulnerable to terrorist attacks. For this reason, he suggested the withdrawal of troops from Somalia and a direct engagement in dialogue with the terrorists. In this way, violence, he argued, would be forestalled.[41]

The spirit of the suggestion seems quite consistent with the goals of virtue-based pacifism. The challenge to be faced, however, if this suggestion were to be followed through, is how to locate the terrorists and invite them for dialogue, and whether either party could trust the other not to sustain a violent aggression. Whether or not the politician intended to propagate principles consistent with those of virtue-based pacifism remains unclear to this day. The point to note here is that relevant authorities remain capable of creating such forums.

CONCLUSION

The argument of this chapter is that a society in which all of its members are morally mature in terms of their character formation stands the best chance of overcoming the threat of terror; and this chance improves if all, or nearly all of the members find themselves committed to virtue-based pacifism. Only the kind of virtue-based pacifism identical or similar to the one described by the apostle Paul as the fruit of the Spirit makes this kind of peace possible. This kind of peace has a supernatural origin, namely, the Spirit of God, and is, therefore, possible only through developing a relationship with someone higher than us—namely, God.

41. Oeri, "Raila Calls for KDF Exit from Somalia." The article refers to Prime Minister Raila Odinga.

REFERENCES

Abbott, Lyman. *Christianity and Social Problems*. Boston: Houghton, Mifflin, 1897.

Ferre, Nels F. "A Christian Perspective on Pacifism." *Religion in Life* 38 (1969) 47–54.

Fiala, Andrew. "Pacifism." In *The Stanford Encyclopedia of Philosophy* (Winter 2014 edition). http://plato.stanford.edu/archives/win2014/entries/pacifism/.

Geisler, Norman L. *Christian Ethics: Options and Issues*. Grand Rapids: Baker, 1989.

Hollinger, Dennis P. *Choosing the Good: Christian Ethics in a Complex World*. Grand Rapids: Baker Academic, 2002.

Howden, Daniel. "Terror in Westgate Mall: The Full Story of the Attacks That Devastated Kenya." http://www.theguardian.com/world/interactive/2013/oct/04/westgate-mall-attacks-kenya-terror.

Kant, Immanuel. *A Groundwork for the Metaphysics of Morals*. Translated and edited by Allen W. Wood. New Haven: Yale University Press, 2002.

Kennedy, Thomas D. "Can War Be Just?" In *From Christ to the World: Introductory Readings in Christian Ethics*, edited by Wayne G. Boulton et al., 436–42. Grand Rapids: Eerdmans, 1994.

King, Martin Luther, Jr. "Letter from a Birmingham Jail." In *From Christ to the World: Introductory Readings in Christian Ethics*, edited by Wayne G. Boulton et al., 427–36. Grand Rapids: Eerdmans, 1994.

Kinsella, David, and Craig L. Carr, eds. *The Morality of War*. Boulder, CO: Lynne Rienner, 2007.

Love, Maryann Cusimano. "Effective Ways to Fight Terrorism While Retaining Our Values: The Lord Has Not Given Us a Spirit of Fear." In *Just War, Lasting Peace: What Christian Traditions Can Teach Us*, edited by John Kleiderer et al., 59–77. Maryknoll: Orbis, 2006.

McCarthy, Colman. *I'd Rather Teach Peace*. Maryknoll: Orbis, 2002.

McQuilkin, Robertson, and Paul Copan. *An Introduction to Biblical Ethics: Walking in the Way of Wisdom*. Downers Grove, IL: InterVarsity, 2014.

Moseley, Alexander. "Pacifism." In *The Internet Encyclopedia of Philosophy*. http://www.iep.edu/pacifism.

Northridge, F. S. "Peace, War and Philosophy." In *The Encyclopedia of Philosophy*, edited by Paul Edwards, 6:67. New York: Macmillan, 1967.

Oeri, William. "Raila Calls for KDF Exit from Somalia." *Daily Nation*, 6 June 2014. http://www.nation.co.ke/news/politics/Raila-calls-for-KDF-exit-from-Somalia/1064-2339284-2w1wou/index.html.

Reimer, A. James. *Christians and War*. Minneapolis: Fortress, 2010.

5

Evangelicals and Public Life in Kenya

Julius Gathogo

THIS CHAPTER DEMONSTRATES THAT the various strands of evangelicalism in contemporary Kenya are united in engaging Kenya's public life. While the Afro-Pentecostal wing of the evangelicals was passive and ignorant of public theology during the Kenyatta and Moi eras (1963–2002), the twenty-first century has seen their contributions and influences in public life grow significantly. Why has this changed? How does it manifest itself? In the light of terrorist activities, the Protestant-Evangelical wing of the Kenyan churches has indeed played a critical role in engaging public life in order to work towards a violence-free society.

Evangelicalism is broadly understood as that brand of Christianity emerging from the pietistic stream of the Reformed tradition, and whose emphasis is on salvation through personal encounter with the risen Christ. As Anthony Balcomb explains, this is intended to include both Pentecostal and Charismatic movements, as well as those who do not identify with those movements but "who believe in the need for personal salvation and Christian discipleship through adherence to scripture."[1] It may also include a number of people in the "mainline" or ecumenical churches such as Anglicans, Lutherans, Methodists, and Roman Catholics.[2] Seen in this way, evangelical Christianity is not only seen in the mainline Protestant churches and the Afro-Pentecostal

---

1. Balcomb, "Left, Right and Centre," 146.
2. Ibid.

churches (such as the Redeemed Gospel Church, the Gospel Outreach Church, the Full Gospel Church, and the Apostolic Church among others), but also in the charismatic wing of the Roman Catholic Church, which, like the Protestants, lays more emphasis on spiritual gifts, elaborate worship, deep meditation in prayer, and the "power of the word" of God among other pietistic strands. Afro-Pentecostals, also referred to as the emerging Christianities, are indeed a hybrid Christian model that blends together Pentecostal/Charismatic practices and African religiosity. Certainly, they capture the African ethos of wholeness, especially in the twenty-first century. Nevertheless, the focus of this chapter is on Evangelicals within the Protestant wing of the church and their reaction to terrorism in modern-day Kenya.

Kenyan Evangelicals evidence unique ways of theologizing, especially with regard to public discourse. Their approach to extremist groups cannot be ignored as they have a huge constituency. Indeed, when Kenya's Attorney General, Githu Muigai, in January 2016 proposed a legal clause that would control rogue pastors who are out to con worshippers oblivious to their schemes, Evangelicals came out strongly to assert their theological position. In particular, the Chairman of the Evangelical Alliance of Kenya (EAK), Bishop Mark Kariuki, stated:

> As believers, we know some anointed men of God are like Peter the fisherman, who was called unlearned. However, he later became Peter Cephas the Rock on which God built His church. The call from God is personal, with or without education. . . . We do not reject regulations. We are law-abiding and we submit to the authority of the day. However, it must be reasonable and after proper consultation. If all fails, then we will fight it in court. . . . We will sustain this pressure as long as our issues remain unresolved.[3]

Equally, the chairman of the National Council of Churches of Kenya (NCCK), Canon Peter Karanja, condemned the proposed regulations and warned the Kenyan government to stop provoking the church or be sued.

From the fact that the churches threatened to take the government to court if it insisted on regulating the activities of the church, several in-

---

3. Nderitu Gichure et al., "Main Churches Split on Kenya's Rules on Religion as Muslims Declare Never!" *Standard Newspaper*, 12 January 2016. http://www.standardmedia.co.ke/m/story.php?id=2000187826&pageNo=4.

sights can be drawn. First, there has been a major paradigm shift among the various strands of the Evangelical wing of the church, particularly the Afro-Pentecostals, who were previously seen as conservative and disengaged from the state. Second, by engaging the state in public discourses, the Afro-Pentecostal wing of Evangelical churches in Kenya has positioned itself as the guardian of the people's heritage. Third, in reaffirming their submission to the authority of the day (cf. Rom 13) with conditions, their communication indicates a revision of their earlier position wherein authorities were obeyed absolutely, especially in the Moi era (1979–2002). In other words, they are theologically conscious about church and state relations, their prophetic role, and the power they hold in public life. In regards to terrorism, their silence seems to communicate that they do not object to the ongoing activities that began in 2011 when the Kenya Defence Forces (KDF) were deployed in neighboring Somalia.

EVANGELICALS AND PUBLIC THEOLOGY

The variety of ecclesiastical structures that emerged after the sixteenth-century Reformation in Europe continue to have a strong bearing on Kenya's religious scene even in the twenty-first century. First, we have the episcopal model, where power and authority are vested in the bishop. The Roman Catholic Church and the Anglican Church belong to this category. Second is the presbyterian model, where leadership is largely exercised by the church elders. Third, is the congregational model, where power and authority are largely exercised by the entire congregation. The fourth is the Pentecostal model, where emphasis is on possession by the Holy Spirit, particularly as evidenced by speaking in tongues, rather than on individuals and councils. Fifth is the charismatic model, where the emphasis is on charismatic gifts such as wisdom, knowledge, faith, healing, working of miracles, prophecy, discerning of spirits, speaking in tongues, interpretation of tongues, and so forth. Of course, there is a very thin line between the latter two.[4] In the Kenyan context, the Kenyan evangelical wing is largely seen in the Protestant branch of the church. In post-independence Kenya, the mainline churches (Anglicans,

---

4. I am deeply indebted to Jesse Mugambi's works *From Liberation to Reconstruction*, and *African Christian Theology*, for this categorization of post sixteenth-century ecclesiastical structures.

Methodists, Presbyterians), were indeed the most visible group overtly engaged in public discourses.

In this regard, David Gitari recalls evangelicalism's engagement with public discourses during the Kenyatta era (1963–78). In one instance, the evangelicals publicly opposed the so-called "Kenyatta oath" of 1969. In his book, *Troubled but Not Yet Destroyed*, Gitari explains that following the brutal killing of Tom Mboya, a leading politician from the Luo ethnic group who was thought to harbor dreams of becoming the president of Kenya after Jomo Kenyatta, news started filtering through that "many Kikuyu's were going to the home of [President Jomo] Kenyatta at Gatundu in Kiambu District in their thousands."[5] He says that they were going to have "tea," which really meant participating in the oath of political loyalty, a phenomenon where Kenyan leadership was to remain within the Kikuyu nation of Kenya. Gideon Githiga captures it thus:

> Large numbers of Kikuyu people were to swallow an oath of a goat's meat and blood, a spittoon for the squeamish was provided at ceremonies which catered for the bureaucratic elite in Nairobi. Many ceremonies were held at the President's home in Kiambu, with oath-takers arriving in lorry-loads to have "tea" with the president. The oathing that started as a voluntary event ended in compelling all the members of the House of Mumbi [meaning, Kikuyu ethnic group] to pay allegiance to Kenyatta by taking the Oath.[6]

As Gitari notes, many people went to Gatundu without knowing the real purpose of the visit and were deeply shocked after facing the reality at hand. It was a very humiliating experience.[7] People were made to squat and ordered around by unruly youth and eventually given an unpalatable concoction to drink. Those who resisted were beaten up, and some were killed. In particular, the East African Revival Movement, a pietistic group that cut across the Anglicans, Presbyterians, Methodists, and other mainline churches, endured the worst. They refused the oath, saying that they could not mix the blood of Jesus that washed away their sins with the blood of goats. This was the occasion of the first major conflict of the mainline Protestant wing of the Evangelical church with the government under President Jomo Kenyatta (1889–1978). In September 1969,

---

5. Gitari, *Troubled but Not Destroyed*, 185.
6. Githiga, *Church as the Bulwark*, 53–54.
7. Gitari, *Troubled but Not Destroyed*, 186.

200 Christians signed a covenant against secret oaths. Protests against it came from the African Inland Church, the Presbyterian Church, the Anglican Bishop Obadiah Kariuki (a brother-in-law of Kenyatta), John Cauri Kamau (the then General Secretary of the National Council of Churches [Protestants] of Kenya [NCCK]), the Revd John Mpayeei of the Bible Society of Kenya, the Moderator of the Presbyterian Church of East Africa (PCEA), the Rt Revd Charles Muhoro Kareri, and the then General Secretary, John Gatu, who went to see president Kenyatta and pleaded with him to bring the oath to an end. Additionally, Bishop Kariuki, whose theological position was beholden to the pietistic theology of the East African Revival Movement, convened a special synod of the Diocese of Mt. Kenya where the Synod deplored the "beating, coercion, brutal treatment, and torture resulting to death."[8] Soon after this gathering, the Gatundu and/or Kenyatta oath came to an abrupt end.

In the era of President Daniel arap Moi (1979–2001), Protestants, with the exception of the African Inland Church and several Afro-Pentecostal churches, remained vocal against the excesses of the government. They decried corruption, rigging of elections, dictatorship, and embezzlement of public funds. Some of the evangelical Anglican clerics who spoke loudly against the excesses of the state were the Archbishop David Gitari (who was almost killed by state-hired attackers), Bishop Alexander Muge (who died in a mysterious car accident), and Bishop Henry Okullu. Rev. Dr. Timothy Njoya of the Presbyterian Church was almost clobbered to death by the security forces. It was to assess their contributions that Gideon Githiga published his book *The Church as the Bulwark of Extremism*. He explains in detail how the leadership of the Protestant wing of the church risked their lives by openly speaking out as the voice of the voiceless in an environment where the ruling elites went to extremes to silence dissent.[9]

While the mainline Protestant churches joined in condemning the extremism of the state in matters of governance, politics, education, religion, agriculture, electioneering, gender justice, and so on, the Afro-Pentecostal wing of the Evangelical churches was busy castigating their colleagues for not respecting the "government of the day." They based their view on Rom 13:1–5:

---

8. Githiga, *Church as the Bulwark*, 56.
9. See the various case studies in Gitari, *Troubled but Not Destroyed*.

> Everyone must submit himself to the governing authorities, for there is no authority except that which God has established. The authorities that exist have been established by God. Consequently, he who rebels against the authority is rebelling against what God has instituted, and those who do so will bring judgment on themselves.

They cautioned their colleagues that they were going against Paul's instruction, and that their role was simply to pray for the political leadership, the nation, and the general society. In taking this pro-government position, and in insisting that their roles were purely pastoral and not prophetic, Afro-Pentecostals were misusing St. Paul's words as contained in the book of Romans. Stated more clearly, Afro-Pentecostals were grossly misinterpreting the Bible. Indeed, they failed to address themselves to issues such as torture, political assassinations, dictatorships, and other human rights abuses that can be done by rogue leadership in a country.

In the post-Moi era (2003 and onwards), Afro-Pentecostals changed course and embraced a theological trajectory that embraced public theology, that is, a trend that not only engaged the state and the general society on issues facing society but even progressed to the point of seeking elected posts. I have previously reported examples of Afro-Pentecostal leaders who have successfully sought elected leadership positions in the post-Moi era.[10] They include: Prophetess Mary Wanjiru of Kinangop, 1992–97; Bishop Allan Njeru of Mwea, 1992–97; Rev. Morris Dzoro of Kaloleni, 2002–7; Rev. Moses Akaranga of Sabatia Constituency, 2002–7 and later the Governor of Vihiga, 2013–17; Bishop Margaret Wanjiru Kariuki of Starehe, 2007–12; Rev. Mutava Musyimi of Gachoka, now Mbeere South, 2007–17; and Bishop Robert Mutemi Mutua, 2013–17, as a Wiper Party's nominated MP among others. This novel and recent engagement in public life has led to the two major groups of Evangelicals in Kenya (Afro-Pentecostals and the mainline Protestants) supporting military operations against terrorism.

Since Kenya's defense forces joined the African Union Mission in Somalia (AMISOM) in the war against terrorism, Evangelicals in Kenya have never called for withdrawal of forces from Somalia despite several setbacks on the Kenyan side. Why? One reason is that Afro-Pentecostals' theological articulation has shifted away from a realized eschatology to

---

10. Gathogo, "Ecclesiastical and Political Leaderships."

focus on an unrealized eschatology wherein the church has to find its relevance in the present age as it waits for the end times and the full inauguration of the kingdom. This theological trajectory has been adopted by Protestants especially through the National Council of Churches (NCCK). Clearly, NCCK was instrumental in offering civic education especially during the Moi era (1979–2002). It was here that they taught the rank-and-file of society about the benefits of reviewing the Kenyan Lancaster constitution of the 1960s and ushering in a pro-people constitution that respected ethnic diversity, the bill of rights, multi-party democracy, and gender equity among other considerations.

GIVE US THE GUNS!

In October 2013, two Mombasa pastors asked the government to give them guns so as to protect themselves from terrorist attacks, particularly after killers went into some pastors' residences and shot two of them dead.[11] The two Mombasa pastors were Pastor Charles Mathole of the Mombasa Kisauni Redeemed Gospel Church and Pastor Ibrahim Kithaka of Kilifi East Africa Pentecostal Church. That same month the riots that erupted after the killing of Sheikh Ibrahim, a radical Muslim cleric, led to the torching of the Salvation Army Church at Majengo Estate. On 24 October 2013, the Mombasa Church Forum pastors issued a statement in which they protested the killing of the two pastors and called on the government to intensify security. In reacting to this, Bishop Wilfred Lai, the Chairman of the Mombasa Church Forum, stated: "The Mombasa Church Forum categorically states that no attack on Christians or their church leaders will deter us from our way of worship and our freedom of religion. To the perpetrators of these heinous attacks, we hereby state that we will not be intimidated and will continue to worship our Lord in our churches."[12]

In January 2015, Mombasa Protestant pastors, mainly the Pentecostals, called again for the right to carry guns so as to protect themselves from al-Shabaab attacks. This was immediately after George Karidhimba Muriki, assistant pastor of Maximum Revival Ministries Church, was shot by gunmen who were believed to be members of al-Shabaab. Bishop Lambert Mbela of the Redeemed Gospel Church,

11. www.youtube.com/watch?v=v6AguprnYNo.
12. "2 Pastors Killed in Mombasa."

Bishop MacDonald Kitwa of Good News Evangelical Centre, and Jeremiah Goodison met with Mombasa deputy county commissioner Salim Mahmoud to ask permission to carry guns. And although Alice Wahome, a member of the Administration and National Security Committee in Kenya's National Assembly, rejected the request on the ground that it would "increase lawlessness in the country if everyone is licensed to carry guns,"[13] the general church frustration had been let out for public consumption, consideration, and/or debate. How far should church leaders engage in military offensives? Is pacifism the only way for a Christian? Do Christian ethics allow a Christian to participate in military activities, where killing is a part? Should the above instances of terrorist attacks change a "non-violence" approach, particularly as seen in the early Christian writings? Or should the church now adapt St. Augustine's classical just-war theory?

In the Kenyan case, a blind appeal to pacifism is indeed escapist and unrealistic. To bring peace, Christians must act, for God's peace made with humanity on the cross is not something human beings can grant to each other. This view is increasingly gaining adherents among Kenyan Evangelicals, for support for the classic "just-war" approach appears to be gaining currency in an otherwise conservative society.[14] "Just-war theory" is the doctrine that propounds the view that war is morally and theologically justifiable if a number of criteria are met; if so, the war can be deemed just. The criteria are split into three groups: "the right to go to war" (*jus ad bellum*), the "right conduct in war" (*jus in bello*), and *jus post bellum*, that is, dealing with the morality of post-war settlement and reconstruction.[15] It postulates that while war remains terrible, it is not always the worst option; for there are some situations where genocide and other atrocities can be prevented through war.

St. Ambrose of Milan (AD 339–97) insisted on the need to distinguish between just and unjust wars. In his view, some circumstances might take a nation to war, though as a lesser of the two evils. A war that is designed to punish a wrong-doer, he argued, is necessary; hence not

---

13. Mark Woods, "Give Us Guns and We'll Defend Ourselves, Say Kenyan Pastors." *Christianity Today,* 19 January 2015. http://www.christiantoday.com/article/give.us.guns.and.well.defend.ourselves.say.kenyan.pastors/46265.htm.

14. When Mombasa Evangelical pastors asked for guns, this was a clear sign that they were subtly endorsing the just-war theory.

15. Guthrie and Quinlan, *Just War,* 11–15.

PART 1: Essays

all wars are immoral.[16] Conversely, he rejected the death penalty as a means of effecting religious conformity.

Similarly, Augustine of Hippo (354–430), generally considered one of the greatest Christian theologians, was one of the first to assert that a Christian could be a soldier and serve God without contradicting the two commitments. He affirmed that, while individuals should not resort immediately to violence, God has given the sword to their respective governments for good reason.[17] Even though the state could use violence to suppress evil and defend itself, St. Augustine's fundamental position was that the peacemaker who wielded the Word rather than the sword was following a higher call. In other words, peaceful means, as opposed to violent means, to counter al-Shabaab, is more glorious than slaying men with guns. That being the case, there is still a role for the judicious use of mercy by the state. Hence the offer by Kenya's Interior Cabinet Secretary, General Joseph Nkaissery, on 14 April 2015, when he directed "all individuals who had gone to Somalia for training and wish to disassociate themselves with terrorism to report to the National government offices,"[18] he was within Augustine's approach to war. He said the Government would consider granting amnesty and appropriate reintegration support for those who reported. However, those who failed to heed this call within the prescribed time frame were warned that they would be treated as criminals and would face the full force of the law.

Another commendable gesture by the government of Kenya is the involvement of parents and guardians and the general society in the war on terror. As a Kikuyu saying goes, "a midnight leopard attack is collectively handled by all, including the in-laws" (*Ngari ihitagwo ni mundu na muthoniwe*), who are ordinarily kept in a distance, so as to promote respect. Considering that a number of unsuspecting Kenyan youths have been lured into traveling to Somalia for purposes of receiving militia training over the years, it is also critical that the government appreciate such backgrounds, hence the amnesty call. As Nkaissery noted, "the

16. Lietzmann, *Era of the Church Fathers*, 70.

17. See Rom 13:4.

18. Cyrus Ombati, "Kenya Announces Amnesty and Reintegration to Youth Who Denounce Al-Shabaab," *Standard*, 16 April 2015. http://www.standardmedia.co.ke/article/2000158358/kenya-announces-amnesty-and-reintegration-to-youth-who-denounce-al-shabaab. Accessed 8 Aug 2016.

training is aimed at, among other things, instilling murderous terrorist ideology targeting fellow Kenyans and has led to senseless killing and maiming of innocent citizens."[19] He further noted that the government was aware of the cunning methods used to recruit the youth, with some recruiters being terrorists masquerading as religious leaders. To be rehabilitated, the youths must be de-educated and ultimately instructed with sound socio-religious doctrines that will return them to society. Considering their ages—ranging from eighteen to twenty-five—one can easily understand the vulnerable nature of their adolescence. Seen in this way, a formula that guarantees a return to normal life in society is certainly the better option. Because terrorist recruitment targets young students in secondary schools, colleges, and universities, de-radicalization must be done by society as a whole. An illustration of the kind of young people being lured to terrorist groups is the four nineteen-year-old female university students, Khadija Abdulkadir, Mariam Aboud, Ummulkhayr Abdulla (a Tanzanian), and Halima Aden Ali, who were arrested by Kenya's security officers in El Wak town along the Kenya-Somali border on 3 April 2015 as they were trying to cross into Somalia to join al-Shabaab and become "jihadi brides."[20] Being at the age of discovery but lacking experience, adolescents and teenagers are prone to recruitment by terrorist groups that can easily mislead them. Hence, schools, churches, media, mosques, and public meetings should be seen as forums of deconstructing the terrorist ideologies and ultimately reconstructing the thinking of youths as a rehabilitative measure.

French President Francois Hollande described the Paris terrorist attack of 13 November 2015, which killed 129 people and injured 415 others, as an act of war. This view resonated well with the position of some American Evangelicals, such as Franklin Graham, the head of Samaritan's Purse and son of renowned preacher Billy Graham. Others rejected the "war against Islam" approach. According to Timothy C. Morgan, some Evangelicals favored reconciliatory measures as opposed to military action.[21] Just as in this case, Kenyan Evangelicals are divided on the terrorism question. Nevertheless, the silence of many in the

19. Ibid.

20. "'Al-Shabaab Brides' Denied Bail," *Nairobi News*, 27 May 2015. http://nairobinews.nation.co.ke/news/four-al-shabaab-brides-denied-bail/. Accessed 8 August 2016.

21. Morgan, "War with Islam?"

Kenyan context appears to imply that there is overwhelming support for the retaliatory attacks against the militants. In view of this, Kenyan Protestant Evangelicals have found themselves draw to just-war theory in order to address the terrorist challenge facing the country. The case of the Paris attack reminds Kenyans of their own crisis, and indeed confirms the nature of the attackers, their aims and goals, as well the global nature of the threat of terrorism.

In light of recent events, Joshuah Akali, the Regional Official of the National Council of Churches of Kenya (NCCK) and the Bishop of the Elim Evangelistic Church, Mombasa City, confided to me that he not only supports the call for guns by some pastors who were threatened by the militants but also the continuous deployment of the Kenyan Army in Somalia. In his view, the NCCK fraternity supports this deployment as a means of weakening the basis of the attackers who cross over to Kenya from time to time. As for the guns, he argued that since the vocal Christian clerics will always find themselves on al-Shabaab's wanted list, the issuing of guns to them will slow down the murder attempts. He appreciated that one can still be killed while armed, but the rationale for carrying a weapon was primarily to scare the terrorists and not necessarily to kill. Seen in this light, the Paris attacks have a bearing on the Kenyan attacks; and indeed, all these attacks have demonstrated the changing roles of evangelicals in public discourse.[22]

NO UNIFIED THEOLOGICAL POSITION?

As noted above, evangelical Christianity in Kenya has not provided a unified theological voice to engage issues related to public life. Rather, there have been several diverse attempts by some evangelical Christian leaders to offer theological direction. First, Protestant and/or evangelical scholars like John Mbiti engage the public space through voluminous publications that touch on culture and the gospel, the secular and the sacred, the oral versus written theologies among other concerns. Second, Protestant scholars such as Jesse Mugambi counsel society on the changing theo-social trajectories from an African perspective. Third, it is now in vogue among Afro-Pentecostal leadership, which had hitherto avoided entering the public space on socio-political matters, to oppose or support political policies. Fourth, examples of political activism

---

22. Joshuah Akali, in conversation with the author, 23 January 2016.

can be found among some evangelical leaders, even from the mainline Protestant churches, such as that epitomized by the Rev. Dr. Timothy Njoya, a now-retired Presbyterian cleric. He continues to engage issues vigorously in the public space through the media on issues such as domestic violence, politically instigated violence, ethnic animosities, good governance, corruption, rogue pastors and the need to regulate religious activities, terrorism, and same-sex marriage. Indeed, he and the late Anglican prelate David Gitari vehemently campaigned for the enactment of the new constitution that was preceded by the referendum of August 2010.

In interviews with senior evangelical pastors across the country, some of whom sought anonymity, I gathered that even though there is no one theological and/or biblical position that has been adopted by the Kenyan evangelicals, the sending of the Kenyan soldiers was first greeted with approval by all shades of evangelicals. In other words, as contributors to public discourses, they initially supported the deployment of Kenyan Defence Forces (KDF) in Somalia—an indicator of the changing theo-ecclesial trajectories in an otherwise conservative society. Indeed, evangelicals saw military intervention as the lesser evil, especially when faced by deadly terrorists and/or murderers who are out to destroy families and civilizations. They decided it was right to stop them from destroying Kenyan families by all legitimate means possible. After the killing of about one hundred KDF soldiers at the Town of El-Adde near the border with Kenya by the al-Qaeda-backed Islamist insurgents on 12 January 2016, some of the evangelical support appears to have diminished. In my interview with Pastor Joseph Maina Kinyatta of Upendo Spiritual Church, he noted that the battle against terrorism should now be abandoned as the country pursues new approaches to combat terror. The sentiment was that if Kenya had not erased terrorism in neighboring Somalia after five years (2011–16) of military engagement, then it would be better for the country to pursue other ways of addressing terrorism.[23]

TURNING THE OTHER CHEEK

Many evangelicals in Kenya are worried that if the nation took Matt 5:38–48 literally as a guide for its foreign policy terrorist groups would

---

23. Joseph Maina Kinyatta, in conversation with the author, 23 January 2016.

quickly take advantage of the situation and gain the upper hand. In my opinion, "turning the other cheek" would become an encouragement for evil; and indeed, this is not what Jesus had in mind. The call to "turn the other cheek" was Jesus' way of encouraging his disciples to be motivated by love, to develop deep passion in the love of the "other" without compromising fundamental principles of our very existence.

In Rev. Dr. Timothy Njoya's view, Jesus' teaching in the Sermon on the Mount, and especially the instruction to "turn the other cheek," does not amount to pacifism.[24] Nor does it mean we place ourselves or others in mortal danger. In telling the Christians to turn the other cheek, Njoya argues that Jesus meant that his followers must respond to eminent dangers that may threaten society. Indeed, Jesus' becoming a sacrificial lamb for the sake of the world is a non-pacifist act. Jesus took a peace-maker role as opposed to a peace-loving role, which called for decisive action, especially in handling terrible threats to human existence. As such, evangelicals cannot use Jesus' teaching on "turning the other cheek" to allow terrorists to burn the country to ashes.[25] Njoya, however, regrets that the terrorist activities plaguing Kenya and the rest of tropical Africa are a by-product of unresolved problems from the Cold War. As the Western and the Eastern blocs competed for the overseas market, Kenya became only a pawn in the power plays. Equally, he views the First and the Second World Wars as wars fought for control of an overseas market. In all those wars, much was left unresolved. To an extent, the State of Israel was the consequence of these wars. To Njoya, Israel is the residue of the intra-tribal war of the market. Likewise, terrorism is the unresolved conflict of the market—centered on oil and other commodities. President George W. Bush warned Americans in September 2001 that "this crusade, this war on terrorism will take a while . . . a conflict between the Arab-Muslim world and the West." To avoid a backlash of civilizations, Bush later appeared in an Islamic center in Washington where he assured Americans that "the face of terror is not the true face of Islam."[26] In Njoya's view, the reference to war against terror as a

---

24. Timothy Njoya, expressed in interviews with the author. Njoya deals with this also in his books *Divine Tag on Democracy* and *Human Dignity*.

25. Timothy Njoya, conversation with the author, 23 January 2016.

26. Peter Ford, "Europe Cringes at Bush 'Crusade' against Terrorists," *The Christian Science Monitor*, 19 September 2001. http://www.csmonitor.com/2001/0919/p12s2-woeu.html.

"crusade" in 2001 changed the nature of the war. It shifted from being an ideological war (e.g., the Second World War) to a cultural war. This clash of civilizations was eventually exploited by the militants to pit the Christian and Muslim religions against one another; hence the hatred and mistrust to date. Considering that religion is part of civilization, and a very critical pillar of culture, some militants have tended to exploit it to create disharmony in Kenya and in various spots in the world.[27]

Some evangelical scholars like Njoya view the terror war as an attempt by al-Shabaab and other militants to close the market for the Western world, and an attempt by America, going to Afghanistan, Iraq, Iran, and other places, to ensure that their market remains open.[28] Whether or not this is the case—even if Kenya is fighting a proxy war—it is imprudent to remove the Kenya Defence Forces in Somalia before proper systems are put in place. Certainly, if one's house is on fire, one cannot wait to establish who set it before taking action. Rather, the first thing is to stop the fire. It is most urgent to devise ways and means of extinguishing the terrorist fire. It is folly to think otherwise.

CONCLUSION

When American President Jimmy Carter was defeated by Ronald Reagan, he included in his concession speech the statement, "I have realized [that] in politics the truth is not enough."[29] As Gitari notes, it was a strange statement uttered by a president whose aim was to apply Christian values to his presidency.[30] Yet it captured the compromise and tensions inherent in leading a nation. The polite Kenyan president Kibaki's unexpected sanctioning of the operation against al-Shabaab is a similar instance of the complexity and compromise necessary to lead a nation, and how it is not enough only to speak of peace. Desperate times call for desperate measures.

This chapter set out to address the Protestant evangelical perspective on terrorism. It has demonstrated that even though there is no unified voice, there is a sense in which the "just-war" approach against terror has become in vogue. For even though Kenya may be fighting a

27. Timothy Njoya, in conversation with the author, 23 January 2016.
28. Ibid.
29. Gitari, *Troubled but Not Destroyed*, 278.
30. Ibid.

proxy war where the interests of the Americans, British, Israelis, and other Western nations were initially the main target, allowing Somalia to remain a stateless society for decades contradicts the principle of the love of the neighbor. Certainly, a neighbor's house on fire is a threat to all neighborhoods, as the fear of the spreading fire is indeed alarming. The chapter has also cited several incidents of violence to demonstrate the magnitude of the problem—a problem that evangelicals cannot watch from a distance. Indeed, they have to swim into action and stop the Kenyan boat from capsizing into the deep sea of violence. Certainly, in the case of Mombasa where pastors asked for guns to fight after their colleagues were gunned down by terrorists, the simple communication is that the Protestants have changed tack, especially in matters of public life. In other words, evangelicals in Kenya no longer want to be seen as mere spectators but as participants in redeeming society from these turbulent situations. This is clear especially when we consider the fact that one wing of Kenyan evangelicals (the Afro-Pentecostals) offered minimal participation in public life during the Kenyatta era (1963–78) and the Moi era (1979–2002). With the change of ecclesiastical paradigm, all strands of the evangelicals in Kenya are now engaging public life, even on matters to do with violence.

REFERENCES

Newspapers and Magazines

Christian Science Monitor
Christianity Today
Nairobi News (Nairobi)
Standard Media (Nairobi)

Other

Balcomb, A. "Left, Right and Centre: Evangelicals and the Struggle for Liberation in South Africa." *Journal of Theology for Southern Africa* 118 (July 2004) 145–51.
Gitari, David M. *Troubled but Not Destroyed: Autobiography of Dr. David M. Gitari*. McLean, VA: Isaac, 2014.
Gathogo, Julius. "Ecclesiastical and Political Leaderships in One Armpit: Celebrating the Life of Thomas Kalume." *Studia Historiae Ecclesiasticae* 41, no. 3 (2015) 92–110.
Githiga, Gideon G. *The Church as the Bulwark against Authoritarianism: Development of Church and State Relations in Kenya with Particular Reference to the Years after Political Independence 1963–1992*. Oxford: Regnum, 2001.
Guthrie, Charles, and Michael Quinlan. *Just War: The Just War Tradition: Ethics in Modern Warfare*. New York: Walker, 2007.

Lietzmann, Hans. *The Era of the Church Fathers*. London: Lutterworth, 1989.
Mbiti, John. *Bible and Theology in African Christianity*. Nairobi: Oxford University Press, 1986.
Morgan, T. C. "War with Islam? Evangelicals Ponder Christian Response to Paris Attacks." *Christian Headlines*. http://www.christianheadlines.com/news/war-with-islam-evangelicals-ponder-christian-response-to-paris-attacks.html.
Mugambi, J. N. Kanyua. *African Christian Theology*. Nairobi: East African Educational, 1989.
———. *From Liberation to Reconstruction: African Christian Theology after the Cold War*. Nairobi: East African Educational, 1995.
Njoya, Timothy M. *The Divine Tag on Democracy*. Yaounde: Editions CLE, 2003.
———. *Human Dignity and National Identity*. Nairobi: Jemisik, 1987.
"2 Pastors Killed in Mombasa, Kenya." *Open Doors Singapore* (24 October 2013). https://opendoorssg.wordpress.com/2013/10/24/2-pastors-killed-in-mombasa-kenya.

6

Being Human in Kenya
Theological Anthropology in the Age of Terror

DAVID K. TARUS

THIS CHAPTER EXPLORES CHRISTIAN theological anthropology in response to terror in Kenya. Among key questions it seeks to answer include the following: What resources does African traditional heritage offer in addressing the challenge of terrorist violence? What resources does Christianity offer in (re)shaping a new humanity capable of subverting violence? In what ways might the affirmation of the sacredness of human life rooted in the doctrine of the divine image and of Christ help alleviate violence in Kenya? In order to address these concerns, the chapter begins by underscoring indigenous African anthropology so as to establish a foundation for the study to build on. Then it enunciates a contextualized theological anthropology centered on the doctrine of the image of God and on the doctrine of Christ as the basis for what it means to be human in contexts of violence. The thesis is that the Christian theology of the image of God and Christology in the context of the African *ubuntu* (community) provides resources for an anthropology capable of subverting violence. Thus, this chapter addresses the place of Christianity and especially Christian theological anthropology in the formation of people for peaceful coexistence in the context of terror and other forms of violence.

AFRICAN TRADITIONAL ANTHROPOLOGY

What does it mean to be human? Whereas Christians locate the answer to this question within the biblical notion that all human beings are created in God's image, traditional Africans look within themselves and their everyday experiences to explain or at least make sense of who they are. According to most African communities, a human being is simply a person in community surrounded by other beings. Even though African traditional anthropology is anthropocentric, for everything exists for the sake of human beings,[1] it is nonetheless a theocentric anthropology because, for the African, there is no existence apart from God. John Mbiti, a distinguished Kenyan theologian, in his *African Religions and Philosophy*, asserts that for the African, the existence of God is a given, "and in traditional life there are no atheists."[2] In other words, to say something about humanity is to say something about the God who makes life possible in a world of immense difficulties. Indeed, it is also to say something about existence itself.

Mbiti also argues that though African peoples have a strong notion of God, God is not the center of everything; instead, humans are.[3] Being at the center, however, does not mean that humans are masters of the universe.[4] No one can master the world. The world is complex and some issues, especially those that threaten harmony and well-being, are beyond human comprehension. This incomprehensible nature of the world causes African people to place their fate in the hands of the Supreme Being. Bolaji Idowu is right in his observation that God means everything for the African peoples, and if God did not exist, all things would break down.[5]

African traditional anthropology is a relational and holistic anthropology. Relationality, as opposed to mystical and metaphysical concerns, was and still is the concern of most African peoples. Jesse N. K. Mugambi, a notable Kenyan theologian, observes, "African religious and philosophical heritage is characteristically based on physical experi-

---

1. See Mbiti, *African Religions and Philosophy* (1969), 92; Kapolyo, *Human Condition*, 19.
2. Mbiti, *African Religions and Philosophy* (2nd ed.), 29.
3. Ibid., 92.
4. Mbiti, *Introduction to African Religion*, 39.
5. Idowu, *African Traditional Religion*, 104.

mental perception rather than on mystical contemplation."[6] Thus, an African worldview understands all reality in a holistic sense. Everything is interconnected. Humans exist in an intricate web of interconnected relationships that include visible and invisible beings, the living and the dead, the unborn, God, and nature.[7] To be human is to relate, first, with God, the Great *Muntu*, then to relate with neighbors and with the non-human world.

Using categories derived from the Bantu[8] people of Africa, Alexis Kagame delineates four categories of existence in this relational web of which humans are a part. The first category of existence is *Umuntu*, which includes all the life forces with intelligence, including humans, spirits, and the recently deceased. The second category is *Kintu*, which denotes beings without intelligence such as animals, plants, and minerals that may be used for the benefit of *Umuntu* (humans). The third category is *Ahantu*, the "being" of time and space. The fourth category is *Ukuntu*, which covers the "being" of "mode" and includes quality, quantity, laughter, passion, and so on.[9] Perhaps this African cosmic anthropology has the possibility of liberating Christian anthropology from the Hellenistic, Western, and post-enlightenment worldviews that idolized disembodiment (emphasis on the soul), detachment from the natural world, the autonomy and self-sufficiency of reason, and personal freedom, resulting in individualism, elimination of God from reality, and destructive tendencies towards nature. African indigenous anthropology critiques this Western disembodied, spiritualized anthropology, emphasizing instead that life is a web of intricate relationships.

This relational interconnection is expressed in the terms, *ubuntu/umunthu/botho* (South Africa) or *utu/umundu/ujamaa* (East Africa). Of these words *ubuntu* is the most common. Bishop Desmond Tutu of South Africa popularized the term *ubuntu* when he used it to construct a theology of racial reconciliation. In his *No Future without Forgiveness* he explains what it means to say someone has *ubuntu*:

---

6. Mugambi, *God, Humanity and Nature*, 25.

7. Bujo, *Foundations of an African Ethic*, 5.

8. The term "Bantu" is the plural of the term *muntu*, which means humanity. The Bantu are among the four major racial categories in Africa. The others are the Hamites, the Semites, and the Nilotes.

9. Kombo, *Doctrine of God*, 152; Mugambi, *God, Humanity and Nature*, 22.

> *Ubuntu* is very difficult to render into a Western language. It speaks of the very essence of being human. When we want to give high praise to someone we say, "*Yu, u nobuntu*"; "Hey, so-and-so has *ubuntu.*" Then you are generous, you are hospitable, you are friendly and caring and compassionate. You share what you have. It is to say, "My humanity is caught up, is inextricably bound up, in yours." We belong in a bundle of life. We say, "A person is a person through other persons." It is not, "I think therefore I am." It says rather: "I am human because I belong. I participate, I share."[10]

Similarly, Mbiti observes that the African view of humanity can be summarized in the maxim, "I am, because we are; and since we are, therefore I am."[11] Bénézet Bujo likewise asserts, "for Black Africa, it is not the Cartesian *cogito ergo sum* ('I think, therefore I am') but an existential *cognatus sum, ergo sumus* ('I am known, therefore we are') that is decisive."[12] The Kalenjins[13] of Kenya have an adage *chi ko bik*, "a person is people," which means there is no other way to exist except to be in relationship with others. The Kenyan government adopted the word *harambee* ("together we pull") as the national motto of Kenya, while the Tanzanian government embraced *ujamaa* ("familyhood") as their national ethos. Similarly, the Xhosa of South Africa say, "*Ubuntu ungamntu ngabanye abante*" ("each individual's humanity is ideally expressed in relationship with others") and the Sotho, also from South Africa, say, "*Mothoke mmotho ka botbo babang*" ("a person is a person only through other people").[14] These African maxims bring out the importance of relationality in the Africa worldview.

For the African people, a person is not a fully complete being when alone, but becomes complete through a progressive process of social integration, a process that occurs through naming ceremonies, communal rites of passage, and inculcation of discipline through taboos, norms, values, education, and training.[15] This definition of humanity in terms of

10. Tutu, *No Future*, 31.
11. Mbiti, *African Religions and Philosophy* (2nd ed.), 106.
12. Bujo, *Foundations of an African Ethic*, 4.
13. The Kalenjin are an ethnic community of eight culturally and linguistically related "tribes," namely, Nandi, Kipsigis, Keiyo, Marakwet, Pokot, Tugen, Sabaot (Sabiny), and Terik. The writer of this essay is from the Nandi ethnic community.
14. See Fernandez, *Reimagining the Human*, 187; Battle, *Reconciliation*, 39.
15. Ng'weshemi, *Rediscovering the Human*, 15.

social integration tends to dehumanize people who cannot live up to the standards demanded by the society. This is particularly true of Christians who have made a choice not to participate in some ritual practices and is also true of the disabled, especially the developmentally challenged, who are sometimes treated as second-class citizens because they cannot live up to the demands of whatever characterizes full humanity as defined by the community.

Though the community shapes an individual's identity, it is up to the individual to choose to embrace and practice the virtues characteristic of a human being. Not all people act human; some, especially those who harm people, are considered inhuman (cruel/barbaric) or unhuman (bearing animal-like characteristics). The Kalenjins categorize such inhumane/unhuman persons as *sorin* (*sorik*), "evil" people, or *bik che matinye koroti* (people with no human blood). Also, the Kalenjins put it this way: "*Ma chi chi nengero ko chi ama chi*" ("a person is not a person who does not act like a person"). Thus, a person has to act like a person for him or her to be considered human. In summary, a person is fully *umuntu* (human) when he/she treats other human beings as *abantu* (humans) and not as *infintu* (things).[16] This sacred character of human life coheres with the Christian teaching that all human beings are created in God's image and deserve honor. The following explores a Christian theological anthropology.

CHRISTIAN ANTHROPOLOGY: TWO THEOLOGICAL AFFIRMATIONS

This section affirms two basic yet very crucial teachings: (1) the creation of humanity in the image of God (Gen 1:26–27)—including the reality of evil in the world (Gen 3) and the retention of the image of God after the Fall (Gen 5:13; 9:5–6); and (2) the renewal of the image of God in believers through Jesus Christ (2 Cor 4:4; Col 1:15). The essence of being human is revealed by its end, being formed by the Holy Spirit into the image of Jesus Christ (Rom 8:29).[17] By conforming themselves to the image of God in Christ by the Spirit, human beings are born afresh as people able to manifest ethical qualities such as love and peacefulness in a world characterized by hate and violence. In other words, humanity

---

16. Kapolyo, *Human Condition*, 19–27.
17. Shults, *Reforming Theological Anthropology*, 241.

is enriched when it adheres to and lives out ethical qualities of renewed humanity available in Christ by the Holy Spirit.

Before considering these two teachings and their importance for countering human violence, it is important to stress that humans are creatures totally dependent on God for life and sustenance. This is a humbling reality, especially in a world of immense hubris. To add to this, humans are creatures bearing God's life and dignity; humans differ from non-humans and non-living things. Humans are persons, not things to be used or to be abused. In contexts of dehumanization or the violations of human life, affirming this sacred nature of human life is important. Thus, in addition to sharing a common origin, humans are dependent on God and on one another. Consequently, the self-autonomous individualism of the Western world, which is slowly taking root in Africa, is problematic. Humans are called to be individuals-in-community. Bishop Desmond Tutu says it well: "Our humanity is caught up in that of all others. We are human because we belong. We are made for community, for togetherness, for family, to exist in a delicate network of interdependence."[18] Similarly, Douglas Hall observes: "We are creatures whose being implies relatedness. The solitary, isolated, self-sufficient human being—the 'self-made man' that still exists for us as a rhetorical ideal—is, in fact, a contradiction in terms. To be, to be-in-the-world, is to be with."[19]

Affirming this common origin as well as relationality has implications for life today. Humans are God's creations, bearing God's life in them, and thus any harm directed to human beings is a direct affront to God, the Giver of life. As persons, not things, all humans (male and female, able or disabled, rich or poor) deserve the highest respect and honor. Of course, the fact that humans are creatures means that they belong, as the African traditional cosmology attests, to a big web of relationships. Thus, violence or abuse of God's other creations affects humanity directly or indirectly. However, humans are different from the other creatures of the earth. They alone are made in the image and likeness of God. Because *all* human beings *without exception* bear the image of God, they must be esteemed.[20] The following considers what it means to be created in God's image.

18. Tutu, *No Future*, 196.
19. Hall, *Imaging God*, 119.
20. Gushee, *Sacredness of Human Life*, 41.

CREATED IN GOD'S IMAGE

Scripture affirms that human beings are created in God's image and likeness (Gen 1:26–27; 5:1; 9:6; 1 Cor 11:7; Jas 3:9).[21] The New Testament affirms that Jesus Christ is the image of God (2 Cor 4:4; Col 1:15) and that the restoration of the image of God in believers occurs through Jesus (Rom 8:29; 1 Cor 15:49). Some Christian theologians have argued that the Hebrew words for "image" (*demut*) and "likeness" (*tselem*) were not synonymous. Origen, for example, asserted that human beings were created in God's image but they achieve divine likeness through their own efforts.[22] Similarly, Irenaeus saw a sharp distinction between "image" and "likeness" of God, arguing that the "image of God" was something static and essential to human nature and could not be lost, while the "likeness of God" was something dynamic and accidental to human nature and was lost after the Fall into sin.[23] Biblical scholars have established through a study of the ancient Near Eastern societies that there is no evidence that warrants the distinction between these two words.[24] There are four major views on the meaning of "image of God": the substantial, royal functional, relational, and Christocentric views.

The Substantial View

This view argues that the image of God is some specific inner substances or capacities that an individual human being possesses. According to Paul Ramsey, the substantial (or structuralist)[25] view "singles out something *within* the *substantial form* of human nature, some faculty or capacity man possesses, and identifies this as the thing which distinguishes man from physical nature and from other animals."[26] In addition to reason, theologians have identified conscience, aesthetic sense, dominion, spiritual awareness, immortality, freedom, personhood, and moral capacity

---

21. Psalm 8:4–6 also alludes to the image of God. Additionally, the Apocryphal writings allude to the image of God in Wisdom of Solomon 2:23–24; 7:25–26; and Ecclesiasticus (Sirach) 17:1–12.

22. Fairbairn, *Life in the Trinity*, 60.

23. See Shults, *Reforming Theological Anthropology*, 221. It is important to point out that this point is debatable. Finch, "Irenaeus on the Christological Basis," 87–90, argues convincingly for their synonymous interchangeability.

24. See specially Middleton, *Liberating Image*.

25. Brunner, *Christian Doctrine*, 59.

26. Ramsey, *Basic Christian Ethics*, 250.

as the substantial characteristics of human nature that are the "stamp" of the *imago Dei*. The substantial view dominated Western theological anthropology until the Reformation.[27]

The substantial view is problematic for several reasons. First, it leads to individualism because in this view, the image of God is all about what an individual human being is endowed with. Second, this view devalues non-human creation by creating an irremediable dichotomy between humans and non-humans. This may lead to abuse of creation. Third, its emphasis on inward possessions (inner capacities of human nature) denigrates the physical body. Contrary to this disembodied emphasis, Scripture affirms that it is the whole human person who is created in the image of God, who is special in God's sight, and who is being sought for redemption by God. Furthermore, the incarnation and the resurrection of our Lord Jesus affirms the importance of embodied existence. Thus, the emphasis on "inner capacities" and on the soul as the "true" part of what it is to be human is a serious distortion of Christian anthropology.[28] Fourth, its emphasis on reason as the epitome of true humanity dehumanizes human beings who cannot live up to this desired goal, for example, the mentally handicapped.[29]

The Royal Functional View

In the royal functional view, what is underlined is the stewardship of God's creation that humans carry out on behalf of God. Thus, being created in the image of God does not imply possession of substantial qualities of human nature as the substantial view asserts, but the function of humanity as God's representatives on earth. Richard Middleton asserts, "on this reading, the *imago Dei* designates the royal office of calling of human beings as God's representatives and agents in the world, granted authorized power to share in God's rule or administration of the earth's resources and creatures."[30] Being created in the image of God is to act

---

27. Ibid. For more on the influence that the rational view of the image had on Western society, see Cairns, *Image of God*, 110; Hall, *Imaging God*, 93; Middleton, *Liberating Image*, 19.

28. See Wright, *Surprised by Hope*.

29. Thus Gushee, *Sacredness of Human Life*, 43, asks, "Do human beings who lack the designated package of image-bearing capacities stop being human beings, or at least stop being image-bearers?"

30. Middleton, *Liberating Image*, 27.

responsibly in the world. It denotes service or stewardship of God's beautiful ("very good") creation (Gen 1:31).[31]

This functional approach rests on two arguments. Foremost, biblical scholars juxtapose "in our image" and "let them rule" in Gen 1:26, asserting that the later phrase "let them rule" defines the former phrase "in our image." Hence, to image God is to exercise dominion over God's creation.[32] Also, the functional view looks at ancient Near Eastern societies, i.e., the "Mesopotamian (that is, Sumerian, Babylonian, or Assyrian), West Semitic (that is, Canaanite), or Egyptian,"[33] the context in which the Genesis text was written, for clarification of the meaning of "image of God." Christoph Barth explains this extra-biblical evidence that justifies the royal functional view of the image: "Ancient Sumerian, Babylonian, and Egyptian texts speak of kings being shaped in the image of their gods. Mesopotamian kings are hailed as the image of Bel or Shamash, Egyptian kings may boast of being the holy image of Re."[34] Yet the Genesis text expands this image bearing beyond kings; it is all human beings, not just the kings, who are the images (representatives) of God (Gen 1:26–27). Thus, all human beings were made to represent God as God's vice-regents on earth. This act of representing God is not a license for pride and violence in God's world. On the contrary, it involves service and duty, stewardship as a manifestation of God's glory. Indeed, as Calvin noted, stewardship as manifestation of God's glory is stewardship as an act of worship.[35]

The Relational View

The relational view of the image posits that human beings "image" God in an active sense.[36] True, humans possess special qualities or capacities as the functional view posits, but these qualities are not definitive of who they are. In other words, humans are human because they relate. Thus Thomas Reynolds writes, "So the image of God in humankind is not a stable substance or identifiable trait embedded in everyone so much as

---

31. Schwarz, *Human Being*, 23–24.
32. Cortez, *Theological Anthropology*, 22.
33. Middleton, "The Liberating Image," 18.
34. Barth, *God with Us*, 27. See also Clines, *On the Way to Postmodern*, 2:475–80.
35. Calvin, *Institutes* (1559), 1.15.3.
36. Ramsey, *Basic Christian Ethics*, 254. See also Grenz, *Social God*, 162.

a dynamic correspondence to God that plays out variously in relationship to other creatures."[37] Reynolds also adds that humans are relational beings who respond to divine and human address; "We are responseable: responsive, opened up to engage God and other creatures freely."[38] Relationship with God shapes the other relationships because humans are fallen creatures and are not able to unselfishly relate with others unless God helps them to do so.

In addition to arguing for the restoration of relationship between humans and God, the relational view also accentuates the damage that sin caused to the image of God when humans disobeyed God and were banished from the Garden (Gen 3). It argues that the Fall caused a serious deformity of the image of God. Furthermore, sin led to noetic depravity (rationality, understanding, and will are fallen); it damaged the relationship that humans enjoyed with God; and it destroyed the relationship between humans themselves and between humans and non-human creation. Yet all is not lost. The image of God can be repaired, restored, renewed, and set towards obedience to God. Without this restoration of the image of God, humans are incapable of truly fulfilling their God-given mandate to be God's representatives on earth. Jesus Christ is the restorer of the damaged image of God, the restorer of all that human beings lost because of the Fall.

The Christocentric View

The Christocentric view of the image of God defines "image of God" in terms of the ultimate vision of salvation in Christ Jesus. Thus, it connects "image of God" to "image of Christ" and "created image" to "re-created image." For this view, Genesis 1 should be read alongside Genesis 3, and indeed alongside the New Testament Christo-anthropological texts such as Col 1:15 and the texts that underscore the restoration of the image of God in believers such as Eph 4:13.[39] Stanley Grenz, like Paul Ramsey, argues that to understand what it means to be in the image of God, we should appreciate what the New Testament says about it.[40] Grenz adds, "Consequently, the humankind created in the divine image is none other

---

37. Reynolds, *Vulnerable Communion*, 180.
38. Ibid., 182.
39. See Ramsey, *Basic Christian Ethics*, 282, 284.
40. Grenz, *Social God*, 204; Ramsey, *Basic Christian Ethics*, 259.

than the new humanity conformed to the *imago Christi*, and the *telos* toward which the Old Testament creation narrative points is the eschatological community of glorified saints who have joined their head in resurrection life by the power of the Spirit."[41] For Grenz, God's intention in creating human beings in his image was that human beings could exist in community with God in Jesus Christ.[42]

THE IMPLICATIONS OF THE IMAGO DEI FOR SUBVERTING VIOLENCE

Genesis 9:6 and Exod 20:13 affirm the sacredness of human life by firmly prohibiting murder, understood as direct intentional killing of an innocent person.[43] Genesis 9:6 says, "Whoever sheds human blood, by humans shall their blood be shed; for in the image of God has God made mankind." Exodus 20:13 simply says, "You shall not murder." David Gushee offers several possible interpretations of the Gen 9:6 prohibition, among them (1) it could mean that to murder another person is "to come as close as we humans can to killing the God each of us resembles as son or daughter, like Seth resembled Adam (5:1)";[44] (2) it could mean the abuse of our God-given mandate of dominion over God's creation; humans were never created to dominate other humans; (3) it could mean the ultimate rejection of God's sovereignty—by murdering another human life, humans are installing themselves as the givers and takers of life.[45] Gushee also adds that Gen 9:5–6 is not limited to murder only, but expands to include such offenses as "assault, rape, or torture."[46] Rather than devalue human life, we are reminded that human life is sacred and must be respected, even revered.

Gushee also provides a comprehensive Christian definition of what it means to say that human life is sacred:

> This means that God has consecrated each and every human life—without exception and in all circumstances—as a unique, incalculably precious being of elevated status and dignity.

---

41. Grenz, *Social God*, 231–32.
42. Ibid., 332.
43. Gushee, *Sacredness of Human Life*, 49.
44. Ibid.
45. Ibid.
46. Ibid., 51.

Through God's revelation in Scripture and incarnation in Jesus Christ, God has declared and demonstrated the sacred worth of human beings and will hold us accountable for responding appropriately.[47]

Gushee goes on to show the implications of an affirmation of the sacredness of human life. He writes:

Such a response begins by adopting a posture of reverence and by accepting responsibility for the sacred gift that is a human life. It includes offering due respect and care to each human being that we encounter. It extends to an obligation to protect human life from wanton destruction, desecration, or the violation of human rights. A full embrace of the sacredness of human life leads to a full-hearted commitment to foster human flourishing.[48]

From Gushee's definition, it is clear that human life, with its dignity and value, is a gracious gift from God. This reminder is important especially for Kenya. Kenya is a country greatly affected not only by terrorist and ethnic violence, but also by wanton destruction of lives through lynching (mob justice) of those accused of alleged crimes, and other forms of violence.[49] After studying over 1,500 cases of lynching in Kenya from August 1996 to August 2013, Robert Guy McKee laments that lynching in Kenya has been accepted "for better or for worse, as part of [the] national culture."[50] Unfortunately, even the media appears to treat this matter casually. McKee asserts,

Similarly, lynchings are seldom front-page news; they are likely, rather, to be reported as briefs, or as regional or local news, or as non-headline items in crime roundup articles. When reported as one of however many briefs—as, e.g., in a narrow vertical column of such—a lynching brief might appear anywhere from top to bottom in the column; when reported as a non-headline item in a crime roundup, the lynching item is often introduced—consistent with its relative lack of salience in the roundup—by a sentence beginning with "Meanwhile, . . . " or "Elsewhere, . . . "

---

47. Ibid., 33.
48. Ibid.
49. Mckee, "Lynchings."
50. Ibid., 4.

The text of some newspaper lynching reports is no longer than a single sentence.[51]

Contrary to this wanton destruction of human life, Kenyans, especially Christians, should engender an alternative way of being human, an alternative appropriate to those created in God's image and whom God dearly loves. This means that terrorists and those suspected of having ties to terrorism are also precious in God's eyes because they too are created in God's image. Viewing them this way does not mean condoning what they do, but advocates treating them, especially when arrested, as human beings, and allowing them to undergo a judicial process of justice. In summary, Kenyans should question the wanton destruction of human life and instead oppose it. The next section explores a Christ-centered anthropology, which is the second theological affirmation.

A CHRISTO-CENTRIC ANTHROPOLOGY

Several scholars highlight the significance of Jesus as the true definition of what it means to be human. Describing Jesus as the "true humanity,"[52] the "perfect realization of true humanity,"[53] "what human nature is intended to be,"[54] these Christ-centered anthropologies show that Jesus is the standard for what it means to be human. In these anthropologies, Jesus is the true embodiment, the archetype, the pinnacle of what it means to be human. He is the image of God *par excellence* and the *telos* (goal) of humanity. In other words, Christ exemplifies what humans are called to be—and destined to be. For Kenyan Christians, Jesus is the authentic person who truly lived out what Kenyan people are unable, on their own, to live out. He displayed qualities of humanness that Kenyan people long for. All the virtues espoused in African traditional life such as hospitality, courage, heroism, and more, were clearly visible in Christ's own life. Even more important is that Jesus redeemed humanity from the evil that prevents them from being truly human. In other words, Jesus Christ enables the overcoming of the condition of sin that hinders us from living as God intended. Thus, Jesus exists not just to model or

---

51. Ibid., 6.
52. Sherlock, *Doctrine of Humanity*, 18.
53. Cortez, *Christological Anthropology*, 20.
54. Erickson, *Christian Theology*, 532.

exemplify good humanity, as if he was merely playing the role of a good village chief, but instead, he is the Savior of fallen humanity.

Jesus Christ is the builder of community. The Fall distorted all relationships; the relationship between humans themselves and between humans and the non-human world was utterly corrupted and distorted (Gen 3:12–13; Rom 8:19–22). But in Christ all social relationships are mended and shaped into more God-glorifying relationships. The church is the place where this shaping and formation of relationships occurs. Though imperfect, the church is the community of God's people, a visible manifestation of a new humanity being born.[55] Therefore, Christians are, or ought to be, agents of Christ's redemption (2 Cor 5:18, 20). Christians should embody the fruit of the Spirit: love, joy, peace, forbearance, kindness, goodness, faithfulness, gentleness, and self-control (Gal 5:22–23). The fruit of the Spirit is but a taste of the reality of being in Christ. Yet this Christian formation or transformation into Christ's image is an ongoing process (Rom 8:29; 12:2; 2 Cor 3:18; Gal 4:19). Having experienced the benefits of being in God's family, the church should live out those benefits so that those who are still outside God's family may be drawn to come in and be a part of it. The more the church faithfully lives out what it means to be a New Humanity born of Christ, the more the circle of evil in the world is broken. The New Humanity in Christ is a powerful healing force in a world of hatred and violence.[56]

The life of Christ illustrates the finitude and vulnerability of human existence. This point is very necessary for Kenyans to grasp (not only because of the threat of terrorism, for terrorism shows the fleeting nature of human life) but because Kenyan people generally abhor weakness and vulnerability. For the African people, the world is centered on power and the use of power for personal, social, and spiritual purposes.[57] In such a worldview, the prevalent choice is strength not weakness. Evidences for such a power-centered worldview are available in the world of Kenyan politics where it is all about capturing power, staying in power, using all means to get to the top, and amassing as much wealth as you can when you get to the top of the power chain.[58] Sadly, Kenyan politicians

55. Fernandez, *Reimagining the Human*, 154.
56. See Grenz, *Social God*, 224–52; Fernandez, *Reimagining the Human*, ch. 8.
57. See Okesson, *Re-Imaging Modernity*.
58. For more on Kenyan politics, see Gifford, *Christianity, Politics and Public Life in Kenya*.

capitalize on ethnic affiliations to capture and/or retain power. Contrary to this dangerous ethnocentric power politics, Scripture attests that Christians are to transcend ethnic divisions.[59] Also, contrary to this power-centered worldview, Christ shows that weakness and vulnerability are not deficiencies; they are the source of a different more effective power. Even Christ himself was not powerful in the way of this world. Rather, he was weak. "He had no beauty or majesty to attract us to him, nothing in his appearance that we should desire him" (Isa 53:2). He was broken, "despised and rejected by mankind, a man of suffering, and familiar with pain" (Isa 53:3).

Acceptance of finitude and vulnerability can be liberating in various ways. At the outset, it will help in fully accepting the humanity of people who may seem to be imperfect in human eyes, such as the disabled and the mentally ill.[60] In addition, it subverts the quest for worldly power and rule that often leads to inhumanness. In other words, an understanding of what it means to be human from the lens of frailty helps tame the dragon of lust for power that sometimes drives humans to commit unimaginable atrocities. Likewise, recognition of finitude and vulnerability deepens our longing for God. Paul exclaimed in worship, "For when I am weak, then I am strong" (2 Cor 12:10).

Christ's response to violence is a necessary reminder of the necessity to embrace life in fullness. Jesus prohibited violence as a way to deal with personal conflicts and attacks (Matt 5:38–48; 26:51–52; Luke 9:54–55). He showed his followers alternative ways of peace and forgiveness, even when confronted with seemingly destructive forces of violence (Matt 5:23–24; 18:22).[61] Because of this courageous and radical alternative to violence, followers of Christ can now truly say that they do not have to be slaves of violence nor can they perpetrate evil, for indeed, even upon the cross Jesus chose the way of forgiveness to his tormentors instead of hatred and revenge (Luke 23:34). Therefore, Jesus' extreme suffering on the cross was an affirmation of the value of life. Christian Duquoc captures this truth when he says:

---

59. See, for example, Acts 1:8; 2:17–18; Rom 1:16; 10:12, 13; 9:9–29. Furthermore, the Bible envisions, at the end of this age, all people groups worshiping together before God's throne (Rev 5:9; 7:9).

60. *Christian Perspectives on Theological Anthropology*, 36.

61. Gushee, *Sacredness of Human Life*, 87.

> Jesus did not die on a cross to prove the truth of the ascetic ideal, to justify or glorify suffering or to denigrate the love of life. He died to show how seriously respect for others and the liberation of the weak should be taken. He died so that justice may come into the world; his violent death bears witness to the inhumanity of our social systems and shows up the illusion of believing that it is possible to live in a secure oasis of happiness and well-being provided one cares nothing for others or allows them to be exploited.[62]

Hence, in Christ, Christians can work at being more peaceful, intentionally committing to fostering human flourishing, and to cultivating honor and respect for human life.

Christ affirms the power of forgiveness in the face of violence. Christ confronted violence through love, forgiveness, and compassion. Hanging on the cross, he looked down on those torturing his body and did not demand vengeance from his followers. He knew that vengeance is corrosive, even destructive, and only robs people of their humanness. By choosing the way of forgiveness, Christ freed himself (and ourselves) from violence's tight grip. On Calvary, Christ showed that evil does not have the last word. Bishop Tutu lends weight to this point: "For us who are Christians, the death and resurrection of Jesus Christ is proof positive that love is stronger than hate, that life is stronger than death, that light is stronger than darkness, that laughter and joy, and compassion and gentleness and truth, all these are so much stronger than their ghastly counterparts."[63] Therefore, Christians are called, not only to affirm and embody the sacredness of human life, but to engender an alternative lifestyle; instead of violence and hatred, peace and love. Christians must also foster alternative practices of peace. They should seek the welfare of their neighbors. They should, like Christ, help the needy, call for justice, protect men, women, and children from abuse, and foster basic human rights.

CONCLUSION

Despite the challenge of terrorism in Kenya, there is a paucity of theological responses to it. More needs to be done to address all forms of violence in Kenya and to foster human dignity. This chapter does not

---

62. Duquoc, "Folly of the Cross," 72.
63. Tutu, *No Future*, 86.

claim to be the entire answer that Kenyan Christians have been looking for in their quest to make sense of their lives in the context of terror, but it is a response aimed at initiating conversations. The chapter proposes a contextualized theological anthropology rooted in the Christian theology of the image of God, the Christ event, and the African concept of *ubuntu* (community). It shows that in affirming these two Christian tenets within the African ethos of community, Christians in Kenya will not only affirm the sacredness of human life but will also seek to model their lives after Jesus, the authentic man, who shows all humans how to be human, especially in response to hatred and violence.

REFERENCES

Barth, Christoph. *God with Us: A Theological Introduction to the Old Testament*. Edited by Geoffrey William Bromiley. Grand Rapids: Eerdmans, 1991.

Battle, Michael. *Reconciliation: The Ubuntu Theology of Desmond Tutu*. Cleveland: Pilgrim, 2009.

Brunner, Emil. *The Christian Doctrine of Creation and Redemption*. Translated by Olive Wyon. Philadelphia: Westminster, 1952.

Bujo, Bénézet. *Foundations of an African Ethic: Beyond the Universal Claims of Western Morality*. New York: Crossroad, 2001.

Cairns, David. *The Image of God in Man*. London: SCM, 1953.

Calvin, John. *Institutes of the Christian Religion*. Edited by John T. McNeil. Translated by Ford Lewis Battles. 2 vols. Library of Christian Classics. Philadelphia: Westminster, 1960.

Christian Perspectives on Theological Anthropology. Faith and Order 199. Geneva: World Council of Churches, 2005.

Clines, David J. A. *On the Way to the Postmodern: Old Testament Essays, 1967–1998*. 2 vols. Journal for the Study of the Old Testament, Supplemental Series 293. Sheffield: Sheffield Academic, 1998.

Cortez, Marc. *Christological Anthropology in Historical Perspective: Ancient and Contemporary Approaches to Theological Anthropology*. Grand Rapids: Zondervan, 2016.

———. *Theological Anthropology: A Guide for the Perplexed*. New York: T. & T. Clark, 2010.

Duquoc, Christian. "The Folly of the Cross and the 'The Human.'" In *Is Being Human a Criterion of Being Christian?*, edited by Jean-Pierre Jossua and Claude Geffré. *Concilium* 155 (1982) 65–73.

Erickson, Millard. *Christian Theology*. Grand Rapids: Baker, 1998.

Fairbairn, Donald. *Life in the Trinity: An Introduction to Theology with the Help of the Church Fathers*. Downers Grove, IL: IVP Academic, 2009.

Fernandez, Eleazar S. *Reimagining the Human: Theological Anthropology in Response to Systemic Evil*. St. Louis, MO: Chalice, 2004.

Finch, Jeffrey. "Irenaeus on the Christological Basis of Human Divinization." In *Theosis: Deification in Christian Theology*, 1:86–103. Cambridge: James Clarke, 2006.

Gifford, Paul. *Christianity, Politics and Public Life in Kenya*. London: Hurst, 2009.

Grenz, Stanley J. *The Social God and the Relational Self: A Trinitarian Theology of the Imago Dei*. Louisville, KY: Westminster, 2001.

Gushee, David P. *The Sacredness of Human Life: Why an Ancient Biblical Vision Is Key to the World's Future*. Grand Rapids: Eerdmans, 2013.

Hall, Douglas John. *Imaging God: Dominion as Stewardship*. Grand Rapids: Eerdmans, 1986.

Idowu, Bolaji E. *African Traditional Religion: A Definition*. London: SCM, 1973.

Kapolyo, Joe M. *The Human Condition: Christian Perspective through African Eyes*. Carlisle: Langham Global, 2005.

Kombo, James Henry Owino. *The Doctrine of God in African Christian Thought: The Holy Trinity, Theological Hermeneutics and the African Intellectual Culture*. Leiden: Brill, 2007.

Mbiti, John S. *African Religions and Philosophy*. London: Heinemann, 1969.

———. *African Religions and Philosophy*. 2nd ed. London: Heinemann, 1990.

———. *Introduction to African Religion*. London: Heinemann, 1975.

Mckee, Guy Robert. "Lynchings in Modern Kenya and Inequitable Access to Basic Resources: A Major Human Rights Scandal and One Contributing Cause." *GIAL Special Electronic Publications* (2013). www.gial.edu/documents/McKee_Lynchings.pdf. Accessed October 14, 2015.

Middleton, Richard J. "The Liberating Image? Interpreting the *Imago Dei* in Context." *Christian Scholar's Review* 24 (1994) 8–25.

———. *The Liberating Image: The* Imago Dei *in Genesis 1*. Grand Rapids: Brazos, 2005.

Mugambi, Jesse N. K. *God, Humanity and Nature in Relation to Justice and Peace*. Geneva: World Council of Churches, 1987.

Ng'weshemi, Andrea M. *Rediscovering the Human: The Quest for a Christo-Theological Anthropology in Africa*. New York: Peter Lang, 2002.

Okesson, Gregg A. *Re-Imaging Modernity: A Contextualized Theological Study of Power and Humanity within Akamba Christianity in Kenya*. American Society of Missiology Monograph Series. Eugene, OR: Pickwick, 2012.

Ramsey, Paul. *Basic Christian Ethics*. New York: Scribner, 1950.

Reynolds, Thomas E. *Vulnerable Communion: A Theology of Disability and Hospitality*. Grand Rapids: Brazos, 2008.

Schwarz, Hans. *The Human Being: A Theological Anthropology*. Grand Rapids: Eerdmans, 2013.

Sherlock, Charles. *The Doctrine of Humanity*. Downers Grove, IL: InterVarsity, 1996.

Shults, F. LeRon. *Reforming Theological Anthropology: After the Philosophical Turn to Relationality*. Grand Rapids: Eerdmans, 2003.

Tutu, Desmond. *No Future without Forgiveness*. New York: Doubleday, 1999.

Wright, N. T. *Surprised by Hope: Rethinking Heaven, the Resurrection, and the Mission of the Church*. New York: HarperOne, 2008.

7

"We Have No More Cheeks to Turn"
Christian and Muslim Responses to Terrorism in Kenya

Joseph Wandera

While the twentieth century was the most violent in recorded history, the twenty-first century has begun with genocides and acts of violence seemingly on every side.[1] Since 2010, incidents of violence with religious, ethnic, or sectarian dimensions appear to be on the increase. This would seem to be a reversal of a steady overall decline in armed and, more generally, identity-based conflict that characterized the post-Cold-War era.[2] In 2014 alone, violence along ethnic lines in Iraq, Syria, the Central Africa Republic, Myanmar, and Ukraine captured media headlines, reflecting troubling scenarios of mass atrocities. Such tragedies replace situations of peaceful coexistence with deep tensions and conflict along religious, sectarian, or ethnic lines.

Kenya, like many countries in the world, is struggling with the pressing challenge of terrorist attacks. These attacks can be understood through the lenses of international, regional, and local networks, including al-Qaeda, the Islamic State of Iraq and Levant (ISIL), Boko Haram, and al-Shabaab. As a frontline state in the war against terror in the Horn of Africa, Kenya has suffered numerous attacks during the last decade. These attacks increased dramatically after the October 2011 deployment of Kenya's Defense Forces in Somalia for a coordinated operation chris-

---

1. See Rummel, *Death by Government*.
2. Cox, Osborn, and Sisk, "Religion."

tened Operation Linda Nchi (Swahili for "secure the country") against the al-Shabaab insurgents in southern Somalia. By mounting this military operation, the Kenyan government hoped to degrade the capacity of al-Shabaab to launch attacks in Kenya. Since then, a spate of attacks has destabilized a swathe of Kenya's rural counties, and brought terror into Nairobi, Kenya's capital, with its more than six million inhabitants. Violence and insecurity have spread, as has fear, combined with ethnic, religious, and regional divisions, and profiling. For example, in Eastleigh, Nairobi's busy suburb inhabited mainly by Somalis, a grenade explosion in a Kariobangi-bound *matatu* (taxi), killing several people and injuring others, shattered the otherwise quite fragile community relations and sparked inter-ethnic violence against the dominant Somali group in Eastleigh.[3]

There is often an assumption that religious actors speak with one voice and can help stem hostilities. This chapter examines the discourse of select church leaders who preside over extensive congregations and who wield significant influence. It is demonstrated in this chapter that every religious tradition expresses "multi-vocality," evidence of social differentiation within Kenyan churches and also between Christian leaders and their Islamic counterparts. However, a clear sectarian theme characterizes responses from the church leaders, with the possibility of negatively impacting interfaith relations. Thus, religion can play the highly ambivalent role of exacerbating exclusion and jeopardizing cohesion in the various contexts. Christian responses to the attacks become more salient when examined within the larger context of engagement with the state and public life. While numerous studies have been carried out on terror attacks globally and locally,[4] very few have focused specifically on the responses of Christian religious leaders and their effects on Christian–Muslim relations.

DISCOURSE ANALYSIS

Religion has often been studied as a system of symbols that exists independently of the actors.[5] However, more recently scholars of religion are paying increasing attention to individual actors and, significantly,

---

3. Mayabi, "Inter-ethnic Clash."

4. See, for example, Holloway, 9/11 *and the War on Terror*, and Ward, *Law, Text, Terror*.

5. Geertz, *Interpretation of Culture*, 470.

to the dialectical relationship between systems and actors.[6] In this approach, the focus is on individual religious actors (leaders) within a discourse with the objective of gaining insight into the relationship between religious discourse and inter-faith cohesion. As artifacts of a political culture, the respective discourses reveal prevalent public opinion on particular issues with direct or indirect effects on members of society.

Generally, discourses within the church regarding terror attacks have centered on key themes such as *Jihad* by Muslims against Christians and perceptions among Christian leaders that Muslim religious leaders have lacked commitment to inter-religious relations. Such discourse fragments Christian–Muslim relationships. Yet other observers have seen terror attacks as products of misguided criminal persons, not as acts of religiously motivated players. The latter offer the possibility of improved inter-religious relations. The analytic premise assumes that the way individuals speak about others can create and recreate a positive social reality within which to view others. In other words, the construction of society provides for the articulation of differences, rendered as generalized meanings though only within specific symbolic systems. In that sense, discourse (language) is a form of social praxis and an agent of social transformation. The critical discourse perspective provides a framework within which to address the lingual-cultural ideas and practices that generate disharmony.

LOCATING KENYA

Kenya shares a 682-kilometre border with Somalia.[7] The political instability in Somalia, triggered by the collapse of the government in 1991, greatly impacted the political and economic situation in Kenya.[8] Demographically, Kenya's population totals approximately 40 million people, of which 45 percent live below the poverty line. Religious demographics are highly contested, with Muslims claiming that government statistics on the number of Muslims in the country are deliberately understated, thus marginalizing Muslim presence in the country. Although the country is predominantly Christian, a substantial and vocal minority are Muslims. Estimates regarding the number of Muslims in Kenya

---

6. Asad, *Genealogies of Religion*.
7. Fakude, "Can Kenya Avoid a Sectarian Conflict?"
8. Ibid.

range from a conservative 10 to 15 percent to approximately 20 percent.[9] Today, religious demographics are not reflected in the national census.

Kenya is also a country of great ethnic and linguistic diversity. However, ethnic and sub-national groups such as the Nubian and Somali minorities often claim marginalization with regard to political representation and resource allocation. Somali Kenyans have historically inhabited the North Eastern province bordering present-day Somalia. Contestation of whether the North Eastern province should continue to be part of Kenya has skewed the country's relationships with Somalia and the Somali ethnic group within Kenya until today. In an article titled "Rendering Difference Visible: The Kenyan State and Its Somali Citizens," Emma Lochery examines the history of Somalis in Kenya through the lens of a screening exercise organized by the government in 1989, ostensibly to distinguish citizens from non-citizens,[10] especially during the early period of Kenya's independence. Lochery argues that "dynamics of inter-ethnic and intra-ethnic competition shape the production of citizenship in Kenya."[11] In this context, Kenyan Somalis claim to have difficulties in accessing citizenship papers, compared to other Kenyans.[12] Although suspicion, tension, and conflict have plagued Kenya's history from the beginning, these dynamics have increased in recent years, occasioned by a variety of factors such as political and economic stress. Linguistic minorities such as the Terik, the Sengwer, and the Suba are challenged by the near extinction of their respective languages.

MUSLIM–CHRISTIAN ENCOUNTERS IN AFRICA

Muslim–Christian encounters in Africa south of the Sahara from the fifteenth to the twentieth centuries could be characterized as encounters between European Christians and Muslims.[13] These encounters were adversarial and competitive in nature with each group seeking political dominance, commercial possibilities, and converts.[14] This general ap-

---

9. Oded, *Islam and Politics in Kenya*, 1.
10. Lochery, "Rendering Difference Visible." See also Murunga, "Cosmopolitan Tradition," 473, among others.
11. Lochery, "Rendering Difference Visible," 3.
12. Ibid.
13. Azumah, "Church and Islam in Africa."
14. Ibid.

proach towards Muslims had far-reaching effects on Christian–Muslim relations that are still in evidence today.

There were trading contacts between East Africa and Western Asia even before the coming of Islam. The East African coast formed part of the western side of the Indian Ocean and was an important destination in the monsoon-based trade.[15] It was in this context that Islam entered the coast of East Africa. Archaeologists have discovered a mosque and Muslim burial sites at Shanga in the Lamu archipelago (off the eastern coast of Kenya) dated between AD 780 and 850.[16] Trading activities on the coast reached a climax between 1000 and 1500.[17] By 1300 Islam had transformed and incorporated the East African coast into the Islamic religious and cultural world. When Ibn Battuta visited it during the fourteenth century, Kilwa, one of the Swahili towns on the coast, was occupied by Muslims and ruled by a Sultan.

The broader context of the entry of the Portuguese to the coast was due in part to the competition between Christians and Muslims. The Portuguese were inspired by Henry the Navigator's goal of conquering Muslim lands. The Arabs resented this encounter and regarded the Christians as "infidels." Thus, according to Baur, "encounters between Portuguese and Arabs on both sides of the Indian Ocean took place in the spirit of crusade and *Jihad*, the holy wars of Christians and Muslims."[18]

Christian–Muslim encounters during the second phase of missionary work in East Africa were similarly disputatious between agents of the two faith traditions, interspersed with some moments of mutuality. Dr. Johann Ludwig Krapf, a Lutheran missionary from Germany working with the Church Missionary Society (the Anglican CMS), arrived at the Sultan's palace in Zanzibar in 1844 and moved to Mombasa "to convert the unbelieving world."[19] Although the CMS was the first of the modern mission organizations to work on the East African coast, it had no intention of working among Muslims, nor was Islam mentioned as a motivation for working with people of the interior. This was due largely to the fact that members of the mission thought that Islam in the region was stagnant and posed no threat to their work. As the organi-

15. Horton and Middleton, *The Swahili*, 72–78.
16. Pouwels, "East African Coast."
17. Ibid., 253.
18. Baur, 2000 *Years of Christianity in Africa*, 86.
19. Ibid., 224.

zation expanded inland, and as missionaries observed Muslims in the region, its attitude and strategies toward Islam shifted towards a more proselytizing approach. By the end of the nineteenth century, concern regarding the growth of Islam had become one of the main motivations for mission work in East Africa. By the 1890s, a clear change in strategy and rhetoric concerning Islam had taken place. During the twentieth century, the missionaries regarded Islam as a serious threat to the spread of Christianity that needed to be curtailed. Later, this general approach to Islam was to characterize discourses and relationships between Christians and Muslims in many parts of East Africa, including Kenya. Scholars soon made the observation that Muslims were marginalized within the body politic of Kenya in a variety of ways.[20] Others scholars confirm that Muslims have been marginalized throughout Kenya's history, but from a different perspective.[21] Kresse, for example, cites President Moi's threat in the early 1980s to eliminate the Kadhi courts.[22] Other scholars have confirmed this marginal position of Muslims, but note, on the other hand, how some Muslims benefitted from the post-colonial state. For example, Constantin has documented a common pattern of Muslim accommodation to post-colonial East African states.[23]

During the rule of Kenya's second president, Daniel arap Moi, Christian symbolism pervaded the body politic in support of his authoritarian rule. Not all religious minorities could be accommodated by the accepted symbolism.[24] It was common during that era to see the then president attending church service each Sunday, sometimes commenting on spiritual and social questions over an open Bible after the worship services. It was also common to hear the president refer to the Muslim community as "slave" merchants. Ironically, Moi's tenure as president was also characterized by economic decline, infrastructural collapse, and ethnic and religious tension, thus reducing the vast majority of Kenyans to socio-economic and political subservience.

There have also been studies on developments since the 1990s demonstrating how the global revival of Islam has noticeably impacted Kenyan Muslims. The Supreme Council of Kenya Muslims (SUPKEM)

20. Mazrui, "Ethnicity and Pluralism."
21. Kresse, "Muslim Politics," 76–86.
22. Ibid.
23. Constantin, "Leadership, Muslim Identities."
24. Mazrui, "Ethnicity and Pluralism."

became more assertive, challenging the erstwhile accommodation of politics of the day.[25] Generally Muslims have become more fervent practitioners of religious obligations, such as prayer multiple times a day. Nairobi and its suburbs are dotted with numerous mosques that regularly announce the Muslim calls to prayer.

"WE HAVE TURNED THE OTHER CHEEK, BUT NOW THE CHEEKS HAVE RUN OUT": NARRATIVES AND THE CONSTRUCTION OF THE "OTHER"

The terror attacks have demonstrated and exacerbated the deep suspicion and tension between some Christians and Muslims in contemporary Kenya. The most disturbing characteristic of contemporary Christian–Muslim relations is attitudes prejudicial to the "other." For example, today it is commonly assumed that Muslims are associated with violence. In Kenya, prejudicial thoughts, ideas, and expressions with regard to Muslims are evident in the public sphere. Today when Christians comment on the terror attacks they ask, "Why do all terrorists profess the Islamic faith?" "Why were only Christians killed during the attacks?"

However, the terror events have also led to differences within both Christian and Islamic traditions, with religious leaders espousing varying positions with regard to the challenge of terror. Some Christian leaders want to resort to extra-biblical measures, such as being equipped with guns, thus undermining the central Christian teaching of "turning the other cheek." It was a shift similar to adopting the security measures deployed by secular governments during moments of crisis. The resort to declaring security measures was the product of leading theorists of the so-called Copenhagen School, led by Ole Wæver and Barry Buzan, who generally referred to the declaring of security measures as a successful speech act "through which an intersubjective understanding is constructed within a political community to treat something as an existential threat to a valued referent object, and to enable a call for urgent and exceptional measures to deal with the threat."[26] Within this security matrix, religious leaders resorted to extraordinary, even extra-biblical measures as responses to the attacks.

---

25. Oded, "Islamic Extremism in Kenya."
26. Buzan and Wæver, "Regions and Powers: Summing Up and Looking Ahead."

Ironically, the frustration of church leaders expressed in their appeal to extra-canonical resources to meet the challenge of terror clearly paralleled the concerns raised by human rights activists when government resorted to extra-judicial killings, unlawful arrests, and renditioning (government sponsored abduction and extra-judicial international transfer of persons) in the wake of terror attacks. Meanwhile the Kenyan National Commission on Human Rights (KNCHR) issued a report titled, "The Error of Fighting Terror with Terror," advocating that the fight against terror be "pursued in compliance with the law and with the utmost respect for the rule of law, democracy, human rights and fundamental freedoms."[27] Some Pentecostal religious leaders have called upon the government to provide them with guns for security, while others appeared to reject the biblical injunction to "turn the other cheek."[28]

The rhetorical statement "We have no more cheeks to turn," attributed to the General Secretary of the National Council of Churches of Kenya (NCCK), represented the deep anger and frustration of some church leaders with what they perceived as an incessant and well-planned campaign against Christians. In the wake of the attacks on Garissa University College, some church leaders in Kenya accused Muslim scholars of half-hearted condemnation of radicalization. Evangelical leaders and leaders of other mainline Protestant churches allied to the National Council of Churches (NCCK) issued a joint statement: "The attack was committed by people professing the Islamic faith, but we have noted a marked indifference by the Muslim leadership to addressing the challenges of Islamist radicalization in the country in a forthright manner."[29] Reading from the same statement, the General Secretary of the National Council of Churches of Kenya, Canon Peter Karanja, appealed to biblical texts (Luke 6:29; Matt 5:39) when he stated: "We have often turned the other cheek, but with the massacre of Christian students at Garissa University College, the cheeks have run out."[30] In effect, Canon Karanja appeared to threaten revenge in response to the terror attacks. It was not clear though, whether such revenge would target al-Shabaab opera-

---

27. Kenyan National Commission on Human Rights, "The Error of Fighting Terror with Terror," 2, quotes this Article 238 (2) b of the Kenya Constitution.

28. Beja, "Church Leaders Demand Guns."

29. Bishop Julius Wanyoike, Anglican Church of Kenya, quoted in Kithogo, "Churches Accuse Muslim Scholars."

30. Kithogo, "Churches Accuse Muslim Scholars."

tives or Muslims in general. Not surprisingly, a Christian commentator responded, "Let them borrow some cheeks from Jesus!"[31]

On the one hand, one can understand the broader context of the statement as an expression of frustration by Christian leaders in the wake of the attacks and their appeal for the use of extraordinary measures to bring the attacks to an end. On the other hand, there is concern regarding the possible effects on social cohesion of statements coming from an influential church body in Kenya. While the deep anger following the attacks was not in doubt, the general mood in the country should have inclined religious leaders to moderate their public statements, thus fostering a sense of calm and, more importantly, reducing the possibility of inter-religious tension and violence. In commenting on tragic events of this nature, one is morally bound to speak truth while being sensitive at the same time to the social consequences of an untoward utterance. While it is true that some Muslims leaders have not spoken out against acts of terror, many others have roundly condemned the attacks. The central Christian teaching on maintaining peace and not responding with evil to unjust treatment must never be compromised. This teaching closely resembles the Islamic tradition of *amr bil ma'aruf nahy anil munkar* (enjoining what is good and forbidding what is evil).[32]

Another statement released by the Christian Leaders' Consultative Forum after a one-day consultative meeting on terror was dated 15 April 2015 and titled "Standing with the Christian Faith." The statement was produced by the General Secretary of NCCK, Canon Peter Karanja, Bishop Mark Kariuki of the Evangelical Alliance of Kenya (EAK), and Fr Charles Odira (KCCB), among others. The leaders stated: "It is naïve for anyone to imply that the so-called terrorism in Kenya is anything other than *Jihad* against Christians." Once again, this was an irresponsible statement coming from the Christian leadership in Kenya that could easily have led to violent encounters between Christians and Muslims. The leaders' interpretation of *Jihad* in purely militaristic terms was an attempt to frame Islam as a violent religious tradition. It overlooked the spiritual meaning of *Jihad* elucidated in the Qur'an and in the teaching of Muhammad.[33] In general, mainline Protestant and Catholic leaders who participated in interreligious convocations in the past have tended

---

31. Conversation with Caleb Likhanga, Nairobi, 6 December 2015.
32. Cook, *Commanding Right*.
33. Ali and Rehman, "Concept of *Jihad*."

to be more tempered in their statements and mostly displayed a more gracious attitude towards Muslims, while leaders from the Pentecostal traditions tended to be more harsh and judgmental toward Muslims. However, a shift of positions can be detected, with leaders from mainline churches who ordinarily tended to be accommodating in their outlook regarding interreligious relations now moving toward less charitable modes of engagement.

ALTERNATIVE VOICES

> You show that you are a letter from Christ delivered by us, written not with ink but with the Spirit of the living God, not on tablets of stone, but on tables of human hearts (2 Cor 3:3).

Human faces are living letters in inter-religious relationships. Not all Christian leaders, and certainly not all Christians, were in agreement with calls for arming pastors with guns. Similarly, in the face of the terror attacks, not all Christians expressed an inability or perhaps the impracticality of upholding the biblical injunction of "turning the other cheek." Many Christians restrained themselves from describing the attacks as violent *Jihads* targeting Christians. Instead, they made a deliberate choice to be conciliatory, demonstrating that even during the most trying moments, friendship was possible. Such leaders helped shape positive attitudes of Christians towards Muslims and vice versa. It is to those voices that our analysis now turns.

Fr Wilybard Lagho, Catholic Archdiocese vicar-general, together with a segment of Muslim clerics in Mombasa, distanced themselves from the call to arm religious leaders, arguing that such action would be counterproductive. Instead, Fr Lagho appealed to Christian leaders to use what he termed "inclusive language" while preaching, to promote religious cohesion.[34] Fr Lagho said, "We do not support the Redeemed Church's request to the government to arm Christian preachers with guns because that is contrary to the nonviolence Christian teaching."[35] He pointed out that de-radicalization of militant religious extremists should be the main concern. Such statements from religious leaders attempted to move beyond the immediate tragedy of the moment and seek possible underlying motivations for the attacks. Similarly, despite

34. "Catholics Oppose Call to Arm Preachers."
35. Ibid.

the attacks in Garissa, the Coadjutor Bishop of the Catholic diocese of Garissa, Bishop Joseph Alessandro, emphasized the good relations between Christians and Muslims in Garissa, citing various initiatives toward peaceful coexistence prior to and following the terror attacks. Unlike the earlier statements from some evangelical church leadership and the NCCK, the Catholic bishop deliberately cited the efforts by Muslim leaders in Garissa to reach out to the church to express solidarity with those affected by the attacks.[36]

In focusing on positive interreligious engagements, the bishop was demonstrating alternative, more constructive approaches to interreligious dialogue. He deliberately chose not to describe the entire Muslim faithful negatively and instead focused on the positive gestures of friendship and solidarity that were extended by the Muslims. The teaching of the Second Vatican Council that strongly encouraged interreligious relations might explain the comparatively charitable attitude that emerged from the Catholic Church leadership at this time.

It is no longer adequate for members of various religious traditions to merely talk about their respective beliefs. Practical joint gestures of goodwill must accompany active bridge building. Other symbolic gestures of friendship and solidarity between Christian and Muslim leaders have followed terror attacks. For example, in an event organized by the Interreligious Council of Kenya, a coalition of all major faith communities in Kenya, together with the council of Imams and Preachers of Kenya, church leaders from around Nairobi joined Muslims for Friday prayers at the *Jamia* Mosque, arguably the largest mosque in Kenya. Participating church leaders came from a broad range of denominations. During this visit, the Christian leaders were first taken on a tour of *Jamia* Mosque and then observed the Friday prayers from a place reserved for them. Later they shared lunch with their Muslim hosts. They agreed to visit each other's places of worship as expressions of solidarity, thus discouraging intolerance among their adherents.[37] In a statement to the media, an official of *Jamia* Mosque stated: "Our brothers and sisters are here as a gesture of cooperation and understanding that should exist between us. Where there is understanding, there is tolerance."[38] This

---

36. Onyalla, "Bishops in Kenya Emphasize Good Relations."
37. Kiplagat, "Church Leaders Now Visit City Mosque."
38. Ibid.

visit and the accompanying symbolic gestures by Christian and Muslim leaders were incarnating the words of Pope Francis:

> Meeting each other, seeing each other face to face, exchanging the embrace of peace, and praying for each other, are essential aspects of our journey . . . All of these precede and always accompany that other essential aspect of this journey, namely, theological dialogue. An authentic dialogue is, in every case, an encounter between persons with a name, a face, a past, and not merely a meeting of ideas.[39]

By visiting *Jamia* Mosque the Christians were sending a powerful message of the churches' esteem for the followers of other religions, thus strengthening bonds of friendship. Practitioners in the field of peacemaking have emphasized the importance of dramatic action as a means of reducing conflict.[40] In this regard, the transformative nature of a handshake with the enemy, whether real or feigned, inspires the other to re-consider any feelings of animosity.

Positive discourse from the Muslim leadership was also in evidence. The Council of Muslim Scholars in Kenya appealed for restraint, urging Kenyans not to be divided along religious or ethnic lines.[41] The Muslim scholars called upon the government to move expeditiously and to address the factors that precipitate radicalization, such as discrimination, unemployment, historical injustices, marginalization, corruption, and harassment by police and other state security agencies. Sheikh Mohamed Dor, secretary-general of the Council of Imams and Preachers of Kenya, asked the leaders to relinquish negative postures and critically re-examine insecurity in Kenya. "We are all victims because many of our clerics have been killed mysteriously. If the Church leaders' agitation for arms is based on the number of their killed colleagues, then Muslim leaders deserve priority," said Sheikh Dor.[42]

It is noteworthy that those Christian leaders who expressed charitable sentiments were mainly those working in parts of the country where there are large numbers of Muslims, such as Garissa and Mombasa. Their statements may have been influenced by the religiously pluralist reality on the ground and by their close engagements with Muslim communi-

39. Vatican Radio, "Pope Francis: I Seek Communion with Orthodox Churches."
40. Brunson, "The Art in Peacemaking," 15.
41. Sheikh Dor, quoted in "Catholics Oppose Call to Arm Preachers."
42. Ibid.

ties for extended periods of time. It is also possible that such leaders may have been more sensitive to the damage that negative statements had on their ministries in Muslim-majority areas.

ANALYSIS OF CHRISTIAN DISCOURSES REGARDING TERROR ATTACKS

The discourses analyzed reflect a range of discussions among Christians in Kenya in the wake of terror attacks. From the statements issued by the leaders, it is not possible to characterize the attitudes of Kenyan Christians in general. Individual religious leaders do not necessarily reflect the attitudes of the larger groups to which they belong. Hence the importance of approaching Christian leaders as individuals. There were clear differences in the manner in which leaders from various churches discussed the tragic attacks. Even within the same faith tradition, there was considerable variety in the way leaders engaged with the phenomenon, sometimes assuming divisive postures, at other times appearing more conciliatory. Thus it can be concluded that the relationship between religion and social cohesion is deeply contextual and constantly evolving.

However, on the whole, the respective discourses suggest strong feelings expressed in antagonistic posturing between Christian and Muslim representatives. Such discourses deployed various rhetorical strategies to establish polemic relationships between Christians and Muslims. Christians portrayed "Muslim" leaders as enemies of peace and uncommitted to interfaith relations, and they paraphrased biblical texts using them in novel ways. They also used the media to publicize their statements to a wider audience. However, there were other more conciliatory discourses focused on building bridges between the two religious communities, deploying speech and symbolic action—such as visits to mosques—to build interfaith relations during the crisis.

The variegated nature of the discourses points to the fact that while religious groups in Kenya continue to play constructive roles towards better Christian–Muslim relations, there are voices within the churches that clearly limit meaningful religious engagement in the public sphere. For example, the call for guns, among other utterances, by some Christian leaders showed that they could not direct or guide public deliberations in positive ways. Such voices, which command considerable following in the country, pitted Christians and Muslims against each other in adversarial ways, thus negatively influencing the relations between members of the two faith traditions. Their rhetoric revealed as much as it obscured, while Kenyans were hoping for better security and social relationships. Discourses by some of the Christian leaders showed that they regarded the public sphere as a space for competition with Muslims. While Christians may continue to make a constructive contribution to public life, their efforts may be rendered ineffective because of their desire to dominate the public sphere. In the wake of divisive discourses, some Christian leaders offered alternative narratives. While not discounting the tragic effects of the attacks, they called for calm and inclusivity within and between the Christian and Muslim communities. Beyond mere rhetoric, they demonstrated through praxis their vision of an inclusive community by arranging for joint visits to mosques and churches to stem suspicion and hostility, thereby building bridges for better relations.

TOWARDS A BIBLICAL RESPONSE TO TERROR

The advocates of inter-religious dialogue are often told that they are naïve idealists and that dialogue does not work when religious groups are set against each other, sometimes violently. Are there any biblical injunctions for Christians, urging them to extend hands of friendship to perceived foes, even during violent times?

The New Testament appeals to believers to extend a hand of peace even in a context of violence. Indeed, the life and mission of Jesus can be understood as God's initiative toward a sinful and rebellious humanity. It is in this regard that the apostle Paul writes: "All have sinned and fall short of the glory of God" (Rom 3:23). In Paul's own words again, "While we were still sinners Christ died for us. . . . While we were still enemies, we were reconciled to God through the death of his Son" (Rom 5:8, 10). The initiative of God in the above biblical texts should form an important basis for Christian responses towards violence. To this end, Paul in his letter to the Romans exhorts his Christian audience not to become trapped in a cycle of violence and revenge, but instead to be active by repaying evil with good:

> Bless those who persecute you; bless and do not curse them. Rejoice with those who rejoice, weep with those who weep. Live in harmony with one another; do not be haughty, but associate with the lowly; do not claim to be wiser than you are. Do not repay any-

one evil for evil, but take thought for what is noble in the sight of all. If it is possible, so far as it depends on you, live peaceably with all. Beloved, never avenge yourselves, but leave room for the vengeance of God; for it is written, "Vengeance is mine, I will repay, says the Lord." No, "If your enemies are hungry, feed them; if they are thirsty, give them something to drink; for by doing this you will heap burning coals upon their heads." Do not be overcome by evil, but overcome evil with good. Rom 12:14–21 NRSV

Peace cannot be built on the foundation of injustice. Indeed, peace and justice are intimately related as dimensions of the biblical understanding of *shalom*. Both point to right and sustainable relationships, not only within and between human communities, but also with the earth as God's creation.

CONCLUSION

Although the roots of Islamist terror groups are found outside of Kenya, especially in Somalia, there is evidence that the philosophies of these groups appear to be gaining growing acceptance among traditional African communities. Within the framework of Christian–Muslim relations in Kenya, historical socio-political grievances feed into strained relations between members of the two faith traditions. Violent conflicts are in significant measure the result of injustice within the larger society. Christians have a prophetic responsibility to speak out against any form of injustice wherever it may be found. The terror attacks in Kenya have presented Christian leaders with both opportunities and limitations of remedial, redemptive responses. The history of Christian–Muslim encounters in Kenya is characterized by suspicion and competition, albeit with some moments of mutual collaboration; unfortunately, a section of Christian leaders has engaged in a similar mode of polarizing discourses. Such discourse has the effect of sharpening boundaries between members of the two faith traditions. However, while all religious groups in Kenya must continue to play constructive roles towards better Christian–Muslim relations, there are voices within the churches that clearly demonstrate the limitation of religious engagement in the public sphere. Religious actors in conflicts must engage the situations in a myriad of ways, ranging from highly individualized to deeply communal, and from ideological to religio-ethnic modalities in the quest for mutually edifying relationships between Muslims and Christians.

REFERENCES

Ali, Shaheed Sarhar, and Javaid Rehman. "The Concept of *Jihad* in Islamic International Law." *Journal of Conflict and Security Law* 10, no. 3 (2005) 321–43.

Asad, Talal. *Genealogies of Religion: Discipline and Reasons for Power in Christianity and Islam*. Baltimore: Johns Hopkins University Press, 1993.

Azumah, John. "The Church and Islam in Africa." *Evangelical Interfaith Dialogue* 2, no. 3 (2011) 3–5.

Baur, John. 2000 *Years of Christianity in Africa: An African History*. Boston: Pauline, 1994.

Beja, Patrick. "Church Leaders Demand Guns to Protect Faithful from Attacks." *Standard Media*, 26 March 2014. http://www.standardmedia.co.ke/article/2000107832/church-leaders-demand-guns-to-protect-faithful-from-attacks. Accessed 4 August 2016.

Brunson, Russell, Zephryn Conte, and Shelley Masar. "The Art in Peacemaking: A Guide to Integrating Conflict Resolution Education into Youth Arts Programs." Springfield, IL: National Centre for Conflict Resolution Education, 2002. https://www.arts.gov/sites/default/files/ArtinPeacemaking.pdf.

Buzan, Barry, and Ole Wæver. "Regions and Powers: Summing Up and Looking Ahead." In *Regions and Powers: The Structure of International Security*, by Barry Buzan and Ole Wæver, 445–60. Cambridge Studies in International Relations. Cambridge: Cambridge University Press, 2003.

"Catholics Oppose Call to Arm Preachers." *Daily Nation*, 4 November 2013. http://mobile.nation.co.ke/counties/Catholics-oppose-call-to-arm-preachers/-/1950480/2058620/-/format/xhtml/-/nynj4q/-/index.html. Accessed 4 August 2016.

Christian Leaders Consultative Forum. "Press Statement: Standing with the Christian Faith." www.ncck.org/newsite2/index.php/information/news/389-Christian-leaders-consultative-forum-press-statement. Accessed 7 December 2015.

Cook, Michael A. *Commanding Right and Forbidding Wrong in Islamic Thought*. Cambridge: Cambridge University Press, 2001.

Constantin, François. "Leadership, Muslim Identities, and East African Politics: Tradition, Bureaucratization and Communication." In *Muslim Identity and Social Change in Sub-Saharan Africa*, edited by Louise Brenner, 36–58. London: Hurst, 1993.

Cox, Fletcher D., Catherine Osborn, and Timothy D. Sisk. "Religion, Peace Building, and Social Cohesion in Conflict-Affected Countries." www.du.edu/korbel/sie/media/documents/faculty_pubs/sisk/religion-and-social-cohesion-reports/rsc-researchreport.pdf. Accessed 11 December 2015.

Fakude, Thembisa. "Can Kenya Avoid a Sectarian Conflict?" http://studies.aljazeera.net/en/reports/2015/05/2015514124231134280.htm. Accessed 12 December 2015.

Geertz, Clifford. *The Interpretation of Culture*. New York: Basic, 1973.

Holloway, David. *9/11 and the War on Terror*. Edinburgh: Edinburgh University Press, 2008.

Horton, Mark, and John Middleton. *The Swahili: The Social Landscape of a Mercantile Society*. Oxford: Wiley-Blackwell, 2001.

Kenyan National Commission on Human Rights. "The Error of Fighting Terror with Terror. Preliminary Report of KNCHR Investigations on Human Rights Abuses in the Ongoing Crackdown against Terrorism. September 2015." http://www.knchr.

org/Portals/0/PressStatements/Press%20statement%20on%20Error%20of%20 fighting%20terror%20with%20terror.pdf?ver=2015-09-15-122506-727. Accessed 4 August 2016.

Kiplagat, Jeremiah. "Church Leaders Now Visit City Mosque for Prayers." *Daily Nation*, 10 September 2015. www.nation.co.ke/news/Church-leaders-now-visit-mosque-for-prayers/-/1056/2876586/-/drmle7z/-/index.html. Accessed 10 December 2015.

Kithogo, Wachira. "Churches Accuse Muslim Scholars of 'Inaction' over Attack." *University World News*, 24 April 2015. http://www.universityworldnews.com/article.php?story=20150423163242805. Accessed 4 August 2016.

Kresse, Kai. "Muslim Politics in Post-Colonial Kenya: Negotiating Knowledge on the Double-Periphery." *Journal of the Royal Anthropological Institute* 15 (2009) 76–94.

Lochery, Emma. "Rendering Difference Visible: The Kenyan State and Its Somali Citizens." *African Affairs* 111 (2012) 615–39.

Mayabi, Lordrick. "Inter-ethnic Clash in Nairobi after Bus Attack." *Capital News* (Nairobi). www.capitalfm.co.ke/news/2012/11/inter-ethnic-clashes-in-nairobi-after-bus-blast/. Accessed 11 December 2015.

Mazrui, Al Amin. "Ethnicity and Pluralism: The Politicization of Religion in Kenya." *Journal of Muslim Minority Affairs* 14, no. 1 (1993) 191–201.

Murunga, Godwin Rapando. "The Cosmopolitan Tradition and Fissures in Segregationist Town Planning in Nairobi, 1915–23." *Journal of East African Studies* 6, no. 3 (21 June 2012) 463–86. http://dx.doi.org/10.1080/17531055.2012.696896.

Oded, Arye. *Islam and Politics in Kenya*. Boulder, CO: Lynne Rienner, 2000.

———. "Islamic Extremism in Kenya: The Rise and Fall of Sheikh Khalid Balata." *Journal of Religion in Africa* 26, no. 4 (1996) 406–15.

Onyalla, Fr Don Bosco. "Bishops in Kenya Emphasizes Good Relations between Christians and Muslims after Varsity Terror Attacks," 9 April 2015. www.canaafrica.org/index.php?option=com_content&view=article&id. Accessed 10 December 2015.

Pouwels, Randall L. "The East African Coast c. 780 to 1900 CE." In *The History of Islam in Africa*, edited by Nehemia Levtzion and Randall L. Pouwels, 251–71. Athens, OH: Ohio University Press, 2000.

Rummel, R. J. *Death by Government*. New Brunswick, NJ: Transaction, 1997.

Vatican Radio. " Pope Francis: I seek Communion with Orthodox Churches." http://en.radiovaticana.va/news/2014/11/30/pope_francis_i_seek_communion_with_orthodox_churches/1113017. Accessed 4 August 2016.

Ward, Ian. *Law, Text, Terror*. Cambridge: Cambridge University Press, 2009.

8

Reconciliatory Peace in the Face of Terror
A Personal Appeal for Quaker Peace Building in Kenya

ESTHER M. MOMBO

Someone can't forgive with a broken heart, we need first to heal our wounds. Then start the work of peace and reconciliation. Sometimes when you are still living with your deep wounds it is not easy to forgive. And without forgiving it is not easy to love someone. They need to heal then forgive then love.

—CÉCILE NYIRAMANA[1]

All this is from God, who reconciled us to himself through Christ, and has given us the ministry of reconciliation; that is in Christ God was reconciling the world to himself, not counting their trespasses against them, and entrusting the message of reconciliation to us.

—2 COR 5:18–19

KENYA HAS WITNESSED DIFFERENT forms of violence over the last ten years spanning from post-election violence to terror attacks. Attempts at peace and reconciliation have become crucial, but have been complicated by the nature of ethno-religious conflict. This chapter seeks to outline some Quaker peace and reconciliatory initiatives and how

1. Lederach, *This Light*; Mombo and Nyiramana, *Mending Broken Hearts*.

they are influenced by biblical teaching. These initiatives are an important lesson for other initiatives on peace and reconciliation in Kenya.

Historically the Quakers are known as one of the peace churches, for peace building is embedded in their faith and practice. Quakers and other peace churches are known to reject any active participation in military service, along with the swearing of public oaths. On peace building, Quakers follow the tradition of quiet diplomacy with a focus on grassroots initiatives to develop positive, nonviolent approaches to resolving human conflict, and facilitating paths toward reconciliation. Quakerism was introduced to Kenya in 1902 when the first mission station was established in Kaimosi. Since that period, Quakers have been associated with social development—particularly education, vocational training, and the provision of health services. On matters of peace, they seek to develop positive, nonviolent approaches to resolving human conflict and facilitating paths toward reconciliation. Several of the initiatives on peace building have been employed to bring together ethnic communities that have in the past been at war with each other.

The above quote from Cécile Nyiramana, a Quaker herself, sums up the ways in which Quakers have gone about dealing with issues of peace and reconciliation. Quakers embarked on peacebuilding to help reconcile people to God, to neighbor, and to nature. Some of the peace initiatives include programs such as the Alternative to Violence (AVP), a program initiated by American Quakers in 1975, and Turning the Tide (TTT), an initiative of British Quakers. Both these projects are nonviolent training initiatives for social change. Turning the Tide "aims to help people use the power of nonviolence to 'turn the tide' of injustice, oppression and disempowerment and to build an inclusive, sustainable and fair world."[2]

The work of Quakers begins with dealing with the hurt at the individual level, which then spreads to dealing with hurt in the wider society. This is needed because the conflict in Kenya and other regions is rooted in the politics of exclusion in which people find themselves denied their identity, their freedom, or resources. The root causes of conflict include a destructive style of ethnicity, denominationalism, poor political and economic leadership, corruption, and poverty, to name just a few. These causes are both internal and external and they are both historical and contemporary. In working towards reconciliatory peace, one does not

---

2. "Turning the Tide."

shy away from naming the historical grievances around cultural ethnic tensions that continue to rock communities. In addressing the legacies of historical injustice, peacebuilders are engaged in deeper dialogue about recurring intergroup tensions and are rebuilding trust. Forgiveness precedes reconciliation which then leads to creating new relationships, and this begins with healing past hurts and framing a vision for a better future. The conviction to work towards reconciliatory peace emanates from Jesus' teachings as recorded in the biblical text which for many Quakers in Kenya is a guiding principle.

PEACE AND RECONCILIATION FROM THE BIBLE

Peace and reconciliation have a central place in God's plan for creation and Christ's work within that plan. In the Old Testament, peace is described in various ways. First, peace means wellbeing, that is, physical health, economic security, and sound relationships with others. It is to be cultivated and preserved as part of the universal order. Second, peace is not merely conformity to a law that is coeternal with cosmic law and social order. Rather, it is a gift from a personal God who intervenes on behalf of his chosen people. Third, peace is conditional: it is a gift from God and can only be fully realized through obedience. Peace is a result of a covenant, the effect of a personal relationship between God and God's people. In order to enjoy peace, Israel had to "make peace" by carrying out its part of the covenant. Peace, then, is a comprehensive term. It means not only being-well, but also doing well (Isa 32:17).

When one looks at the New Testament, the new covenant was founded in an act of peace that is neither *shalom* nor non-belligerence. It was God's offer of friendship to people, who consciously or unconsciously had rejected justice. It is peace as reconciliation; the kind of "making peace" that is not limited to laying down arms but that also creates a new relationship in which people are enabled to do justice. New Testament peace is that peace that works justice, so that justice may work peace. Peace has a dual meaning: reconciliation given by God, and wellbeing in all its fullness. Justice is the fruit of the first and the cause of the second. It creates the new person as mediator between God's act and the world's identity.

One cannot create a new world order without re-creating the order among human beings, just as one cannot bring the world to its fullness without bringing all people to a new friendship. Total peace and contractual peace regard the other as the enemy, whereas reconciliatory peace seeks to turn the other into a friend. In the Beatitudes, Jesus says, "Blessed are the peacemakers, because they will be called the children of God" (Matt 5:9).

The peacemaker agrees with the ultimate goal of the unrealized total peace, but disagrees with it in not identifying self with justice and in not seeing self as the sole bearer of peace. Jesus made a distinction between the peace that God wants, and the peace that the world wants (John 14:27). The peace that God wants is a peace that is based on truth, justice, and love. The peace that the world offers is a peace and unity that compromises the truth and covers over injustices—usually because of thoroughly selfish purposes. Jesus destroys this false peace and even highlights the conflicts in order to promote a true and lasting peace. There is no question of preserving peace and unity at all costs, even at the cost of truth and justice. Rather, it is a matter of promoting truth and justice at all costs even at the cost of creating conflict and dissension along the way. For reconciliatory peace to occur, people need to be involved at all levels, not because of what they can get as peacemakers but for restoring what false peace has destroyed. Reconciliatory peace involves making oneself a friend and regarding the other as potential friend even in situations of conflict.

In the Pauline text quoted at the beginning of this paper, and in other texts as well, Paul raises several points as far as reconciliation is concerned. Reconciliation is an act of God, or it is initiated by God. It is God in this case who reconciles humanity to God's own self. It is not a human achievement. Reconciliation then is not a process that only we initiate or achieve, but we discover it already active in God through Christ (2 Cor 5:18–19). Paul takes the imagery connected with the usage of the term in his time—of enmity and friendship—to explain our relation to God.

The means of reconciliation is the death of Christ. Death on the cross was a very shameful and humiliating death as understood in Paul's day. This means of reconciliation not only takes us to the limit of human existence, it also takes us into the very core of violence. Christ's descent to the dead presents another image of going to the limits, but one that shows more the consequences of violence than the encounter with violence directly.

The shedding of blood on the cross was a means of reconciliation. Blood is a paradoxical metaphor in the Hebrew Scriptures and in other cultures. It is a symbol of both life and death. Writing about reconciliation, Paul develops the paradoxical nature of the cross as well (1 Cor 1:18; Phil 3:18). The paradoxical character of the symbol helps mediate the move from death to life in the reconciliation process. The symbols make possible a firm way to acknowledge violence, suffering, and death, but also provide the means for overcoming them. They do not escape the confrontation with violence, and they do not become hopelessly mired in it. They provide a vehicle for overcoming and transcending, preparing the basis for reconciliation. For Paul, the death, the cross, and the blood of Jesus are powerful symbols for reconciliation. They contain rich strands of meaning that might seem in themselves contrary or even self-contradictory, but are still held together in a conceptual network that makes sense in people's reconciliation to God.

Paul applies his teaching on reconciliation by dealing with the reconciliation of Jews and Gentiles. The Jews who were chosen people of God have been offered the saving message of Jesus, but most have chosen to reject that message. These people who were supposedly friends of God, as it appears, had become enemies of God, and those at greatest enmity had been reconciled to God. Apart from accounting for how God reconciles Jews and Gentiles, and how God reconciles past and present covenants, the Pauline literature reflects another approach in which the relative priority of Jew or Gentile is not the concern, but rather how God is making one people out of Jews and Gentiles. This is clear in Ephesians and Colossians, which, whether or not of Pauline authorship, still bear the imprint of his theology (for example, see Eph 2:12–16; Col 1:22–23). From these insights, we can deduce that reconciliation is not such a simple task in societies that have suffered violence and oppression. It is a complex and challenging task. However, from the biblical passages, we can draw lessons for this decade to overcome violence. Certainly, the Pauline theology of reconciling Jews and Gentiles gives a framework of reconciliation among different groups.

LESSONS ABOUT RECONCILIATORY PEACE

From the above descriptions of the nature of peace and reconciliation, one can draw insights for building peace through reconciliation. From the peace aspect, it is important to note that peace in modern times is not understood as fullness and harmony but as the absence of war. What exists today is a contractual peace that is not lasting and hence leads to the ethnoreligious tensions that have been witnessed. This kind of peace is unsatisfactory because it is limited in its claim and does not rest on a genuine will of peace. This type of peace appears to be tactical or instrumental and does not deal with the issues that breed conflict. This is because it aims at defending one's interests against the threat that comes from others. The underlying will for war remains, and this warlike spirit submits to peace without genuine conversion.

Reconciliation is at times misunderstood to mean several things, including truce, hasty peace, a quick-fix solution, or a managed process. It is in those contexts that some people say we must be fair, we must listen to both sides of the story, and there is always a right and wrong on both sides if we could only get people to talk to one another to sort out their misunderstandings and misconceptions of one another. This may sound very Christian but it is only half the truth because it elevates reconciliation into an absolute principle that must be applied in all cases of conflict. But conflicts are not the same, for instance in some conflicts one side is right and the other side is wrong, one side is being unjust and oppressive and the other is suffering injustice and oppression.

Reconciliation from the Pauline writings is not a hasty peace where the victims are expected to let go quickly of their painful past. A kind of quick-fix does more harm to the victim and does not help the perpetrators of violence come to a realization of what they have done. Nevertheless, many a time the quick-fix reconciliation is called for either by the perpetrators or by those that have been outside the violence situation. James Cone in this regard has observed that "Such calls for reconciliation not only trivialize and ignore the sufferings that African Americans have undergone, but also ignore the source of the sufferings—namely, those who oppress and do violence to African Americans of one and the same group; white people."[3] Trivializing or ignoring any history of suffering is a false attempt at reconciliation that actually underscores how far the situation still is from genuine reconciliation. Sadly, church leaders are often victims of the appeal of this kind of "reconciliation" because they think it is the Christian way. They stress correctly the theme of forgiveness but are ignorant of what forgiveness will entail. To overcome violence in this decade it is important for all who are involved

---

3. Cone, *Black Theology*, 143–52.

in the reconciliation process to note that it takes time to heal and begin a new life. But at the same time root causes of violence should not be glossed over but faced and tackled. The structures that have perpetuated violence need to be brought to light and dealt with even though sights of violence remain; they should be a reminder that violence should not be repeated.

Reconciliation is also viewed as a managed process, and this can be seen in the increase of literature and courses on conflict and reconciliation. For instance, in the mission statement of such groups as non-governmental organizations trying to create peace, reconciliation is often treated as a managed process.[4] In such cases, reconciliation is confused with conflict mediation, a process whose goal is to lessen conflict or to get the parties to accept and live with the conflict. Reconciliation is seen as being brought about by a disciplined process in which a skilled mediator helps the conflicting parties recognize the issues at conflict as representing different interests and values that have to be negotiated. Reconciliation becomes a process of bargaining in which both sides are expected to compromise some of their interests in order to reach an end to the conflict. The process acknowledges that both sides have legitimate interests, but that both sets of interests cannot be met concurrently. Consequently, a balancing process must be undertaken that will require both sides to give something up, to an extent that the conflict does not flare up again.

When reconciliation is viewed or treated as a managed process, there is an acknowledgment that people can come into conflict trying to maintain legitimate interests and values, but that these interests and values can put them hopelessly at odds with each other. Likewise, the managers of the process assume that a minimum sense of human dignity for all parties in the conflict must be acknowledged, so that claims by the parties may be taken seriously. This approach also assumes that reconciliation is not a quick process and that certain conditions must be met if the conflict is not to occur again. But reconciliation as a managed process fails because we do not bring about reconciliation, especially in the profound and complex situations described above. It is God who reconciles. This is not said to create an attitude of acquiescence in the face of violence or fatalism in the midst of political oppression. It is,

---

4. Getui and Kanyandogo, *From Violence to Peace*; Assefa and Wachira, *Peacemaking and Democratisation*. Cf. *The Mediator*.

rather, to acknowledge the enormity of the task of reconciliation in situations where the social order has shifted radically and dramatically.

It is a mistake to reduce reconciliation to a board room technique by people who are not affected, or by those using only "book knowledge," or by people offering skills to manage an issue. Reconciliation is not a skill to be mastered, but rather something discovered—a certain kind of power. It comes as a stance assumed before a broken world rather than a tool to repair that world, or, to put it in more theological terms, reconciliation is more spirituality than strategy. To see reconciliation as a form of learned technique or a mere skill is to reduce reconciliation to mere talk, and it may not work in situations of conflict.

Reconciliation is also not a hasty process. It requires respecting and often restoring human dignity. Take, for example, violence in the home. The spouses who have been violent to each other should not be coerced into tolerating each other or forced to forgive each other and live with each other for the sake of maintaining the status quo or because it is "Christian."[5]

In bitter situations where a violation has been committed, the victims would be rightly asking themselves how they can forgive those who have violated them and society at large. As Nyiramana observes in the quote at the beginning of this paper, "Someone can't forgive with a broken heart, we need first to heal our wounds." In reconciliation, as discussed by Paul, the question is not how one can forgive, but rather how survivors of violence can discover the mercy of God welling up in their lives and where this leads them to. Reconciliation is not a process that we initiate or achieve, it begins with the survivor's healing of their wounds, not always that their pain and anger has gone, but that they have made much progress in the healing process.

Quaker peacebuilding work in Kenya has paid more attention to the grassroots than to board room meetings. Using the methods of Alternative to Violence and Turning the Tide, the members of the grassroots community are empowered to make informed choices and not to be manipulated to cause conflicts. The situation of terrorism in Kenya has caused rifts between communities blaming each other. One church leader was quoted as saying, "Christians have no other cheek to turn,"

---

5. Mombo, "*Vumilia* Theology." *Vumilia* is a Kiswahili word that means "endure"; in this section, it is used to mean passive endurance. While Christians are asked to endure, it is not enduring acquiescing to wrongs or injustice.

as a result of all the terror attacks. In interfaith situations, the Christian means of reconciliation, that is, through the death of Jesus Christ, could be a source of unrest rather than peace. But I would argue that there is room for reconciliation through dialogue. In dialogue one is not outdoing the other but listening and acknowledging the other. In this sense, then, reconciliatory peace can achieve peace much better than "contractual peace."

REFERENCES

Assefa, Hizkias, and George Wachira. *Peacemaking and Democratisation in Africa: Theoretical Perspectives and Church Initiatives*. Nairobi: EAEP, 1996.
Cone, James. *Black Theology and Black Power*. New York: Seabury, 1969.
Getui, Mary, and Peter Kanyandogo, eds. *From Violence to Peace: A Challenge for African Christianity*. Nairobi: Acton, 1999.
Lederach, John Paul. *This Light That Pushes Me: Stories of African Peacebuilders*. London: Quaker, 2014.
The Mediator: Fostering Godly Peace in Africa. Nairobi: Peace Building, Healing and Reconciliation Programme, 2002.
Mombo, Esther. "*Vumilia* Theology." In *Anglicanism across the World*, edited by A. Wingate et al., 219–22. London: Mowbray, 1998.
Mombo, Esther, and Cécile Nyiramana. *Mending Broken Hearts, Rebuilding Shattered Lives: Quaker Peacebuilding in Eastern Africa*. Swarthmore Lecture, 2016. London: Quaker, 2016.
"Turning the Tide." http://www.quakersintheworld.org/quakers-in-action/238. Accessed 24 February 2017.

9

Gender, Women, and Children, and Al-Shabaab Terrorism in Kenya
A Christian Response

Eunice Karanja Kamaara and Simon Gisege Omare

The US Department of Defense defines terrorism as "the unlawful use of violence or threat of violence to instill fear and coerce governments or societies. Terrorism is often motivated by religious, political or other ideological beliefs and committed in the pursuit of goals that are usually political."[1] It is also usually in response to perceived or actual injustice, and in the context of this chapter, this is the point we want to underscore. Terrorist attacks from Islamic fundamentalist groups have become a defining characteristic of the globe since the September 2001 attack in New York. The groups have emerged in various contexts to pursue various agendas but with the common goal of establishing Islamic States.

In Africa, one of the worst hit countries is Kenya. Towards the last quarter of the 1980s, the Somali civil war broke out in Somalia in opposition to Siad Barre's rule. The Somali crisis began as a cold war before deteriorating into civil war (1988 to 1991). This led to the collapse of the Somali state, the consequent clan war and famine (1991 to 1992), and

---

1. Joint Chiefs of Staff, US Department of Defense, Joint Publication 3-07.2, "Antiterrorism." 24 November 2010. http://www.bits.de/NRANEU/others/jp-doctrine/JP3_07.2(10).pdf. Accessed 11 August 2016.

eventual interventions by international humanitarian groups.[2] Over the years, a number of Islamist armed rebel movements seeking to establish an Islamic state in Somalia have emerged, among them, the Union of Islamic Courts (UIC), which controlled most of the main towns in Somalia. After their defeat in 2006, the UIC split into several groups, among them, al-Shabaab, a youth wing. al-Shabaab, estimated to have between 7,000 and 9,000 members, has emerged as a deadly Islamic extremist liberation group affiliated to al-Qaeda. It has attracted jihadists from all parts of the world sympathetic to their cause to support them in and outside Somalia. Many countries, including the UK and the USA, have identified al-Shabaab as a terrorist group and banned it.

Al-Shabaab largely controlled the main Somali town of Mogadishu. In 2006, the UN-backed Transitional Federal Government of Somalia with its Ethiopian allies started flushing out al-Shabaab, eventually capturing Mogadishu in 2011. In 2011, the Ethiopian troops exited Somalia and the Kenya Defence Forces (KDF) entered. Their coordinated military operation was dubbed Operation Linda Nchi ("protect the country") under the command of then president Mwai Kibaki. The initial motivation for Kenyan military troops to enter Somalia was supposedly al-Shabaab's kidnapping of foreign tourists and aid workers in Kenya's refugee camps near the Somalia border.[3] It was expected that Operation Linda Nchi would quickly give al-Shabaab the last death blow and bring an end to both Islamic insurgency and the Somali civil war. However, close to ten years after the conquest of Mogadishu, al-Shabaab continues to be a formidable force. In response to the invasion of Somalia by the KDF, al-Shabaab has since consistently attacked Kenya for siding with the Western nations in their "global struggle against Islam."[4]

Kenya is overwhelmingly Christian in terms of numerical strength. Since its invasion of Somalia in October 2011, the country has suffered various terrorist acts killing over 200 people and maiming hundreds of others. Probably more tragic is the cost of continued erosion of the harmonious coexistence that Kenyan Muslims and Christians had nurtured over previous decades. As in any unsystematic war targeting civilians, al-Shabaab terrorism causes most havoc to vulnerable populations, es-

---

2. Bradbury and Healy, "Endless War," 10.

3. International Crisis Group, 2012. http://www.banadir.com/ICGTheKenyanMilitaryInterventionIinSomalia.pdf. Accessed on 18 August 2016.

4. Hansen, *Al-Shabaab in Somalia*, 130–31.

pecially Christian women and children, who have become targets of terrorists. Kenyan Christians have not responded with physical violence to Muslims amid attacks by al-Shabaab but various antagonizing responses have been registered.

While Muslim leaders, with good reason, have constantly warned against treating al-Shabaab as a Muslim group and regarding these attacks as religious violence, there is no denying that these attacks have religious connotations. Against this background, we examine gender relations in Kenya to show how these relate to the continued threat and reality of al-Shabaab and the attendant vulnerability of women and children. We adopt a postcolonial feminist theological perspective to engage in constructive dialogue, discussing not so much how the church in Kenya has responded to al-Shabaab but more proactively how the church could respond in future.

GENDER AND WOMEN IN THE CHURCH

We begin with a brief discussion on gender and the church. According to Hazel Ayanga:

> The term gender tends to evoke certain emotions in both the user and the hearer of the term. For men in particular, it conjures images of militant women who forcefully and emotionally want to become like men. These women want to "wrench" the power in its various dimensions from the rightful "owners" who in this case are the male human species. For some women, the term gender describes therefore fellow women who have lost direction and who want to destroy the God given mandate to be submissive and indeed only follow their husbands' direction.[5]

Yet, gender is nothing more than the roles, attributes, and expectations that society assigns to men and women in specific cultural contexts. Although gender is defined as if it is derived from sex (maleness and femaleness) and as if it is natural, it is not. Gender is a socio-cultural construct that varies from one society to the other and from time to time.

According to Thomas O'Dea and Janet O'Dea, religion has been described as:

---

5. Ayanga, "Inspired and Gendered."

something unimportant and evanescent, something peripheral to the genuine business of human life. Yet, the facts point to something else . . . Religion has been characterized as embodying the most sublime of human aspirations; as being a bulwark of morality, a source of public order and inner individual peace; as ennobling and civilizing in its effects upon (hu) mankind. It has also been accused of being a stubborn obstacle retarding progress and of promoting fanaticism and intolerance, ignorance, superstition, and obscurantism. The record reveals religion to be among the strongest buttresses of an established social order. It also, however, shows it is capable of exhibiting profound revolutionary tendencies, as in the peasant war in sixteenth century Germany.[6]

O'Dea and O'Dea seem contradictory, but their observation is accurate. Such are the contradictions of religion. In Africa, religion remains an indispensable institution, an important aspect of culture. As in any other place, religion in Africa is a paradox in that it buttresses gender inequality and yet it is regarded as a source of morality. Numerically, Christianity is the major religion in Kenya; over 75 percent of Kenyans claim to be Christian. The Christian tradition has had a great impact on gender relations in Kenya. Within the constraints of this chapter, we give a brief history of gender relations in Christianity before analyzing gender relations in contemporary Kenya.

A cursory look at the history of Christian tradition suggests that gender relations have shifted over the years toward more egalitarianism, but not significantly. The dominant opinion of the early church was that women are inferior to men and therefore should suffer subjugation.[7] This view received little dissent. Within the medieval church, a debate on gender emerged. Among the major proponents of the view that women are inferior was Augustine of Hippo. Augustine is referred to as the

> Master of Medieval thought, for through him, the Middle Ages were furnished with a framework of ethical reference in the area of sexuality and conjugality. Right up to the twelfth century, theologians, jurists, and moralists systematically referred to him when discussing these ethical issues.[8]

---

6. O'Dea and O'Dea, *Sociology of Religion*, 3.
7. Chadwick, *Early Church*, 39.
8. Fuchs, *Sexual Desire and Love*, 115.

According to Joseph Kambo, Augustine is "renowned of all times because of his clear and well synthesized theology which is the foundation of Christian doctrine."[9] Sadly, Augustine believed that women are inferior to men by nature because they are not made in the image of God. He pronounced:

> The woman, together with her husband is the image of God, so that the whole substance may be one image; but when she is referred separately to in her quality of help-meet, which regards the woman herself alone, she is not in the image of God; but as regards the man alone, he is the image of God as fully and completely as when the woman too is joined with him in one.[10]

Within this Augustinian thinking, gender becomes a sexual issue in that a woman needs to unite with a man if she is to ever bear the image of God.

Prior to Augustine, theologians such as St. Ambrose and St. Basil believed and propounded that women and men are equal. Ambrose wrote: "Everybody, man and woman, must know that he bears God's image and likeness," while Basil declared: "the woman, no less than the man possesses the privilege of being created after God's image. Both sexes have the same dignity, both the same virtues."[11] In spite of these comments, the negative attitude to women carried the day. In spite of the critique of the church's moral teachings by the renowned Reformers of the sixteenth century, the attitude that women were inferior to men prevailed. Martin Luther, who spearheaded the Reformation, subscribed to the thinking that women suffer subjugation as punishment for the original sin.[12] How did this view influence how women were treated in the post-Reformation eras?

Christian thinking with regard to gender relations in contemporary times indicates some shift from the thinking of the early church, the medieval church, and the Reformation. A strong counter-reaction has arisen, particularly from feminist theologians. This advocates for a positive attitude to women and for gender equality. Nevertheless, the

---

9. Kambo, "Integral, Personal and Sexual Development," 202.
10. Augustine, *On the Holy Trinity*, 12.7.10.
11. Quoted in Peschke, *Christian Ethics*, 1:383–84.
12. Ruether, "The Western Religious Tradition," 33.

traditional thinking that women are inferior continues to hang o
patriarchal attitudes continue to govern the church.

At face value, it would appear that the contemporary Kenyan
Christian church believes in the equality of men and women. But this is
only at the theoretical level. In practical terms, men continue to dominate women as they defend their superior positions. This writer concurs
with Paul Avis that churches remain "the willing tool of patriarchy, the
instrument of oppression and the sustainer of exploitation to a vast
scale."[13] Patriarchal attitudes characterized by male dominance and
female subordination continue to govern gender relations in contemporary Christianity.

The clearest manifestation of discrimination of women in the
church in Kenya today is that in spite of women being critical members
in terms of membership and socio-economic support, their participation is limited to the quantitative level. Generally women participate in
the cleaning of the church building and property, making provisions for
the upkeep of the clergy, visiting the old and the sick, attending church
services and small Christian group meetings, and holding prayer sessions. Rarely are women engaged in positions of influence and control
such as those of ordained ministers, bishops, preachers, pastors, choir
masters, catechists, and lay leaders.

Unlike the Roman Catholic Church, many Protestant bodies such
as the (Anglican) Church of the Province of Kenya and the Presbyterian
Church of East Africa have come to accept the ordination of women as
members of the clergy. Despite this, there is not a single female bishop in
Kenya except Bishop Margaret Wanjiru, the founder and spiritual head
of the charismatic movement Jesus Is Alive Ministries (JIAM).

From the foregoing, it seems clear that gender relations in the
church in Kenya are characterized by male dominance and female subordination. This is in spite of various efforts by feminist theologians both
within and outside the country.

THE FAMILY, CHURCH, AND ISLAMIST TERRORISM

Some literature is available on the impact of al-Shabaab on women and
children, much of it pointing to the obvious vulnerability of women and
children in civil violence. Basically, women and children are treated as

13. Avis, *Eros and the Sacred*, 12.

tools of violence; in the case of al-Shabaab as in many cases of civil war, women and girls suffer sexual violence in incidents of rape or worse when they are captured to become "wives" and sexual tools of pleasure for the militants. The abduction of 276 girls from a secondary school in Chibok in north-eastern Nigeria on 14 April 2014 by Boko Haram remains fresh in our minds, but only because so many girls were abducted in one instance. Girls and women are constantly being abducted or seduced to become tools of sexual pleasure for terrorists.

Similarly, boys and young men are abducted or seduced and brainwashed to join terrorism essentially to carry out the dirty work of bombing and indiscriminate killing, often at the expense of their own lives. In nearly all situations where terrorists have been identified or killed, they have been young men. Women have been widowed and left in deep agony when their husbands and male children are killed or injured in incidents of terror or their female children are abducted. The suffering of women and children can never be overestimated. Men too suffer deaths and injuries when they are directly attacked or recruited as well as deep agony when their children, both male and female, join al-Shabaab willingly or by coercion. Both men and women, girls and boys, are vulnerable to terrorist attack. Nevertheless, in this chapter, we focus away from these manifestations of vulnerabilities, which we consider to be symptoms rather than the root causes of the suffering, to engage in a deeper analysis of gender violence in the contemporary Christian family in Kenya with the aim of finding a proactive response to the al-Shabaab crisis, not just in Kenya but in Africa as a whole. We associate the al-Shabaab crisis with the crisis of gender relations in the family in Kenya.

Any student of sociology appreciates that the good of the family ultimately translates into the good of society. The family in Kenya, as in many other parts of the world, is faced with rapid and dramatic changes that threaten its fundamental values and, therefore, its wellbeing, and by extension the wellbeing of the entire Kenyan society. Unequal gender relations at the family level in post-colonial Kenya complicate the effects of the ever-growing influence of neoliberal capitalism.

Within Christian doctrine, especially as documented and clarified in the Roman Catholic Church, the family, which is the basic social unit in any human society, is the smallest unit of the church, the immediate church for every individual. The family is expected to provide love, care, and security to individuals within it as it meets its basic functions:

companionship, reproduction, and production. In Kenya, while the family has been undergoing diverse changes in all spheres of life, the value of the family is still regarded as basic, with high expectations for its benefits. But the gap between the expected provisions and the actual provisions seems to increase every day with the family becoming one of the most oppressive and brutal institutions, especially with regard to gender violence.

In pre-colonial African societies, women and men were equipped to manage their environment despite the limitations placed on each sex. Various checks and balances were in place to protect each gender from abuse. For example, in the traditional set-up where land was the basic resource and source of livelihood, individual ownership of land was unknown. It was communally owned with clear female usufructuary rights to grow certain crops and keep certain animals. Women had full control of these resources in as far as production and distribution was concerned.

During the colonial period, this traditional economic system based on communality and reciprocity disintegrated with changes in the forces of production. With re-defined modes of access to resources, antagonism between men and women emerged. Alienation of land combined with the need for money generated by the imposition of taxes, for example, forced men to seek employment away from home. With the migration of men to urban areas in search of labor, women were left as the functional heads of families. They had to take up what were previously men's roles and responsibilities. For example, they had to manage familial farms in which traditional crops were being replaced with cash crops, due to the demand for money. The introduction of title deeds brought in a new concept of ownership of land. Men, under whose names the lands were registered, got exclusive ownership and control of not just the lands but of the tools of production and the products of the land. In due course, women ended up as tools of labor with no access to or control of land and its products.[14]

A relatively new phenomenon in post-colonial Africa is women in wage employment. Could this be signifying economic independence of women and changed gender relations? S. B. Stitcher carried out a study

---

14. For more details of these changes in the family, see: Kilbride and Kilbride, *Changing Family Life*.

in Nairobi, Kenya in 1988 among 317 families,[15] the findings of which suggested that wage employment of middle-income women does not necessarily translate into economic independence or autonomy, due to the husband's dominance in financial decision-making.[16] Close to thirty years later the scenario has dramatically changed. More and more women are becoming economically independent as they increasingly gain control of economic decision-making, not only through wage employment but also through entrepreneurship.

> A few women would raise money for one person to go and shop in London. The goods would be distributed between the women, according to their contributions, for onward sale at their individual tables. "Freemark" became a fashion trend-setter for the growing middle-class.

Today, some pioneer Freemark women own the sizeable upmarket shops in Nairobi's malls. They regularly hop from Nairobi to Guanghzou to Istanbul and Dubai, exploring trading partners that Kenya never had in its decolonizing years.

> They have mastered the mechanics of importation and short term borrowing that eluded the generation of their parents in the early 1970s. Without any prior design or donor-funded proposal, Freemark has been one of the most successful gender empowerment programmes in Kenya![17]

Even on sex and reproduction, demographers, anthropologists, epidemiologists, among others, indicate that women are increasingly gaining control. But the most conspicuous gain for women in Kenya is their economic empowerment. It would be expected that with so much activity on gender empowerment, gender violence would be reduced. Paradoxically, gender inequality manifests not so much in gender discrimination but in gender exploitation, and gender violence is on the increase.

But what is the relationship between gender relations, women's economic empowerment in Kenya, and al-Shabaab? Analysis suggests

---

15. Stitcher, "Middle Class Family."
16. Mugenda, "Female Education."
17. Joyce Nyairo, "We Were Not Always Businessmen, but We Have Learnt Fast." *Daily Nation*, 21 November 2015. http://www.nation.co.ke/lifestyle/weekend/KENYANS—not-always-businessmen-learnt-fast-NYAIRO/1220–2964836-b1yodb/index.html. Accessed 13 August 2015.

that with support from gender empowerment programs and the attendant economic independence, more and more women are becoming the sole breadwinners as well as the sole homemakers of their families as they take up traditional male roles.[18] Unfortunately, there are no gender empowerment programs for men and, therefore, as women take up traditional male roles, nobody is encouraging men to take up traditional female ones. The result is gender exploitation of women, whereby many of them are shouldering all familial responsibilities single-handedly, whether they are married or not. Consequently, many men are increasingly losing self-value, confidence, and esteem as they continually become irrelevant and "absent" from the family.[19] This amounts to gender discrimination and violence against men. Many men have resorted to violence against women, especially their wives, as well as against their own devalued selves by resorting to drinking cheap brews. True to the assertion that violence begets violence, some women are responding to violence from their husbands with even more violence—especially when men come home physically drained after drinking. Indeed, violence against men is becoming a common phenomenon in Kenya among couples less than thirty years old, probably signaling the time (female) gender empowerment programs began to take root in Kenya.

Within the Eastern African region, post-colonial Kenya stands out as the most neo-liberal capitalistic state, as well as a regional "superpower." Women are part of the equation here as they more and more assume the position of "super powers" as they perfect capitalistic entrepreneurship in the public sphere and become the bread earners, bread owners, and bread breakers at the family level. Murithi Mutiga, advocating for the withdrawal of KDF from Somalia, notes:

> My view on this is shaped by the question a professor in London posed, which sent the whole class into silence. Would terrorism exist if superpowers did not exist? It was a veiled reference to the fact that the principal grievances of groups such as al-Qaeda and ISIS seem to be tied to the policies of the major global powers in the Middle East and the presence of their armies there.[20]

18. Silberschmidt, "Women Forget that Men Are the Masters."
19. Silberschmidt, "Have Men Become the Weaker Sex."
20. Murithi Mutiga, "Rise of ISIS Should Prompt Rethink of Kenya's Strategy against Terrorism." *Daily Nation*, 22 November 2015. http://www.nation.co.ke/oped/Opinion/ISIS-should-prompt-rethink-of-Kenya-strategy/440808-2966452-kqn0pxz/index.html. Accessed 13 August 2016.

Within a neo-liberal capitalistic environment characterized by materialism, individualism, and consumerism, with competition as a hallmark of capitalism, gender inequality has assumed the form of competition between men and women. As women seek more and more material resources for more and more consumption at the individual and family level, they too become physically absent from their families, sometimes for weeks and months. The case of international business women doing circuits (from Nairobi to Dubai to Istanbul to Hong Kong to Beijing, to Bangkok, to London and back to Nairobi) referred to earlier by Nyairo, offers a perfect example. But even women in salaried employment are combining their jobs with side businesses in an effort to get enough resources to ensure that their children are well fed and afforded the best education and health facilities. The result is that many women often arrive home late, well after their children have gone to sleep, and leave early before the children have woken up. Subsequently, children are growing up with little interaction or time with their parents and many a parent would confess that they do not know their children or their children's friends well enough. Against this background, the central value learnt within the family is that success is measured by how many material resources an individual accumulates, no matter how. This value is learnt so early that at primary school, children are already choosing careers on the basis of what translates to a lot of money in the shortest time possible. This thinking, coupled with absent fathers and absent, overworked mothers provides al-Shabaab with an easy target in boys and girls. The lure of making huge amounts of money without having to work as hard as their mothers or without becoming as irrelevant as their fathers is bound to overcome children who have no fundamental family values. Besides, with absent fathers and mothers, children are left unsupervised for long hours, opening up opportunities for their recruitment not only in schools but also right inside their homes. In the context of this chapter, the result has been a lose–lose situation—men lose and women lose and children lose—to al-Shabaab.

Amina H. Ibrahim, a Muslim mother who is also a gender, adolescents, and educational consultant, asserts the connection between gender relations at the family level and al-Shabaab. In a lengthy comment she writes:

> The recent terror attack in Garissa has shaken our souls . . . particularly those of us with teenage children. There are hushed

discussions and shocking narratives from neighbourhood tales in reaction to the recent pictures of the young men turned terrorists. These could have been anyone's children. Mothers with young adults and teenagers in or outside of learning institutions, regardless of whether they live in posh suburbs or in rural north eastern villages, whether they are housewives or top executives, educated or illiterate, rich or poor, the buzz is how indiscriminate this radicalisation has become and how nobody is safe anymore. Our hearts are shaken. Our new reality is constructed by the fact the recruitment process seems to be right in the midst of the circles of our own children. In my case, I am asking myself: How much closer could this get? The young lawyer who was involved in the Garissa University College attack was in the same high school with my younger brother; he is the son of our well-respected chief for Bulla Jamhuria, Mandera County—our childhood neighbourhood and where our parents reside.... Recently, one of my close friends was watching TV airing the story and pictures of the three young women from Mombasa who were arraigned in court for allegedly planning to join Al-Shabaab when her daughter said: "I know one of the girls so-and-so, she is in my university." My friend was shocked and anybody can guess how many questions were running through her mind.... Mothers of young adults are worried and asking questions whether we actually know our children, who they associate with, listen to, chat with and who is influencing their worldview more than us?... The changes within our household structures may also be re-examined more keenly. For example, a common phenomenon in a good number of Somali households globally is the fact that mothers are single-handedly raising their sons even when the father is around. Somali father-son relationships were traditionally educative, authoritative and served as an effective channel for instilling family values and order but this has recently been eroded and become almost non-existent. Father-son dialogue, where it exists, is now short, and instructive rather than conversational, where boys can pick up skills from their fathers. This change in family relationships and socialisation of boys is not only overwhelming for mothers but is also subconsciously confusing boys with regard to their roles in society. Could this new father-son relationship be a contributor to radicalisation where the emotional void created is giving an opportunity to dangerous male figures to easily step in?

More than ever before, parents require a new roadmap to journey with youngsters in this changed world with deeper communication, dialogue and vigilance at home, at school and in our neighbourhoods if we are to save ourselves from the pain that has torn us apart in the past one week. [21]

We concur with Ibrahim to argue that a relationship exists between gender, women, and children on one hand, and al-Shabaab on the other. Notice that Ibrahim makes radicalization of youths a concern for mothers, which leads one to ask: where are the men?

Having presented the relationship between gender and al-Shabaab and the fact that Islamic fundamentalism is right in our midst as professionals, as mothers, as fathers, and as Christians, we devote the following section to suggesting what we consider to be a sustainable approach for Christians to respond effectively to al-Shabaab, and any other form of terrorism for that matter.

FIGHTING AL-SHABAAB WITH UNITY: AN UPSTREAM APPROACH[22]

As we worked on this chapter, and as the news of the Paris terrorist attacks[23] reverberated across the globe, one of us received an email message from Bernie and Farsijana Adeney-Risakotta, a Christian couple from Indonesia, with the subject, "Upstream Solutions and Terrorism." Bernie and Farjisana are actively involved:

> in "up-stream solutions," to prevent hatred and violence from ever occurring, rather than just dealing with the anguish after tragedy strikes, like it did in Paris. By the grace of God we are trying to bring reconciliation, justice and peace to our Muslim neighbors. Women and children in one of the poorest villages in Indonesia are gaining hope and learning that Muslims and Christians can love and help each other. Indonesia has 220 million Muslims, more than the whole Middle East put together. Yet very few Indonesian Muslims are going to Syria to fight with ISIS. Ironically, far more Europeans than Indonesians are joining the

---

21. Amina H. Ibrahim, "Mothers," *Daily Nation*, 11 April 2015. http://www.nation.co.ke/oped/Opinion/-/440808/2682822/-/3nqeggz/-/index.html. Accessed 11 August 2016. For details of the Garissa attack, see "Kenya Attack: 147 Dead in Garissa University Assault." *BBC News* 13 April 2015. http://www. bbc.com/news/world-africa-32169080. Accessed 11 August 2016.

22. The expression "upstream approach" is borrowed from our friend Bernie Adeney-Risakotta.

23. See *BBC News*, 16 November 2015, "Paris Attacks: What Happened on the Night." http://www.bbc.com/news/world-europe-34818994. Accessed 11 August 2016.

terrorist ranks of ISIS. There are many reasons for this, including that many Indonesian Muslims and Christians consider each other brothers and sisters, not enemies. Another reason is that many Muslims in Indonesia have hope for the future. <u>Violence and death is not an attractive life plan, if you have hope.</u>[24]

In the email, though from a different context and from a different faith, Bernie and Farsijana share the concern of Ibrahim, quoted in the previous section, that Islamic terrorism is very close to our families. Sharing on the broader ISIS in Indonesia, the couple observe:

> Still, ISIS and other radical groups are trying to recruit in Indonesia. One of my former students from the State Islamic University was involved with a notorious Islamic school which has graduated many terrorists, some of whom were put to death for involvement in the Bali bombing. When he came for dinner at our home, he introduced himself to Farsijana as "Bernie's terrorist student." His son went off to fight for ISIS and was killed in Syria a few months ago. My former student is trying to distance himself from radical Islam and has reached out to me again, asking when we can meet. How do I feel about this? We will meet soon. Perfect love casts out all fear. I love him, although not yet perfectly.[25]

The church as a community of believers in Jesus Christ has adopted various responses to the al-Shabaab crisis ranging from cooperation (continuum) (with some Christians joining al-Shabaab in both word and deed)[26] to advocating violence against al-Shabaab as a Christian way of actively resisting evil. In between are other Christians in Kenya who naively assume that al-Shabaab is weakening and will soon be eradicated if only the government of Kenya focuses "on finding suitable approaches to de-radicalize the small number of Muslims who have been lured into extremism in Kenya."[27] The church in Kenya needs an effective and sus-

---

24. We are grateful to Bernie and his wife Farsijana for allowing us to quote the email in this paper.

25. Ibid.

26. Not that Christians are joining al-Shabaab, but some are sympathetic to their grievances. There is a rare case of a 14-year-old from a Christian family found participating in an al-Shabaab cell. See "Police Holding Boy, 14, Rescued from Al-Shabaab Training." *Daily Nation*, 10 October 2015. http://www.nation.co.ke/news/1056-2908226-jp3rlaz/index.html. Accessed 18 August 2016.

27. Kipkoros, "Towards a Christian Response."

tainable "upstream" approach to al-Shabaab terrorism in Kenya: gender equality at the family level and unity at the religious level.

The church more than ever before needs to offer guidance, but one cannot offer what one does not have. The immediate task of the church is to understand the context within which al-Shabaab is operating in Kenya. Some of the responses of the churches in Kenya suggest that part of the church confuses Islam and Muslims with Islamism and Islamists. In so doing, churches are being hypocritical, given that history is awash with examples of religious violence in the name of religion, including Christianity. An understanding of al-Shabaab necessarily informs the church that in condemning Islam and Muslims, the church falls into the very pitfalls that al-Shabaab wishes it to. Understanding al-Shabaab is critical. As Sheikh Mohamadu Saleem of the National Imam's Council of Australia observed, Muslims should be more understanding of other religions, but "at the same time Christian groups and other religions must overcome their prejudice to Muslims and Islam."[28] Such an understanding will include the need for the churches to join with Islam and all other religions to build a cohesive and harmonious Kenyan society that would be difficult for al-Shabaab or any other terror group to infiltrate.

To build society, it is essential to understand the blocks with which society is built and create unity in these blocks before we expect unity in the whole. This calls for unity of Christians with Muslims towards establishing and strengthening the fundamental value of family and relationships against neoliberal capitalistic values of materialism, individualism, and consumerism. This would be a common rallying ground for Muslims and Christians. For religion, be it Islam or Christianity, reminds us "of human finitude and weakness, also enjoins us not to place our ultimate hope in this passing world. Man is 'like a breath, his days are like a passing shadow' (Ps 144:4)."[29]

Gender equality emerges as one of the ways of ensuring the value of family and relationships. In trying to dig into the root causes of the

28. Cited in "Pope Urges All Faiths to Unite," *CBC News*, 18 July 2008. http://www.cbc.ca/news/world/pope-urges-all-faiths-to-unite-1.724685. Cf. *BBC News*, 16 July 2008. "Saudi King Appeals for Tolerance." http://news.bbc.co.uk/2/hi/europe/7510208.stm.

29. Benedict XVI, "When Religious People Quarrel, Extremists Have Met Their Goal." *Kearney Hub*, 19 July 2008. http://www.kearneyhub.com/news/opinion/when-religious-people-quarrel-extremists-have-met-their-goal/article_f5839c12-e65a-5ab4-bbbb-6c11fe32f246.html. Accessed 13 August 2016.

success of al-Shabaab in Kenya, the breakdown of the family unit resulting from unhealthy competitive gender relations emerges as a facilitator rather than controller of radicalization of young people into al-Shabaab. The way to effectively respond to Islamic terrorism, or any other terrorism, therefore, is to strengthen the Kenyan family. The opening statements of Pope John Paul II remain accurate, current, and inspiring:

> While building up the Church in love, the Christian family places itself at the service of the human person and the world, really bringing about the "human advancement" whose substance was given in summary form in the Synod's Message to Families: "Another task for the family is to form persons in love and also to practice love in all its relationships, so that it does not live closed in on itself, but remains open to the community, moved by a sense of justice and concern for others, as well as by a consciousness of its responsibility towards the whole of society."[30]

The Pope is clear that the wellbeing of the human society is dependent on the wellbeing of the family unit. Reiterating the message of the Synod of Bishops, the Pope spells out the task of the family as that of forming persons in love and practicing love in all its relationships. This calls for families to adopt healthy gender relations that will translate into the formation of children in love, and also into healthy relationships that can then radiate across the human society.

The affirmation that we put forth in this chapter is that the family remains the determining core of all social relationships at all levels. Further, we argue that gender relations at the family level are the central theme around which all forms of justice revolve. The scenario in Kenya calls for a reconstruction of gender relations and revision of gender approaches from competitiveness to complementarity for the benefit of men, women, and children. We affirm that there should be no competitive efforts in the struggle for justice, for no one should gain rights by denying them to another. From a theological and natural perspective, men and women are different for complementary purposes. Indeed, the cooperation of men and women is critical to the basic instinct of human survival, perpetuation, and development. A reconstruction of gender towards complementarity recognizes the need to encompass a wider ex-

---

30. John Paul II, *Familiaris Consortio*, §64. See also Synod of Bishops, Fifth Ordinary General Assembly, "Message to Christian Families in the Modern World" (24 October 1980), 12.

periential base that produces a whole, necessary for sustainable human development. Gender complementarity then has to be understood as a societal need rather than a women's need, for it will benefit both men and women. The fact that what are conventionally labeled as masculine and feminine (social attributes) are found in every man and woman and the inability of men and women to operate biologically independent of one another indicates that if we are to exploit human resources to the full, we must stress gender complementarity and discard any traits of gender competitiveness. This necessarily calls for embracing the values of family and relationships for eventual building of a lasting harmonious human society away from materialism, consumerism, and individualism. This calls for unity of men and women, which necessarily translates to unity of all human persons.

CONCLUSION

Meeting al-Shabaab terrorism, like any other form of terrorism, with violence complicates an already difficult scenario. While governments may be justified responding to terrorism with violence since the security and safety of citizens is directly entrusted to it, churches cannot afford to respond in like manner, not only because it is not a viable response but more so because it is not theologically permissible.

In this chapter, we argue that the continued attack on Kenyan Christians by al-Shabaab compels the churches in Kenya to respond by first seeking to understand al-Shabaab as a group of Islamists and not of Muslims. The next step involves understanding the Kenyan context that al-Shabaab effectively exploits to successfully carry out terrorist attacks. This chapter contributes towards an understanding of the situation of the family in Kenya. This situation, we argue, is characterized by unequal gender relations that leave women overburdened by family responsibilities as they take up nearly all traditional male gender roles on top of their traditional gender roles. As they lose their traditional gender roles, some men become "absent" fathers as they resort to drinking and, in turn, to violence to cope with their situations of irrelevance. Unfortunately, as women achieve economic independence, many have embraced the values of neoliberal capitalism to focus almost exclusively on the accumulation of material resources for individual consumption at the expense of the emotional wellbeing of their children. The impact of this on the family is there for all to see: "absent" mothers and absent fathers; unguided children—a situation that provides fertile ground for al-Shabaab to thrive. The way forward is to seek religious unity for societal unity. This necessarily begins at the family level, and so we propose promotion of the family and healthy relationships as high values, which can then radiate beyond the family to the entire nation. With strong family values across society, al-Shabaab will die a natural death for lack of recruits.

REFERENCES

Newspapers and Online News

BBC News
CBC News
Daily Nation
Kearney Hub

Other

Avis, Paul. *Eros and the Sacred*. London: SPCK, 1989.
Ayanga, Hazel H. "Inspired and Gendered: The Hermeneutical Challenge Teaching Gender in Kenya." In *Men in the Pulpit, Women in the Pew? Addressing Gender Inequality in Africa*, edited by Jurgens Hendriks et al., 85–92. Stellebosch: African Sun Media, 2012.
Bradbury, Mark, and Sally Healy. "Endless War: A Brief History of the Somali Crisis." In *Whose Peace Is It Anyway? Connecting Somali and International Peacemaking*, edited by Mark Bradbury and Sally Healy, 10–14. Accord 21. London: Conciliatory Resources, 2010. http://www.c-r.org/downloads/21_Somalia_2010_ENG_F.pdf. Accessed 11 August 2016.
Chadwick, Henry. *The Early Church*. London: Penguin, 1967.
Fuchs, Erich. *Sexual Desire and Love: Origins and History of the Christian Ethic of Sexuality and Marriage*. New York: Seabury, 1963.
Hansen, Stig Jarle. *Al-Shabaab in Somalia: The History and Ideology of a Militant Islamist Group* 2005–2012. Oxford: Oxford University Press, 2013.
John Paul II. *Familiaris Consortio*. http://w2.vatican.va/content/john-paul-ii/en/apost_exhortations/documents/hf_jp-ii_exh_19811122_familiaris-consortio.html. Accessed 15 August 2016.
Kambo, Joseph A. "The Integral, Personal and Sexual Development of Future Parents: The Responsibility of Kikuyu and Nandi Christian Families." DPhil thesis, Catholic University of East Africa, 1993.
Kilbride, Philip L., and Janet C. Kilbride. *Changing Family Life in East Africa: Women and Children at Risk*. University Park: Pennsylvania State University Press, 1990.
Kipkoros, William C. "Towards a Christian Response to Al-Shabaab's Terror Attacks on Kenyans." *Journal of Philosophy, Culture and Religion* 11 (2015) 25–33.
Mugenda, Olive. "Female Education in Kenya: A Status Review." In *AAWORD Strategies to Action*, 39–60. Nairobi, AAWORD, 1995.

O'Dea, Thomas, and Janet O'Dea Aviad. *Sociology of Religion*. Englewood Cliffs, NJ: Prentice-Hall, 1993.

Peschke, Karl H. *Christian Ethics: Moral Theology in Light of Vatican II*. Vol. 1, *General Moral Theology*. 3rd ed. Eugene, OR: Wipf & Stock, 1979.

Ruether, Rosemary R. "The Western Religious Tradition and Violence against Women in the Home." In *Christianity, Patriarchy, and Abuse: A Feminist Critique*, edited by Joanne C. Brown and Carole R. Bohn, 31–41. New York: Pilgrim, 1989.

Siberschmidt, Margrethe. "Have Men Become the Weaker Sex? Changing Life Situations in Kisii District, Kenya." *Journal of Modern African Studies* 30 (1992) 237–53.

———. "'Women Forget that Men Are the Masters': Gender Antagonism and Socio-economic Change in Kisii District, Kenya."1999. http://www.diva-portal.org/smash/get/diva2:276982/FULLTEXT01.pdf. Accessed 18August 2016.

Stitcher, S. B. "The Middle Class Family in Kenya: Change in Gender Relations." In *Patriarchy and Class: African Women in the Home and the Workforce*, edited by S. B. Stitcher and J. L. Parpart, 187–211. Boulder, CO: Westview, 1988.

10

Missions to Muslims
A Kenyan Experience

Joseph K. Koech

The issue of Christian mission to the world finds its roots in the Bible. Both the Old Testament and the New Testament provide a framework for carrying out mission work among various communities of the world. Various questions touching missions to Muslims need to be explored in the present Kenyan context as a result of challenges brought about by recent terrorist activities. This study briefly examines the theological basis of mission work from the New Testament, and the historical evidence about challenges in Christian relations to Muslims. First, the understanding of the meaning and implications of mission in Christianity from theological and New Testament perspectives is examined. Second, Christian contact with Islam in the past and the present is explored, touching areas of mutuality, cooperation, tensions, and reasons for such. Third, an overview of the church's role in missionary activity among Muslims in the context of terrorist activities is given, and experiences of missionaries are evaluated with the intent of providing impetus for future academic discourse and practical application. Some individuals from one unnamed Protestant church are interviewed to explore the practice of mission to Muslims in Kenya, focusing on preparation, approach, field experiences, and recommendations.

THE MEANING OF MISSION(S)

The term "mission" eludes a simple definition, for it has been used to indicate a diversity of activities involving almost any service, especially cross-cultural work done by Christians. Biblical scholars note that from biblical revelation, mission is understood within the overall context of salvation history. God calls persons individually or collectively and sends them out with a clear mandate. Mission has been used to mean many things in the past. Bosch has identified several of them including:

> (a) the sending of missionaries to a designated territory, (b) the activities undertaken by such missionaries, (c) the geographical area where the missionaries were active, (d) the agency which dispatched the missionaries, (e) the non-Christian world or "mission field," or (f) the center from which the missionaries operated on the "mission field" . . . In a slightly different context it could also refer to (g) a local congregation without a resident minister and still dependent on the support of an older, established church, or (h) a series of special services intended to deepen or spread the Christian faith, usually in a nominally Christian environment.[1]

It has also been used to mean evangelism, expansion of God's rule, conversion to Christianity, and planting new churches. According to Johnannes Hoekendijk, mission encompasses what he calls *kerygma*, *koinonia*, and *diakonia* (proclamation, fellowship, and service).[2] His model is drawn from the Acts of the Apostles, where the apostles proclaimed the gospel, founded churches, and were engaged in *diakonia*. Mission is also defined as unity and as *indigenization* or *inculturation* of the gospel.

Some scholars have emphasized the holistic dimension of mission, that it should focus not just on spiritual concerns but also on physical and social needs, going beyond the individual to a societal focus.[3] However, the danger of over-stressing the physical aspects must be guarded against by providing a balanced view.

The apostolic commission, as couched in the terms of the experience of the early church, is very clearly presented in the four Gospels.

---

1. Bosch, *Transforming Mission*, 28.

2. Hoekendijk, "Notes," cited in Glasser and McGavran, *Contemporary Theologies of Mission*, 17.

3. Glasser and McGavran, *Contemporary Theologies of Mission*, 28.

The church acts in consonance with the commission that Jesus received, a commission that is universal in its scope. All Christians are commanded to preach the gospel to all nations, baptizing them in the name of the Father and of the Son and of the Holy Spirit (Matt 28:19–20). Therefore, mission is primarily *missio Dei* (the mission of God) implying that it is a God-centered activity, not people-or church-centered. Mission is an on-going process involving the entire Trinity from beginning to end.

In a definition more applicable to what this chapter is discussing, Glasser and McGavran define mission as "carrying the gospel across cultural boundaries to those who owe no allegiance to Jesus Christ, and encouraging them to accept Him as Lord and Savior and to become responsible members of His church, working as the Holy Spirit leads at both evangelism and justice, at making God's will done on earth as it is in heaven."[4] The goal is for the target group to become disciples of Christ, form churches or join one, and live lives as Christ would have them live. However, approaches such as education, literacy programs, agriculture, medicine, presence, dialogue, proclamation, and social action can be employed.

The Great Commission (Matt 28:16–20), Luke's writings (in his Gospel and Acts), and the writings of Paul provide our impetus for missions. The perspectives of Matthew and Luke are highlighted here. The focus of Matthew is on the discipleship of all nations. Matthew was writing to a predominantly Jewish church urging them to reach out in mission activity to other, non-Jewish communities. Matthew's concern for mission can be summarized in the following statement by Michael J. Wilkins:

> The offer of discipleship found in the Great Commission broke down the same barriers that Jesus broke down all through his earthly ministry. Restrictions on the basis of gender, ethnicity, social status, and religious practice were abolished so that now women and men, Jew and Gentile, rich and poor, clean and unclean are all called to be Jesus' disciples.[5]

Luke presents the message of mission activity from a more universal perspective. The tone of the entire Gospel and Acts of the Apostles is that of reaching out to all communities even in the face of hostility (Luke

---

4. Ibid., 26.
5. Wilkins, *Matthew*, 34.

24:47; cf. Acts 1:8). According to Bosch, Jesus' rejection at Nazareth sets the entire understanding of the mission of Jesus across racial boundaries in the face of persecution. He states that "in Luke's mind, the Nazareth episode has a clearly Gentile mission orientation and serves to highlight this fundamental thrust of Jesus' entire ministry at his very first appearance in public."[6] Jesus' mission is not just to the Jews but also to the Gentiles.

Some scholars have shifted their attention from the Great Commission text of Matt 28:16–20 as the primary mandate for mission to the writings Luke depicting the ministry of Jesus in Luke's Gospel and of the church explained in the book of Acts. Bosch's presentation of important lessons gleaned from Luke provides an overview of dimensions of mission work.

In the first place, Luke highlights the need for the empowerment of the Spirit in carrying out mission work (Luke 24:49; Acts 1:8). Second, Luke seeks to highlight the similarities of God's concern for both the Jews and the Gentiles. The ministry of Jesus in Luke's Gospel and of the disciples in Acts shows that God treats both Jews and Gentiles in the same way (Acts 10:38 cf. Acts 15:6–11). The continuity of the *missio Dei* from the Jews to the Gentiles is noted in Luke's writings. Third, the goal of the gospel is repentance and living a life acceptable to God (Acts 2:36–40). Fourth, mission work relates to a salvation defined in a holistic manner touching economic, social, political, physical, psychological, and spiritual concerns.[7] Jesus' declaration made in the Nazareth synagogue sermon was a universal message of liberation by the Spirit. Joseph Koech notes, "Luke 4:14–30 is programmatic for the entire ministry of Jesus, that is in its scope and character. It is the ministry of Jesus presented in a nutshell. The success, reactions, character, and even rejection are encapsulated in the narrative."[8]

The fifth point is that Luke presents missioners as people practicing non-violent resistance to evil. Jesus and the disciples did not retaliate in the face of persecution but readily forgave their opponents (Luke 23:34; Acts 7:60). Sixth, the church as a community is non-sectarian and inclusive, uniting Jews and Gentiles into one new community through the power of the Spirit (Acts 15:6–11). Seventh, mission work is expected

---

6. Bosch, *Transforming Mission*, 89.
7. Ibid., 117.
8. Koech, *Holy Spirit as Liberator*, 92.

to be accompanied by challenges and sometimes serious opposition. Persecutions sometimes resulting in death are expected outcomes. Luke uses the term "witness/testifier" (Greek, *martus*), meaning in one sense "martyr," to describe the role of a disciple (Acts 1:8; 7:1—8:8). Jesus suffered for those who would follow him, setting an example for those who would take his message to others (Luke 24:27). Mission work had to be carried out even in hostile territories.

Luke provides an all-encompassing missionary paradigm, holistic in nature and all-inclusive in its perspective. The attitude of the missionary finds its paradigm from Luke, especially that of readiness to face persecution and death in the face of a hostile environment. The African context, particularly the Kenyan one, is currently one of hostility, especially involving targeted terrorist activities. Luke's perspective provides a paradigm for facing the Islamic fundamentalist challenge.

THE CHALLENGE

The present challenge for the church in Africa is first to correctly define and understand its mission through the religio-cultural heritage of the African people and with heightened sensitivity to their economic and socio-political dynamics and concerns.

The ethnic composition in Kenya poses great challenges due to the ever-present conflicts resulting from social, economic, and political factors. Religious pluralism also plays a role, especially the relationship between Christians and Muslims. This is a potential point of contention and conflict, but can also be an area of engagement in constructive dialogue. The rise of religious fundamentalism resulting in terrorist activities by those who purport to represent Islam has made it difficult for Christians to relate to Muslims. Terrorist activities have made some communities somewhat suspicious, and have resulted in a greater challenge to mission activities by the church. Such religious fundamentalism in Kenya is making mission activity difficult, especially as it relates to reaching those of the Islamic faith.

Muslims in Kenya

Kenya's population is approximately 42 million according to current estimates by the Kenyan government. Christians comprise approximately 80 to 85 percent, while Muslims range between 8 and 10 percent of the population. The rest either belong to other religions or follow African Traditional Religion. Muslims are dominant in the Coastal region and the north-eastern parts of Kenya. Their presence is also felt, though less, in the Western region around the Mumias area and also in the major towns.

Some studies have been carried out regarding Islam and Muslims in Kenya but mostly within the context of East Africa[9] or Sub-Saharan Africa.[10] Scholarly work is still ongoing regarding the origin and characteristics of Islam in the coastal regions of Eastern of Africa. Some scholars have argued that the type of Islam in this region of Africa, including that of Kenya, has peculiarities differing from the Islam introduced from Arabia and Persia.[11] Accordingly, addressing the issue of mission to them requires an understanding of these peculiarities. Contextual issues resulting from historical, cultural, economic, and even political factors must be considered.

Mbiti has argued that both Christianity and Islam are indigenous in Africa in the sense that they both have a long history in the African continent.[12] Kim describes Islam among the Swahili in Kenya as peculiar because it has integrated into it the traditional African culture of the locals.[13] This can be termed an African expression of Islam.[14]

The collection of papers from a national seminar on contemporary Islam in Kenya held in 1995 gives insight into various aspects of Islam in Kenya, such as historical issues, the perception of Muslims by the wider society, economic issues, social change, and education.[15] Baraza wrote on Muslims among the Bukusu people in Western Kenya, expounding the history, penetration of Islam into the interior of Kenya, and ways of dialogue between the traditional religion, Islam, and Christianity.[16]

Other studies on Islam among ethnic groups dominated by Islam include those by Faulkner among the Boni at the Kenyan coast,[17]

9. Holt, Lambton and Lewis, *Cambridge History of Islam*.
10. Brenner, *Muslim Identity*.
11. See, for example, Sanneh, *Domestication of Islam and Christianity*.
12. Mbiti, *African Religions and Philosophy*, 229.
13. Kim, *Islam among the Swahili*.
14. Allen, *Swahili Origins*.
15. Bakari and Yahaya, *Islam in Kenya*.
16. Baraza, "Strategies for Developing On-going Dialogue."
17. Faulkner, *Overtly Muslim, Covertly Boni*.

Tablino among the Gabra,[18] and also the Somali in Somalia and Kenya by Lewis.[19] Phillips has also mentioned the existence of Islam among certain Kenyan communities such as the Somali, Oromo, Borana, Gabbra, Garre, Ajuran, and Orma.[20]

Christian–Muslim Relations in Kenya

Various scholarly works discuss relations between Christians and Muslims from diverse perspectives. Some of the approaches are summarized by Michael Dennis Brislen. They include:

> examinations of incidents between Christians and Muslims within a particular African nation, theoretical explanations for why conflict and tensions exist between African Christians and Muslims, discussions of *sharia* and its implications for African Muslims and Christians, histories of Christian missions among African Muslims, and analysis of the influence of African Religion on interreligious relations between Christians and Muslims.[21]

Historically, the relationship between Christians and Muslims in the East African region has not always been hostile. Since the arrival of the Arabs with the Islamic faith on the coast of East Africa the relations with the locals seems to have been positive. Muslims were apparently friendly towards Christians right from the beginning of their presence on the East African coast.

Hassan Mwakimako[22] describes some of the issues of tension in Christian–Muslim relations in Kenya in more detail and points out negative perceptions of the other religious group coupled with mistrust as one of the main evidences of conflict. He evaluates historical peaceful coexistence evidenced by cooperation in trade. Some notable examples are the Omani rulers (from 1840 to 1963) who were open and tolerant to Christians in East Africa, including Sayyid Said (1797–1856), the first Omani Sultan in Zanzibar, who granted permission to Dr. Johann Ludwig Krapf (1810–85) to establish a missionary station at Mombasa

---

18. Tablino, *The Gabra*.
19. Lewis, "Origins of the Galla and Somali."
20. Phillips, *Peoples on the Move*.
21. Brislen, *Christian Perceptions of Islam in Kenya*, 32.
22. Mwakimako, "Christian–Muslim Relations in Kenya," 288.

in 1843, and Ali bin Modehin, a Muslim judge who helped Krapf to develop Kiswahili dictionaries and the translation of sections of the Bible.[23]

Recognition and support of Kadhi courts by the Kenyan government and freedom of worship may promote peaceful coexistence. The inclusion of Islamic studies in public academic institutions encourages positive relations between Christians and Muslims. Islamic religious studies are included in the curricula of primary and secondary schools in Kenya. Kenyan universities have Religion Departments in which Islamic Studies are included with the study of Christianity and other religions as part of the program.

The African idea of community may promote acceptance of people of all religions in one community, positively affecting the relationship between Christians and Muslims. However, relations become strained when there is debate between Muslims and Christians in matters of faith. Terror attacks have also stretched the relations between Christians and Muslims to the limits.

Local Muslim communities in Kenya such as the political leaders, religious leaders, and the Supreme Council of Kenyan Muslims (SUPKEM) have officially condemned terrorist activities and even pledged to support the government in dealing with the problems. Suspicions still continue from those of non-Muslim faiths, especially Christians. Another important result is the increased challenge of reaching Muslims with the Christian message. A new missiological approach must be thought out that will be effective in reaching out to Muslims within this hostile environment. One way could be to create an atmosphere of positive attitudes between Christians and Muslims.

Attitudes of Muslims towards Christianity

As a general rule, Muslims are either hostile to or have a dislike of Christians. Some scholars claim that this could be based on the Qur'an, which discourages close relations with "people of the book," that is, Christians and Jews, as follows:

> Believers, do not seek the friendship of the infidels and those who were given the Book before you, who have made of your religion a jest and a pastime. Have fear of Allah, if you are true believers. . . . Say: "People of the Book, do you hate us for any

---

23. Alio, "Kenyan Christian–Muslim Relations," 113.

reason other than that we believe in Allah and in what has been revealed to us and to others before us, and that most of you are evil-doers?" (Sura 5:381).[24]

Contextual factors may, however, impact the attitude of Muslims towards Christianity. Africans are more accepting towards people of other religions on the basis of communal issues or family closeness when many religions are represented in one family. Muslims would therefore be more accommodating in such a situation, though this is not always the case. However, there are cases in which those who convert to Christianity are shunned even by family members.

Regarding Jesus, Muslims respect him not as a savior but as a prophet. This is a more positive attitude than what they have towards the Christians. But this does not translate to a positive attitude towards Christians and Christianity in general.

ACADEMIC WORK ON MISSIONARY EFFORTS TOWARD MUSLIMS

A study done by Daystar University indicated that among the unreached people groups are those dominated by Islam. They presented this in a report in 1982 showing that among the 26 unreached people groups in Kenya, 12 were predominantly Muslim. The main purpose was to highlight the implications for missionary activity by the church.[25]

Later, in 1995, the Kenya Unreached Peoples Network, Summer Institute of Linguistics and Daystar University presented another report of unreached communities comprising Burji, Maasai, Samburu, Mukugodo, the Giryama, Pokot, and Turkana among others mostly adhering to Islam.[26]

Some academic studies on missiology include a Master of Theology thesis by Braaksma[27] who did a study on missionary activities among Muslim pastoralists such as the Orma in Eastern Kenya, and works on

---

24. English translation from Dawood, *The Koran*.
25. See Kenya Unreached Peoples Network, *A Call to Share*.
26. See Daystar Communications, *Unreached Peoples of Kenya Project*.
27. Braaksma, "Can Christian Development Work Fit."

the Digo by Lundeby (a ThM thesis),[28] Morgan (a DMiss dissertation),[29] and Sesi (a PhD dissertation).[30]

Other existing studies on missionary work among the Muslim communities in Kenya include those by Tablino[31] on the work by the Catholic Church in Northern Kenya, and Kamau's MA thesis, on the ministry methods of a Christian youth center in Eastleigh, a section of Nairobi dominated by Islam.[32] Karuku's MA thesis analyses challenges faced by new Kenyan missionaries in the North-Eastern Province of Kenya, where Muslims predominate.[33] Omollo, in her MA thesis, assesses the mission strategy of the Karen Community Church in Lamu among the Boni.[34] An older MA study by Famonure studied the methods used by three evangelistic ministries among the Muslim communities in Garissa.[35] An MTh thesis by Murumba focused on conversions to Christianity by Borana women in Nairobi,[36] highlighting the seven-stage model of Rambo.[37]

These studies provide a significant contribution to understanding the general situation of Muslims in Kenya. They help us to appreciate challenges faced in any attempt to present the Christian message to places where Islam is dominant. Such challenges are compounded by the wave of terrorist activities in various parts of Kenya.

MODELS OF REACHING MUSLIMS

Various strategy models have been used to reach Muslims with different results. They include the polemical model, the power encounter model,[38] the gospel of work model, involving employing the locals first before converting them (the economic factor associated with Christianity distorts the meaning of faith and has caused a problem, to this day, in

28. Lundeby, *The Digo of the South Kenyan Coast*.
29. Morgan, "Unreached, but Not Unreachable."
30. S. Sesi, "Prayer among the Digo Muslims."
31. Tablino, *Christianity among the Nomads*.
32. Kamau, "A Study of Eastleigh Fellowship."
33. Karuku, "Missiological Study of Culture Shock."
34. Omollo, "Ministry to the Boni of Lamu."
35. Famonure, "Investigation into the Strategies of Evangelism."
36. Murumba, "Study on Conversion from Islam to Christianity."
37. Rambo, *Understanding Religious Conversion*.
38. J. Sesi, "Impact of Christianity," 163.

witnessing to Digo women),[39] and also the crusade evangelism model.[40] Missiologists are now talking about the incarnational model, particularly in attempts to reach communities where cross-cultural barriers exist. The model involves immersing oneself in the target community by identifying with their culture in order to win them.

Within the Kenyan context, a new model is being practiced that seeks to foster positive relations between Christians and Muslims by getting them to talk and understand each other, especially in areas where hostilities have been reported. Basically, this model can be dubbed the dialogue model, as is practiced by St. Paul's University staff and students who have established a center called the Centre for Christian–Muslim Relations in Nairobi to foster peaceful coexistence between Christians and Muslims. The Eastleigh area of Nairobi has been called "little Mogadishu" due to the large Somali Muslim population living and doing business there. This part of Nairobi and some other places in the city have experienced terrorist attacks since the year 2012. The attacks have been blamed on the Somali-based al-Shabaab terrorist group, some claiming that it is operating from Eastleigh due to the presence of a Somali community there. Strained relations between Christians and Muslims have resulted from the terrorist attacks, which are believed to target Christians. Thus, there is need to promote dialogue between people of the two faiths in Nairobi and elsewhere. The general objective of the Centre is to provide a forum for Muslims and Christians to work together through what they call diapraxis, meaning dialogue in practice.

In order to achieve this, the following objectives have been formulated:

- To recognize and overcome stereotypes
- To encourage all parties (Christians, Muslims, other-believers and non-religious persons) to take part in the project
- To demonstrate that, in spite of historical, cultural, and political diversity, scholars, adult educators, students, and guests of the Centre can learn from each other in the processes of the CCMRE activities
- To facilitate, organise, and publish academic research in the field of intercultural and interreligious studies, e.g. seminars, and

39. Ibid., 160.
40. Ibid., 156.

workshops that are made public by academic articles, books, and audio-video materials.[41]

Dialogue for its own sake has some positive impact in the sense of promoting peaceful coexistence between the various communities of difference faiths. It can also foster healthy relationships between Christians and Muslims.

CASE STUDY: MISSION ACTIVITIES BY A PROTESTANT CHURCH IN KENYA

I have selected a certain Kenyan Protestant church[42] for a case study to help provide a practical understanding of the situation in Kenya regarding mission work among Muslims, with special interest in challenges posed by recent terrorist attacks on Christian targets. I sought to address this church's understanding of mission to Muslims. Four key informants from the church were carefully selected and interviewed.[43] The first one, to whom I have given the name "Paul" (not his real name) for purposes of confidentiality, is a trainer of missionaries, especially in the area of reaching Muslims. He is currently a missionary instructor with more than five years' experience. At the time of writing, he holds Master of Theology and MA degrees in Islamic Studies and is learning Arabic. The second informant, "Peter," teaches in a theological institution. Peter has a Master's degree in Religious Studies and is currently a PhD candidate. The third and fourth informants are a missionary family of husband and wife, and we can call them "John and Mary." Both have a Diploma in Theology but the man is currently doing a Bachelor of Theology degree. They have served as church planting/pastoring missionaries for over 15 years in two places, that is, at Madogo area (Tana River coastal region) and at Garissa (North-Eastern Province).

Informants' View of the Church's Understanding of Mission to Muslims

I sought to find out from the informants their church's understanding of mission to Muslims and they all agreed that Muslims are candidates for the gospel. According to Paul, Muslims are part of the mission field that needs to be reached as commanded by Christ. According to the Great

---

41. Peter, Wandera, and Jansen, *Mapping Eastleigh*, 6.
42. The church will be unnamed in this chapter to maintain confidentiality.
43. The interviews were conducted in July 2016.

Commission (Matt 28:19–20) Muslims need to be reached with the message of salvation. The main problem they noted is that many pastors and church leaders have no understanding of Muslim beliefs. Peter stated that the church has not previously adequately trained missionaries going to Muslim regions.

In order to explore the experiences of the missionaries in the field, I interviewed John and Mary. They informed me that they have served as missionaries for fifteen years, including nine years at Madogo before being trained in cross-cultural ministry. After training, they went to Garissa where they served as pastors in the church until they were attacked by terrorists, resulting in the killing of several members of their church.

Their initial ministry training did not give them skills in cross-cultural communication. Currently, they have received some missionary training at diploma level and the man is now pursuing a bachelor's degree in theology.

To them, the mandate to reach Muslims is the Great Commission presented in Matt 28:19–20. Their observation is that the church is lacking an agenda for outreach to Muslims. The focus of the church is missions in general but not specifically to Muslims. However, recent terrorist events have caused the church to begin to act somewhat in that direction. Very few church members are conversant with issues touching Islam. Teaching by the church on outreach is minimal.

John and Mary claimed to have witnessed Muslims convert Christians to Islam in those areas dominated by Muslims. Muslims present arguments against Christianity that many Christians are unable to respond to adequately.

Number of Missionaries

Paul stated that whereas about forty families are involved in missionary activity in general in his church (denomination), only five families are directly involved in Muslim outreach. The main hindrance is lack of training of the missionaries, especially for reaching out to Muslims. Missionaries to Muslims are greatly needed for Muslim areas, such as Mandera and Garissa, which are mainly populated by Somali Muslims, and the Coast, populated by various mostly-Islamic tribes such as the Mijikenda, Swahili, Pokomo, Segeju, Taveta, Taita, and Digo, to name just a few. Paul said that the church has been doing missionary work for about ten years. It was started with a Somali convert who was eventually killed because of propagating the Christian faith.

Kind of Training Offered

Paul explained that the level of training offered by the church's college to those preparing to go for missions is Certificate and Diploma level in Islamic studies. This is mainly because the missionary candidates available have a level of secondary education that does not qualify them initially for a higher level of training such as a degree.

Currently some of the courses being taught include History of Islam, Culture and Worldview of Islam, Women in Islam, Theology of Islam, Muslim Apologetics, and Approach to Muslims. The college also provides refresher courses every year.

All respondents stated that there is need for more concerted academic engagement to address the issue of Muslim outreach, especially in light of the terrorist attacks. Currently there are no public forums to deal with this challenge. Paul stated that he has attended conferences on outreach to Islam in other countries, particularly Turkey and Ethiopia (Addis Ababa), but no such meetings have ever been held Kenya.

According to Peter, the training previously offered was too general to meet the needs of those going to be missionaries in areas dominated by the Islamic faith. In the past, the church did not see the need to equip missionaries to specifically minister to Muslims. For that reason, there was little success by the few missionaries sent to Muslim-dominated communities.

It was not until 2013 when terrorist activities escalated that the church started to think of equipping the missionaries to face the situation. Whereas one general course of three units on Islam had been taught to the missionaries at diploma level, there was then an increase in the number of courses. Since 2013 the courses have been increased to equip missionaries to better understand Islam. At present about twenty-six missionaries have been trained with more emphasis on understanding Islam.

The training targets families (husband and wife) because both are usually sent to the mission field together. It begins at certificate level and continues to the diploma level. A higher level of training is yet to be provided. To Peter, this is a weakness that the church needs to address. There is much to be done, especially in the need to increase courses touching on understanding the Islamic faith. He acknowledged that there is always a refresher workshop of one week a year that the missionaries are invited to attend. During that time focus is on preparing the missionaries to face new challenges in the areas to which they will be redeployed.

Methods of Outreach

There was consensus that open air meetings (usually called "crusades") should be totally avoided because such an approach reminds Muslims of the infamous Crusades. Muslims also shun any attempts to reach them with the Christian message in public settings. Paul noted that one of the best methods is a one-on-one approach, especially through friendship, or even internet conversations and debates. Another important method is the need-based approach, such as provision of health facilities and drilling of borehole wells. Provision of education is another important approach, particularly in the upper coastal region. There is a more recent attempt to use media such as television, radio, and internet websites. In a limited way movies have been employed to try reaching those of the Islamic faith

Peter pointed out that the main method of Muslim outreach currently used by the church is what he called an "incarnational" approach whereby missionaries live among the people they are sent to without necessarily overtly preaching to them. They are encouraged to develop friendships, provide services such as education, veterinary and health services, and water supply among others. How effective is this method? What are the advantages and disadvantages of using it?

The method adopted by John and Mary was incarnational, whereby they first lived among the community in Madogo for about nine years without directly preaching to the people. They started a primary school that is now admitting pupils up to Standard 8. To them the project has been a success and has caused the community to accept them to the extent that local people began inviting them into their homes. They went to Garissa as pastors for an already-existing church. To them this was problematic because most of the membership comprised those people from other parts of Kenya who were in the town either as government workers or on business. None of the local Somali community was ever converted to Christianity during their stay there. Due to the negative attitude by the locals towards them, they would always experience hostility from them. The situation was worsened because they lived in the church compound, so were easily identified as propagators of Christianity, making them objects of ridicule to the locals.

Christian–Muslim Relations

Generally, from Paul's experience, Muslims are very sensitive to any attempts to convert them. They welcome Christian aid for their needs but reject any attempt to preach the gospel to them.

The attitude of most Christians towards Muslims is that of suspicion and fear. As a result of terrorist activities, few Christians would readily socialize with Muslims, let alone relate to them as friends. Paul told a story of how he wanted to see the reaction of Christians in church towards Muslims. He and his wife put on Islamic attire and attended a church service on a Sunday morning in one church. Several members panicked on seeing them. At one point one of the ushers did not permit them to sit towards the front of the church. No one wanted to sit near them. There was palpable anxiety, and peace was restored only when their true identity was known.

Through their encounter with Somali people (mostly adherents of Islam), John and Mary reported that they came to realize that Muslims are all unbelievers and so lost. They accept Christians in general social interactions, but in matters of faith hostility comes to the surface. So long as one does not interfere with their faith they are accommodating. They welcome education, business, health, financial support and any other help from Christians. Their children even attend schools run by Christians but they are intolerant of attempts to introduce the Christian faith to them.

Experiences of Missionaries in Muslim Areas

Paul's view was that even before the advent of terrorism, missionaries had hostile receptions in some areas, especially in Garissa. When terrorist activities began, which coincided with the invasion of Somalia by the Kenyan Defense Forces (KDF), the missionaries became openly threatened. Stones were thrown on the roofs of churches during church services. Some churches were attacked and several Christians killed. Though the attacks were blamed on outsiders, the locals were said to be sympathetic to the attackers. Some missionaries were forced to leave the region because of the events and overt threats to their lives.

Those churches that were attacked faced a decline in numbers for a while but have started growing again. Part of the reason for the decline was that most of the members, being people from other parts of Kenya, left Garissa town after the terrorist attacks. However, some members were emboldened and became more committed in their faith. John and Mary said that the Sunday following the attack on their church, some members who had not been doing so before came to the church early in the morning to pray.

Paul said an important consequence of the attacks was the need to retrain the missionaries about how to approach Muslims in an effective way and also to avoid creating animosity. He also called for new strategies to reach Muslims. Whereas some missionaries experienced fear in the face of the attacks, most stated that they were ready to die in the field.

I asked Paul and the others regarding the identity of the terrorists and their relationship to Islam, and they responded that all terrorists claim to be Muslims. To the terrorists, moderate Muslims are not true Muslims because they are not following the full requirements of the Qur'an. However, not all Muslims are terrorists.

John and Mary's experiences were mixed. At Madogo they received acceptance from the locals basically as a result of the school they started. At Garissa, their experience was initially mild hostility from the locals. Immediately after the KDF invaded Somalia, hostility towards them increased. Soon terrorist attacks started, with churches being targeted. They requested security guards, but one Sunday morning in July 2012 they were attacked, resulting in the death of several church members including one of their relatives. Though John was not physically harmed, his wife Mary was hurt and had to be admitted to hospital for two weeks. The terrorist attacks resulted in the reduction in the number of church members. John and Mary were also forced to leave the town due to threats to their lives and the trauma they experienced. During the interview, it was evident that they were still experiencing pain from the incident.

As to the question of the impact of terrorist attacks on missionary work and church life, the informants stated that several issues arose. Immediately after the attack, many started questioning God in relation to their faith. One of the church members asked the pastor, "What sin have we committed that led to this attack?" Others asked, "Where was God when the terrorists attacked?" Some left the church completely, while a majority left the town, particularly those who were there on business or were government employees. Positively, some members became even more committed in their faith. Currently, possibly due to the improved security situation, the church has grown. A new pastor has also been posted there.

Recommendations for Missionaries and the Church in the Face of Terrorism

Each of the respondents made significant personal observations touching the attitude towards Muslims, mission to Islamic areas, preparation of missionaries, and readiness of the missionaries under the threat of terrorism. It is noteworthy that none of the respondents blamed the government for the terrorist attacks on Christians.

Paul was categorical that the Christians ought to love Muslims and see them as God's creation, though Muslims need to hear God's message of salvation. There is an urgent need to pray regarding the threat of terrorism and future outreach to Muslims. Missionaries should be ready to reach out to Muslims and not fear death.

Peter advised that the church should rethink its approach to reaching Muslims by creating forums for academic discussion. Training should also focus on interfaith dialogue to allow a greater understanding of the other faiths. Seminaries should be more open to other views and not closed to their own perspectives, especially on Islamic outreach. Literature should be produced aimed at helping ordinary Christians to have a greater understanding of the beliefs and practices of other faiths, especially Islam. Scholarly work can also engage Muslim scholars in an effort to foster a better understanding between Islamic and Christian scholars and reduce tension between Christians and Muslims.

CONCLUSION

The foregoing discussion has shown that mission work finds its basis in the Bible, in both the Old Testament and (especially) the New Testament. Challenges posed by terrorist activities can be addressed by reevaluating strategies. By doing so it will be possible to address the negative challenges such as hostilities stemming from the general issues of Christian and

Islamic beliefs, problems caused by terrorism, and the questions caused by cross-cultural barriers. Dialogue and incarnational models may be the most relevant approaches for missionary outreaches in Muslim areas. Training by the church needs to be reevaluated, so that it will address both the lack of understanding of mission work by ordinary church members and the preparation of missionaries. Those intending to serve in hostile areas will find comfort in the ministry of Jesus presented in the Gospels and the work of the early church described in Acts. They should be ready to serve in the face of hostility and persecution and even death.

REFERENCES

Alio, Mohamed Sheikh. "Kenyan Christian–Muslim Relations: Bridging Factors and Persisting Challenges." *International Journal of Education and Research* 3, no. 12 (2015) 111–28.

Allen, James de Vere. *Swahili Origins: Swahili Culture and the Shungwaya Phenomenon*. East African Studies. London: James Currey, 1993.

Bakari, Mohamed, and Saad S. Yahya. *Islam in Kenya: Proceedings of the National Seminar on Contemporary Islam in Kenya*. Nairobi: Mewa, 1995.

Baraza, Patrick Wanakuta. "Strategies for Developing On-going Dialogue between African Traditional Religions, Islam and Christianity within the Context of the Bukusu People of Western Kenya." ThD diss., Graduate Theological Union, 2002.

Bosch, David Jacobus. *Transforming Mission: Paradigm Shifts in Theology of Mission*. Maryknoll, NY: Orbis, 2011.

Braaksma, Debra. "Can Christian Development Work Fit on a Donkey's Back? Rethinking the Approach to Missionary Development Work among Muslim Pastoralists." MTh diss., University of Edinburgh, 1994.

Brenner, Louis, ed. *Muslim Identity and Social Change in Sub-Saharan Africa*. London: Hurst, 1993.

Brislen, Michael Dennis. "Christian Perceptions of Islam in Kenya: As Expressed in Written Sources from 1998 to 2010." PhD thesis, University of Birmingham, 2013.

Dawood, N. J., trans. *The Koran*. London: Penguin, 2006.

Daystar Communications. *Unreached Peoples of Kenya Project: North Coast Report (Including Giriama, Sanye, Swahili/Arab, Bajun, Boni). A Survey Conducted by Daystar Communications for the Committee on Unreached Peoples*. Nairobi: Daystar, 1982.

Famonure, Esther Adenike. "An Investigation into the Strategies of Evangelism among Three Evangelistic Ministries in Garissa." MA thesis, Nairobi Evangelical Graduate School of Theology, 1993.

Faulkner, Mark R. J. *Overtly Muslim, Covertly Boni: Competing Calls of Religious Allegiance on the Kenyan Coast*. Studies of Religion in Africa. Leiden: Brill, 2006.

Glasser, Arthur F., and Donald McGavran. *Contemporary Theologies of Mission*. Grand Rapids: Baker, 1983.

Hoekendijk, Johannes C. "Notes on the Meaning of Mission(ary)." In *Planning for Mission*, edited by Thomas Wieser, 37–48. New York: US Conference for the World Council of Churches, 1966.

Kamau, Wairimu. "A Study of Eastleigh Fellowship Centre's Muslim-Youth Ministry Methods from a Christian Cross-cultural Perspective." MA thesis, Nairobi Evangelical Graduate School of Theology, 2005.

Karuku, Harun Wang'ombe. "A Missiological Study of Culture Shock Experiences of The Sheepfold Ministries' Missionaries in Kenya with Implications for Training at Centre for Missions Training." MA thesis, Nairobi Evangelical Graduate School of Theology, 2006.

Kenya Unreached Peoples Network. *A Call to Share: The Unevangelised Peoples of Kenya. A Project of Kenya Unreached Peoples Network (KUPNet) in Cooperation with Summer Institute of Linguistics and Daystar University*. Nairobi: Daystar, 1995.

Kim, Caleb Chul-Soo. *Islam among the Swahili in East Africa*. Nairobi: Acton, 2004.

Koech, Joseph. *The Holy Spirit as Liberator: A Study of Luke 4:16–30 in the African Context*. Eldoret: Zapf Chancery, 2006.

Holt, Peter Malcolm, Ann Katherine Swynford Lambton, and Bernard Lewis, eds. *The Cambridge History of Islam*. Vol. 2A. Cambridge University Press, 1977.

Lewis, H. S. "The Origins of the Galla and Somali." *Journal of African History* 7, no. 1 (1966) 27–46.

Lundeby, Erling Andreas. "The Digo of the South Kenyan Coast: Description and Annotated Bibliography." ThM thesis, Fuller Theological Seminary, 1993.

Mbiti, John. *African Religions and Philosophy*. Nairobi: Heinemann, 1969.

Morgan, Garry Robert. "Unreached, but Not Unreachable: A Comprehensive Strategy for Making Disciples among the Digo People." DMiss diss., Western Conservative Baptist College, 1995.

Murumba, Pauline Cherop. "A Study on Conversion from Islam to Christianity among the Borana Women in Nairobi, Kenya, with Implications for Christian Witness." MTh thesis, Nairobi Evangelical Graduate School of Theology, 2008.

Mwakimako, Hassan. "Christian–Muslim Relations in Kenya: A Catalogue of Events and Meanings." *Islam and Christian–Muslim Relations* 18, no. 2 (2007) 287–307.

Omollo, Mary Kuyume. "Ministry to the Boni of Lamu: An Evaluation of Karen Community Church's Mission Strategies." MA thesis, Nairobi Evangelical Graduate School of Theology, 2004.

Peter, C. B., Joseph Wandera, and Willem J. E. Jansen, eds. *Mapping Eastleigh for Christian– Muslim Relations*. Limuru: Zapf Chancery, 2013.

Phillips, David J. *People on the Move: Introducing the Nomads of the World*. Carlisle: Piquant, 2001.

Rambo, Lewis R. *Understanding Religious Conversion*. New Haven: Yale University Press, 1993.

Sanneh, Lamin. "The Domestication of Islam and Christianity in African Societies: A Methodological Exploration." *Journal of Religion in Africa* 11, no. 1 (1980) 1–12.

Sesi, Josephine Katile Mutuku. "Impact of Christianity among Digo Muslim Women." In *African Missiology: Contributions of Contemporary Thought*, edited by Stephen Mutuku Sesi et al., 155–76. Nairobi: Uzima, 2009.

Sesi, Stephen Mutuku. "Prayer among the Digo Muslims of Kenya and Its Implications for Christian Witness." PhD diss., Fuller Theological Seminary, 2003.

Tablino, Paul. *Christianity among the Nomads: The Catholic Church in Northern Kenya*. 2 vols. Nairobi: Paulines, 2004.

———. *The Gabra: Camel Nomads of Northern Kenya*. Nairobi: Paulines, 1999.

Wilkins, M. J. *Matthew*. NIV Application Commentary. Grand Rapids: Zondervan, 2004.

Part 2

Responses

11

Response to Joseph D. Galgalo and Joseph B. O. Okello

Gordon L. Heath

THE OLD MAXIM "THOSE who do not learn from the mistakes of the past are doomed to repeat them" should be kept in mind by Kenyan Christians, for their leaders face a crisis that is, in many ways, similar to that faced by Martin Luther roughly five hundred years ago. While certain elements of Luther's response can be commended, there is also a dark and troubling side of the story that he has never lived down—and that is a sober warning for Kenyan church leaders today.

It was dangerous living in German-speaking central Europe in the early 1520s. Roving bands of malcontented and disenfranchised citizens destroyed property and made safe travel difficult. Uncertainty was the order of the day as covert groups plotted their next act of terror. The Peasant's War/Revolt of 1524–25 was a disaster for the region: crops were uprooted, property razed, trade ruined, and up to a quarter of a million peasants perished.

In the midst of the mayhem was the religious reformer Martin Luther, a man who had electrified and polarized Europe with his radical call for religious reform. Citizens and magistrates looked to him for guidance. Luther addressed the unrest in his preaching, as well as in a number of tracts. He passionately spoke out against the unrest and the chaos in its wake, and his most infamous statement of support for the government was in *Against the Murderous, Thieving Hordes of*

Peasants (1525): "Let everyone who can, smite, slay, and stab, secretly or openly . . . nothing can be more poisonous, hurtful, or devilish than a rebel. It is just as one must kill a mad dog; if you do not strike him he will strike you." I would argue that Luther's response to unrest in his day is informative for the Kenyan situation, and provides a helpful foil for Joseph Galgalo and Joseph Okello's chapters on the Just War and Pacifist positions.

Rightly so, Luther, Galgalo, and Okello link systemic injustice with the outbreak of unrest and violence. Before the revolt, Luther prophetically rebuked his princes over a litany of injustices perpetrated by the princes on the peasants, and he urged them to change their harsh and unjust ways before it was too late. In like manner, Galgalo and Okello urge the church in Kenya to offer similar exhortations to the state to ensure and encourage justice for all citizens—Christian, Muslim, and other—with the aim of defusing tensions.

Like Luther, Galgalo and Okello also recognize the role of the church in preaching and modeling peace. Luther initially sought to preach the problem away, and it seems as if Galgalo and Okello hope that the church in Kenya can do likewise. Such attempts are noble, and needed.

For my purposes, the most significant intersection between Luther, Galgalo, and Okello is in the area of the government's use of violence. Luther made it clear in the development of his "two kingdoms" approach that the church was not to use violence to carry out it aims, whereas the state had a responsibility to use violence to protect its citizens. Luther's conviction that the princes had a divine mandate to use the sword (Romans 13) eventually led him to call for the princes to ruthlessly put down the rebellion in order to restore peace. Galgalo, Okello, and the Kenyan church can draw two very important lessons from Luther's robust and excessively harsh response.

First, the state is not to be pacifist, for it is the state's role to suppress evil. It is the historic Christian theological position that the state has a role in using violence to suppress violence, and there is nothing "un-Christian" about calling for the state to use violence—if necessary—to protect innocent civilians and restore peace. Both Galgalo and Okello seem hesitant to declare this outright, but it needs to be said. The church can and should still prophetically preach peace and reconciliation, but there are often limits to preaching's effectiveness. Luther rightly recognized that Christians need not (and should not) take up arms to fight on their own, but rather, when necessary, they must call on the state to do what God has ordained it to do. Likewise, Kenya church leaders should feel no compunction in expecting the state to do what the state is supposed to do.

Second, fear, anger, and hatred can lead to troubling and regretful statements. And the lust for revenge can cloud clear thinking. Luther was deeply disturbed by the devastation he saw as he travelled from parish to parish. As a result, he angrily called on the princes to ruthlessly suppress the violence. However, even his supporters were shocked by his harsh and inflammatory comments. Rather than rethink his exhortation to the princes, Luther went on to defend his comments and published even more harsh statements in support of the suppression of the peasants. For many it is one of the most shameful episodes in Luther's ministry. The lesson is this: while there is danger in not calling on government to suppress violence, there is also danger in advocating for government to use violence. Galgalo, Okello, and the Kenyan churches are right to be wary of calling upon the state to use the sword. Luther's harsh reaction evokes parallels with what postcolonial scholars call the creation of the "other"—a demonizing and dehumanizing of one's enemy that justifies inordinate violence. Kenyan Christians must avoid being so outraged over attacks on churches that they descend into hateful and dehumanizing portrayals of Islamic radicals—portrayals that will justify illegitimate and unbridled government uses of violence. And that violence, among other things, would bring harm now and poison any future national reconciliation, let alone contribute to any positive Christian witness.

Galgalo mentions the church walking a tightrope—an apt metaphor. Christians in Kenya can, in good conscience, call on the government to use force to end terror and establish peace. However, at the same time, they should be very wary, knowing that outrage and anger can lead to a loss of perspective and prophetic voice that justifies violence beyond what is prudent and just. The way forward for Kenyan Christians is neither clear nor easy, and Kenyans would be wise to learn from the trials and tribulations of a by-gone leader who was called upon to chart a way forward under extreme duress.

12

A Response to Julius Gathogo

BRIAN STANLEY

EVANGELICAL CHRISTIANS ARE NO longer marginal to the public life of most African nations south of the Sahara. In countries like Kenya, they are simply too numerous for their opinions and potential political influence to be ignored by the state. Equally, church leaders have become more conscious of the new capacity—and hence, also, the enhanced spiritual responsibility—of the evangelical Christian community to shape the direction of public political discourse and even the direction of government policy. If there is any sense in which it is fitting to attach the disputed label of "the next Christendom" (to borrow Philip Jenkins's well-known phrase) to the expanding Christianities of the southern hemisphere, it is in this quite specific respect. Although the Anglican Church in Kenya does not possess, or even wish to possess, the formal established status that its mother, the Church of England, still retains in England, it is nonetheless the case that the Kenyan churches as a whole—the great majority of which share a fundamentally evangelical theological orientation—feel a responsibility to act as the Christian conscience or compass guiding the nation and to represent to government what they perceive to be the will of God. The church as a composite pan-denominational entity has become more conscious than ever before that part of its divine commission to preach the gospel of the kingdom of God is to address in the name of Christ issues of pressing national concern, whether these be in the area of corruption and injustice, or the increasingly prominent questions posed by the threat of armed terrorism, often yoked to a militant and intolerant version of Islam.

The novelty of this development can, of course, be over-stated. Julius Gathogo has reminded us of the courage displayed by the late Archbishop David Gitari, that wonderfully "turbulent priest" whose fearless preaching rattled the political cages of the government of Daniel arap Moi and put his own life in danger on at least one occasion. The venerable Presbyterian ecclesiastical statesman, John G. Gatu, whom Gathogo mentions, is in his own career evidence that even a product of the East African Revival tradition can transcend the boundaries of a narrow pietism. One can go further back still in Kenyan Christian history to consider the roles of missionary prophets of justice in the colonial era such as Bishop Frank Weston, Handley Hooper, or J. H. Oldham, all of whom challenged white settler power on behalf of African interests. Nonetheless, it is undoubtedly the case that the political temper of Kenyan evangelicalism has become more pronounced in recent years: evangelical church leaders have gained a new confidence to apply the Christian faith in the public sphere, and for that we should all be profoundly grateful. The growing salience of African Christian public theology is a development to be warmly welcomed, as is the gradual retreat of forms of evangelical pietism that refuse to apply the gospel at any level other than that of the individual and her or his relationship to eternity. However, as Gathogo rightly emphasizes, the growth of an evangelical public theology has not necessarily implied a growth in political consensus among evangelical Christians. The increasing prominence of forms of neo-Pentecostalism has complicated the picture. There are Pentecostal leaders in modern Africa such as Ghana's Mensa Otabil who have applied Pentecostal spirituality to the issues of national life to a commendable degree. But there are other strands of neo-Pentecostalism that appear to cut the nerve of political responsibility by their apparent obsession with identifying and combatting the malevolent spiritual forces that are supposed to lie behind the wrongdoing of individual politicians. Although certain predominant emphases in their political theology can be discerned, evangelicals no more agree over politics than they do over ecclesiology or the sacraments. But perhaps that is a good thing, for it saves evangelicalism from the worst excesses of a monopolistic Christendom approach to Christian political responsibility.

This volume as a whole, and Julius Gathogo's important essay in particular, highlight the urgent and uncomfortable ethical challenges posed by the rise of militant Islamic terrorism. He makes appropriate use of the ancient Augustinian tradition of the just war to suggest that the deployment of Kenyan Defence Forces in Somalia against al-Shabaab may be a regrettable moral necessity. However, the relevance of the just war tradition to the other and related development discussed by Gathogo is more dubious. Some Kenyan Christians, including pastors, have begun to claim the right to carry guns in order to defend themselves, their families, and their congregations against the threat of terrorist attack. It is easy for commentators such as myself who live in a peaceful society in which the threat of terrorism is not a daily reality—though recent events in France and Belgium provide a salutary warning against British complacency—to criticize the responses of those who feel their lives to be in peril, but nonetheless some words of caution are appropriate. A society in which individual citizens feel the need to arm themselves to dissuade others from attacking them is a society that meets violence with violence. Many right-wing Christians in the United States in recent decades have adopted precisely this position, defending the right of the individual to carry a gun at almost any time, including in educational institutions and even in churches. That has nothing to do with just war theory, but everything to do with a lack of trust in the transcendent power of the gospel of Jesus Christ, who came to give his life as a ransom for many. If Christians resort to arming themselves, then the terrorists have won, and the message of the Cross is denied. The language of making war on terrorism can easily slide into the language of making war on Islam, and that would take the church back to the enormities of the medieval crusades, whose fateful legacy has hampered Christian witness to both Muslims and Jews for centuries. The command to love our enemies is the most morally challenging of all the words of Jesus. But for that very reason, when Christians take it seriously, even at the cost of their own lives, the potential benefits for Christianity are beyond calculation. The apostle Paul's words in Romans 13, which, as Gathogo reminds us, have been misused by generations of Christian conservatives to justify supine compromises with state-inflicted injustice, are in fact the necessary basis for a responsible theology of combatting evil through properly constituted and appropriately controlled political authority rather than through individual resort to violence.

13

A Response to David K. Tarus

Richard J. Gehman

IN THIS ADMIRABLE ARTICLE, David Tarus touches on all the vital components of a theological anthropology in the context of terrorism in Kenya. His thesis is that a "theology of the image of God and Christology in the context of the African *ubuntu* (community) provides resources for an anthropology capable of subverting violence."

He begins to unpack this by elucidating the meaning and importance of the African concept of *ubuntu*, and this he does comprehensively and effectively. However, he introduces the paper by calling this African anthropology "a foundation for the study to build on." This erroneous assertion is in contrast to what he later calls, and I believe correctly, "the context" of an African anthropology. Human traditions and cultural values cannot form the "foundation" of a Christian Theology; rather they are the "context."

I say this for several reasons. First and foremost, the inspired writings of the Christian Scriptures are the supreme and final authority of faith and conduct. Human traditions should never supplement scriptural authority. Furthermore, *ubuntu*, as an African cultural value, is an imperfect "foundation" to build on because this idealized African community only occurs among peoples of the same tribal identity. Violence between ethnic communities prevailed throughout Africa before the heavy hand of the colonialists brought inter-communal fighting to an end. *Ubuntu* values did not prevent violence.

In addition, *ubuntu* prevailed in a rural setting where people of the same linguistic and cultural community lived together in perpetuity. With the introduction of industrialization and urbanization, peoples from every community are moving into the impersonal cities where individualism takes root. I fear that *ubuntu* philosophy cannot survive the inevitable move toward modernization and urbanization without concerted effort. It cannot be a foundation for African Christian Theology.

However, *ubuntu* is the natural *context* in which African Christians should build a biblical theology to confront terrorism. It is the cultural bridge to biblical truth. The traditional African emphasis on community (*ubuntu*) is more consonant with biblical teaching than the individualism of the West. Indeed, it would be a tragedy if this African emphasis on community should dissipate in the face of modernity. Efforts should be made to hold on to this distinctively African value. But in the end, *ubuntu* is a defective cultural value that can only point to eternal truths.

Turning to a Christian theological anthropology, Tarus lays out a comprehensive theology under two affirmations that subvert violence: (1) creation of humanity in God's image, and (2) the renewal of the image of God through faith in Jesus Christ.

The first plank of his theology is humanity's creation in the image of God, which he expounds quite extensively by explaining the four interpretations of *imago Dei*. Unfortunately, he leaves us hanging without demonstrating which view he believes is correct or why this iteration of different interpretations is important to know.

In my opinion, all the interpretations are biblical. It is not a case of either/or because all four views are valid. The God revealed in Scripture is rational (thinking), volitional (decision making), and emotional (showing love, hate, joy, sadness). The mind, will, and emotions of human beings reflect God's Being. He is the Eternal Spirit, not a physical entity, so God's image has *nothing* to do with our materiality. At the same time, as the Ruler of the universe, God created Adam and Eve as persons to be stewards of creation, to rule over and exercise dominion under the eternal rule of God.

Furthermore, God is a social Being. The three Persons in the Trinity are related to one another in love throughout eternity. Therefore, human beings are relational creatures, intended to live in community, related to one another in love. Jesus Christ, God's eternal Son, is God incarnate. He not only came to rescue us from the dominion of darkness through his vicarious death on the cross, he revealed in flesh and blood what God is like. "He who has seen me," Jesus said, "has seen the Father."

In light of this full meaning of the *imago Dei*, Tarus then narrates the implications of God's image in man with implications for Kenya. Following his discourse on the *imago Dei*, Tarus explores a Christ-centered anthropology. If human beings by their sinful nature are "full of envy, murder, strife, deceit, and malice" (Rom 1:29), then the new birth is essential. Of equal importance is growth in grace, the putting off of the old self and the putting on of the new self, "which is being renewed in knowledge in the image of its Creator" (Eph 4:22, 23; Col 3:10). Tarus makes this insightful statement: "The church is the place where this shaping and formation of relationships occurs. Though imperfect, the church is the community of God's people, a visible manifestation of a new humanity being born. Therefore, Christians are, or ought to be, agents of Christ's redemption." On this issue of the church I would like to make my final contribution.

The tragedy is that Christians, including pastors, have been involved in ethnic clashes that have destroyed property and taken human life. The new birth alone is not sufficient to transform lives, though it is a necessary beginning. As Tarus says, although the church is "a visible manifestation of a new humanity," it is still imperfect, sometimes very imperfect. Systematic, Spirit-empowered teaching of God's Word is essential to grow Christians. We need to "grow up" in our salvation by craving for the pure spiritual milk of God's Word (2 Pet 1:3). And the agency for this teaching and mentoring process is the church, which is mandated by Christ to be light and salt in this world.

I propose two steps in a process of peace and reconciliation. First, church leaders should be thoroughly taught the basic emphases that Tarus outlines: the creation of humanity in the image of God and the consequent value of all human beings, the renewal of that image through faith in Jesus Christ, and the work of the Holy Spirit in reforming this image. These leaders in turn should teach these truths to all Christians; valuing everyone and accepting their dignity is the goal. When Christians recognize that everyone is an image bearer and has dignity, animosity between communities can begin to be replaced with respect and trust.

However, if enmity persists, a second step is essential even if ethnic animosity is only under the surface. After the ethnic clashes in Kenya, hatred and enmity were palpable. The belligerent parties needed to be brought together. This in fact was done through the churches in seminars that arose spontaneously, convened by leaders of Transformational Development. The facilitators represented different communities and had hearts for listening. They displayed a nonjudgmental attitude that encouraged people to talk and share without finding fault or blame. An equal number from each community were invited to the seminars. This prevented either group from feeling overwhelmed. Tribal names were replaced by positive names, such as "blessed" and "holy." This eliminated the negative baggage conveyed by the tribal names. Each small group was mixed so that all parties mingled with one another. It is easy to hate a stereotype whom you do not know. But sitting down and dialoguing, listening to each other's stories and seeking to understand the other, is a powerful change experience. Participants learned to value the "other" and their opinions. With skill, humility, and patience, the trained facilitators cultivated reconciliation. In the cases where this has taken place in Kenya, the belligerents learned to forgive one another. The seminars concluded with tears, hugging, and forgiveness. Reconciliation is never easy, but David Tarus has laid out a firm theological basis and pointed a way forward.

14

A Response to Esther M. Mombo and Joseph Wandera

GREGG A. OKESSON

I AM DELIGHTED TO RESPOND to these two fine essays. Having lived in East Africa for thirteen years, I find the topics explored by Esther Mombo[1] and Joseph Wandera[2] hauntingly familiar. My aim in what follows is to highlight some of the shared discourses between the two chapters, as well as to situate these discussions within the broader context of literature dealing with peace and reconciliation around the world.

THE MULTIFACETED NATURE OF CONFLICT IN KENYA

Let me begin by highlighting the variegated nature of conflict around the world, with specific reference to Kenya. Of course, beginning on this note sounds like invoking a truism of the worse kind—as if there are any simple conflicts! Nevertheless, it is necessary to first exegete the underlying causes of violence in order to know how to respond with anything resembling the peace and reconciliation offered by Jesus Christ. This is not to say that discerning the sources of violence is a pre-condition for reconciliation, only that it unpacks the deeper narratives and helps bring reconciliation to the most important places.

At the most obvious level, Kenya, like all locales around the world, experiences its fair share of bloodshed. I recall the stunned faces and

1. Mombo, "Reconciliatory Peace."
2. Wandera, "We Have No More Cheeks."

slow, measured replies of my Kenyan colleagues following the 2008 post-election violence, as they were saying, "We always thought we were a peaceful people." Of course, Kenya is not the only country to experience such things. There are no peaceful people. However, violence tends to look different around the world. In the United States, where I currently live, we tend to see conflict arise around the subterranean fault lines called race and gun rights. Each of these issues emerges from historic markers that trace back, in some instances, to the very founding of the country. For Kenya, the story requires a different telling that involves pre-colonial Africa, with skirmishes over land, cattle rustling, and conflicts involving tribal identities; the introduction of the slave trade; and the pillage of Africa undertaken by Western peoples under the pretense of colonial expansion; and only then can we proceed to talk about tribal clashes, politically inspired killings, land grabbing by political elites, and the more recent sustained military campaigns against terrorist organizations such as al-Shabaab.

"Social Imaginaries"

This is to argue that violence flows from narratives deeply hidden in the social fabric of a people. Every conflict arises from a story; and the poignancy of the narrative is not just caught up in the world of facts, but runs much deeper into what Charles Taylor refers to as "social imaginaries." Taylor defines "social imaginaries" as "the ways in which [ordinary people] imagine their social existence, how they fit together with others, how things go on between them and their fellows, the expectations which are normally met, and the deeper normative notions and images that underlie these expectations."[3] The task before us is to untangle some of the threads that make up the imaginative fabric of Kenya's social and religious history.

I find it interesting that neither author mentions anything about patron-client relationships. Scholars such as Paul Gifford[4] and Patrick Chabal[5] highlight the prevalence of patrimonialism where "clients" (meaning, everyday people) honor "patrons" (the elites) in exchange for access to vital resources. In the past, such webs of belonging were built

---

3. Taylor, *A Secular Age*, 171.

4. See Gifford, *African Christianity*, and Gifford, *Christianity, Politics and Public Life in Kenya*.

5. Chabal, *Africa*.

upon highly complex accountability relations, where the networks were held together by the honor given to patrons in exchange for ethically obligated generosity to the clients.[6] However, with the introduction of colonialism and then independence, the patron-client relations became "increasingly divorced from the moral and ethical dimensions of pre-colonial rulership."[7] This has led Gifford and Chabal to speak of neo-patrimonialism, where the previous ethical obligations give way to fear, insecurity, and violence as political instruments; or where Gifford explains, "It is not that Kenya doesn't work; Kenya has worked extremely well for the elite who control it—the politicians, civil servants, parastatal bosses and their associates."[8] Hence, disorder functions as a highly effective political tool.[9]

Patron-client relations operate upon a social imaginary, as do broader conflicts in the region, as expressed by one pastor to me in the days following the 2008 post-election violence, where he explained that he had always been told from childhood that a certain tribal people were bad. Such kinds of narratives form the substructure of all kinds of violence, and to the extent that they trade in the currency of images and symbols, they hold greater influence; or as Mombo explains: "the underlying will for war remains."[10]

However, conflict in Kenya is not just about patron-client relations, but arises out of long-standing narratives in the region. Emmanuel Katongole tells the story of *King Leopold's Ghost*,[11] and how colonialism carved deep runes within the landscape of Africa's history, leading to a re-dramatization of the colonial heritage through the scripts of modern-

---

6. Or as John Iliffe says, "Wealth in itself attracted honour, but doubly so if generously distributed." *Honour in African Society*, 334.

7. Chabal, *Africa*, 95.

8. Gifford, *African Christianity*, 29. He goes on to describe disorder as a political instrument: "There is a logic in underdevelopment. There is a logic in widespread insecurity, in which (especially as elections approach) private armies enforce the will of their masters. Millions who are uneducated and scrambling for subsistence will have little time for demanding their rights. Chaos at the ports of Mombasa ensures that none of the barons trafficking drugs will ever be caught. Heightening tribalism will ensure that self-proclaimed champions of the group are re-elected" (ibid., 30).

9. For more on this concept, see Chabal and Daloz, *Africa Works*.

10. Mombo, "Reconciliatory Peace," 6.

11. Hochschild, *King Leopold's Ghost*.

day politics.[12] While neither of the authors I am responding to in this volume trace the origins of terrorism back to colonialism, Wandera explains some of the uneasy history with Kenyan Somalis and the challenges they experience receiving vital services within the country.[13] He further describes how Muslim–Christian relations "were adversarial and competitive in nature with each group seeking political dominance, commercial possibilities, and converts,"[14] leading to a condition where "Muslims were marginalized within the body politic of Kenya in a variety of ways"[15] while Christians "dominate the public sphere."[16] All of this is to say that narratives lie behind the violence Kenya is experiencing.

The Use of Language

Wandera further talks about "Christian symbolism" as a key characteristic of former President Daniel arap Moi's regime, in which Muslims could not function in the country as equals. He explains, "It was common during that era to see the then president attending church services each Sunday, sometimes commenting on spiritual and social questions over an open Bible after the service."[17] He thereafter enters into a fascinating account of language-usage by Christians in response to terrorist attacks in Kenya. The first of these was when the General Secretary of the National Council of Churches (NCCK) in Kenya said, "We have no more cheeks to turn" in response to the horrific killings that occurred at Garissa University College; or where other key Christian leaders stated, "It is naïve for anyone to imply that the so-called terrorism in Kenya is anything other than *Jihad* against Christians."[18] These kinds of statements, Wandera suggests, form a kind of implicit script in the country to justify a turn towards violence.

Language matters, and when symbolic leaders speak thus, they influence, or in some instances, create the social imaginary within the country. This is especially true in light of certain "declarative" predispositions within African Christianity, where a key leader will pro-

---

12. Katongole, *Sacrifice of Africa*, 11.
13. Wandera, "We Have No More Cheeks," 4.
14. Ibid., 5, citing Azuma, "The Church and Islam in Africa."
15. Wandera, "We Have No More Cheeks," 6 citing Mazrui, "Ethnicity and Pluralism."
16. Wandera, "We Have No More Cheeks," 16.
17. Ibid., 7.
18. Ibid., 10–11.

nounce something with the intention of making it true.[19] Thus when the General Secretary of the NCCK says that Christians have "no more cheeks to turn," he is not merely offering a personal opinion, but rather stating what is in fact the case (or what becomes the case after speaking it). Such language builds upon the imagined past to form the prevailing script by which Christians think and act. When such language is spoken, the symbolic person "declares" it to be true, while the religion behind the speech (in this case Christianity) "sacralizes" such language with divine-like intent. These kinds of utterances thus form the "social imaginary" behind Muslim–Christian relations and justify all kinds of "extra-biblical" responses.

THE MULTIFACETED CHARACTER OF RECONCILIATION IN KENYA

If conflict, such as terrorism, arises from such a varied, colorful assortment of reasons, then reconciliation must likewise communicate a similar "thickness" of character. Or to state this in another way: we cannot presume to tackle something as intricate and complex as religious conflict without resources equally as intricate and complex. However, we need not worry; the gospel of Jesus Christ as embodied by communities boasts an abundance of resources by which to engage such thorny problems as terrorism.

The Symbolic

In her essay, Mombo goes to great length to underscore the seeds of peace-making in Scripture as embodied by the Quakers. She talks about the potency of symbols such as "blood" and how such "symbols make possible a firm way to acknowledge violence, suffering, and death, but also provide the means of overcoming them."[20] She later describes how "the death, the cross and the blood of Jesus Christ" "contain rich strands of meaning that might seem in themselves contrary or even self-contradictory, but are still held together in a conceptual network that makes sense in people's reconciliation to God."[21]

---

19. Gifford, "The Bible in Africa."
20. Mombo, "Reconciliatory Peace," 5.
21. Ibid.

Symbols represent a kind of narrative; they speak. Thus reconciliation is not a matter of knowing the appropriate skills, but artistically using symbols and imagination to tell a different story.[22] Wandera says something similar where he describes the use of language as a "form of social praxis and an agent of social transformation,"[23] and says that Christian leaders need to draw upon the resources of the Christian faith to employ symbolic gestures such as friendship, hospitality, and solidarity with Muslims to communicate a different kind of life knitted together across religious divides.

Wandera and Mombo are in good company with such thoughts. Emmanuel Katongole moves in a similar direction. He explains the problems of conflict in Africa in terms of the stories that shape the continent's existence, especially as they arise from the colonial era and flow into the present. "To attend to this task," he says, "the focus of social ethics must shift from the external formalities of nation-state politics to its inner workings or logic, from skills and technical strategies to myths and visions, from a preoccupation with fixing a broken institution to imagining new experiments in social life in Africa," or where he explains more explicitly, "This task of the imagination calls not so much for experts and technical aides, but for storytellers who are able 'to offer people better stories than the ones they live by.'"[24]

Congregations and Doxology

Africa possesses a wealth of narratives. The churches on the continent, in particular, boast all the resources to reshape narratives that have birthed violence. To walk into an African church is to experience rich, textured doxology that oozes out of every pore of the service.[25] People pray God's attributes; they sing his character; and, when people dance, they dramatize God within the everyday vicissitudes of life. What is more, "All the realities of the Christian tradition—the Scriptures, prayer, doctrine, worship, Baptism, the Eucharist, the sacraments—point to and

---

22. This is the central idea behind John Paul Lederach's, *The Moral Imagination*.
23. Wandera, "We Have No More Cheeks," 3.
24. Katongole, *Sacrifice of Africa*, 61.
25. Karin Barber refers to African praise poetry as "Africa's master genre," and I argue that this historical, cultural reality forms the bedrock upon which Christian doxology builds. See Barber, *Anthropology of Texts, Persons and Publics*, 74.

reenact a compelling story that should claim the whole of our lives."[26] All of this is to say that when people leave the church, they take God with them, where doxology seeps like the long, satisfying rains into the rich red, soil.

Of course, this doesn't directly address what to do with militant terrorism, but it does provide vital resources to shape many of the deeper narratives within the country: allowing doxology, sacraments, and liturgy to inform such things as patron-client relationships, or the social memory of colonialism that continues to lurk beneath the surface and give justification to continued domination. It also reshapes how people respond to violence. A people seeped in the liturgies of Jesus' death and resurrection cannot respond to hatred with hatred; neither can those who dance with choreographed movements to Jesus' teachings continue to sow seeds of violence in retaliation for violence. Doxologies such as we find in Kenyan churches allow us to imagine alternatives to the kinds of social existence experienced under contemporary religious fraction.

Structural Elements

Of course, this doesn't answer all of the problems. Kenyan Christianity must take seriously not only the narratives that lie behind violence, but also the existing structures that make such violence possible. Mombo acknowledges this where she says, "The structures that have perpetuated violence need to be brought to light."[27] Yet herein we find a problem. The kind of Christianity brought from the Western missionaries came with its own internal inconsistencies. The missionaries were at once children of the Enlightenment and children of the pietistic revivals; they were simultaneously modern and anti-modern.[28] Thus they imparted to Kenya theological resources that sought to address spiritual *and* material realities, but without integration between the realms. Furthermore, their biblical interpretations of the political realm likewise sent mixed messages to Africans, teaching, at once, that politics was inextricably "secular" in nature and thus something to be avoided; while at the same time "baptizing" such passages as "Touch not the Lord's anointed" (1 Chron 16:22; Ps 105:15) and "The authorities that exist have been estab-

---

26. Ibid., 61–62.
27. Mombo, "Reconciliatory Peace," 7.
28. For more of this, see Okesson, *Re-Imaging Modernity*, 79–84.

lished by God" (Rom 13:1), leading people to believe that the political realm—and thus the structures emerging from the state—correspond to God. Africans subsequently repackaged such views according to their distinct cosmology. Integrative connections between spiritual and material realms, built upon these inherited readings of Scripture, led Africans to see leaders (whether political or otherwise) as residing closer to the realm of the ancestors (or in Christianized version, nearer to God), making any critique against the leaders suggestive of a critique against the spirit realm or deity.[29] Such sacralized readings of politics make it hard, if not impossible, for Kenyans to stand against the structures that perpetuate violence.[30]

The reconciliation offered by the church in Kenya must address these realities with the gospel of Jesus Christ; or as Katongole explains: "The salvation promised by God to God's people, to which the birth, death, and resurrection of Jesus is a witness, is not merely spiritual: it is a concrete social, material, political, and economic reality that is ushered into existence by God's revelation in history."[31] However, stating that the gospel is a "concrete social, material, political, and economic reality" does not mean that it needs to be "secularized"—only that it cannot be spiritualized and thus dislocated from the public realm. Greater energies need to be given to overcome this inhibition of harmony between spiritual and material realities, while at the same time avoiding the other danger of "sacralizing" the authorities.

CONCLUSION

Let me conclude by lauding the fine essays written by Mombo and Wandera. They offer fascinating insights into contemporary conflict in Kenya, while also pointing the reader to the reconciliatory work through the church of Jesus Christ. Along the way, they touch upon key aspects of literature, dealing with such themes as narratives, symbols, and structures, while taking the reader deeper into the complex realities of terrorism in Kenya and highlighting the need for an appropriate Christian response. I have offered some suggestions for how to strengthen their offerings, but with the acknowledgement that no simple, ready-made

---

29. See Bediako, "Unmasking the Powers."

30. There is one noteworthy exception; see Knighton, *Religion and Politics in Kenya*.

31. Katongole, *Sacrifice of Africa*, 59.

solution stands before us, as if we merely need to find the right key to the proper lock.

Mombo tell us that "reconciliation is not a skill to be mastered, but rather something to be discovered—a certain kind of power."[32] To state it this way is not to locate the power high up in the heavens as if we need to become super humans to attain it,[33] nor does this power belong inextricably to the political realm, as if we need to cozy up to "patron" elites in order to reap any benefits. No, this power is in the churches: it is danced, sung, and dramatized by the people of God; it flows through doxology and sacraments; and is thus littered across the Kenyan landscape. This power is Christ, through the Holy Spirit, and before the Father, and the churches have it in abundance. This is where Kenya's hope lies.

REFERENCES

Azuma, John. "The Church and Islam in Africa." *Evangelical Interfaith Dialogue* 2, no. 3 (2011) 3–5.

Barber, Karin. *The Anthropology of Texts, Person and Publics: Oral and Written Culture in Africa and Beyond*. Cambridge: Cambridge University Press, 2007.

Bediako, Kwame. "Unmasking the Powers: Christianity, Authority, and Desacralization in Modern African Politics." In *Christianity and Democracy in Global Context*, edited by J. Witte, 207–29. Boulder, CO: Westview, 1993.

Chabal, Patrick. *Africa: The Politics of Suffering and Smiling*. London: Zed, 2009.

Chabal, Patrick, and Jean-Pascal Daloz. *Africa Works: Disorder as Political Instrument*. Oxford: James Curry, 1999.

Gifford, Paul. *African Christianity: Its Public Role*. Bloomington, IN: Indiana University Press, 1998.

———. *Christianity, Politics and Public Life in Kenya*. London: Hurst, 2009.

———. "The Bible in Africa: A Novel Usage in Africa's New Churches." *Bulletin of the School of Oriental and African Studies* 71, no. 2 (2008) 203–19.

Hochschild, Adam. *King Leopold's Ghost: A Story of Greed, Terror, and Heroism in Colonial Africa*. Boston: Houghton Mifflin Harcourt, 1998.

Iliffe, John. *Honour in African Society*. Cambridge: Cambridge University Press, 2005.

Katongole, Emmanuel. *The Sacrifice of Africa: A Political Theology for Africa*. Grand Rapids: Eerdmans, 2011.

Knighton, Ben (ed.). *Religion and Politics in Kenya: Essays in Honor of a Meddlesome Priest*. New York: Palgrave Macmillan, 2009.

Lederach, John Paul. *The Moral Imagination: The Art and Soul of Building Peace*. Oxford: Oxford University Press, 2005.

Mazrui, Al Amin. "Ethnicity and Pluralism: The Politicization of Religion in Kenya." *Journal of Muslim Minority Affairs* 14, no. 1 (1993) 191–201.

32. Mombo, "Reconciliatory Peace," 9.

33. Okesson, "Are Pastors Human?

Mombo, Esther. "Reconciliatory Peace in the Face of Terror: A Personal Appeal for Quaker Peace Building in Kenya."

Okesson, Gregg A. "Are Pastors Human? Sociological and Theological Implications for Ministerial Identity in Africa." In *Africa Journal of Evangelical Theology* 25, no. 2 (2008) 19–39.

———. *Re-Imaging Modernity: A Contextualized Theological Study of Power and Humanity within Akamba Christianity in Kenya*. Eugene, OR: Pickwick, 2012.

Taylor, Charles. *A Secular Age*. Cambridge, MA: The Belknap Press of Harvard University, 2007.

Wandera, Joseph. "'We Have No More Cheeks to Turn:' Christian and Muslim Responses to Terrorism in Kenya."

15

A Response to Eunice K. Kamaara and Simon G. Omare

CYNTHIA LONG WESTFALL

KAMAARA AND OMARE HAVE three primary concerns that are valid and compelling. First and foremost, they are concerned about the radicalization of the Kenyan youth by al-Shabaab, particularly their young men and boys. Second, they are concerned about the neglect of children and the erosion of families in Kenya. Third, they are concerned about violence in the family. Their priority is that Kenya finds indigenous solutions to these issues that are in continuity with Kenyan traditional culture values. These issues are layered with facts and concerns about the effects of Kenya's recent political history, Westernization, urbanization, and neoliberal capitalism. They are further complicated by other factors including modernization, technology, education, and globalization. Their goal is to find a Christian answer to these challenges that is both indigenous and effective.

The priority of finding Kenyan answers to the problem of the radicalization of Kenyan youth is important. While there are some common determinants and responses that can be instructive, European studies of radicalization deal with some significantly different patterns than those that emerge from Kenyan studies.[1] For example, according to European studies, the internet plays a vital role in radicalization, but in Kenya, peer

---

1. See, for example, Fataliyeva, "Preventing the Radicalisation," and Wright, "Preventing Radicalisation and Terrorism."

relationships play a primary role and the internet is not mentioned as a contributing factor in two studies.[2] Radicalization is occurring among Kenyan nationals rather than among migrant populations navigating a dominant Western culture.[3] While other African nations are facing comparable crises, Kenya has its own unique challenges given recent historical events such as the Somali crisis, and has its own traditions that may serve as a resource.

However, Kamaara and Omare's explanation of the "root cause" of their concerns and their proposed solution raises some questions. They suggest that the root cause is real or perceived changes in women's roles that are at odds with traditional Kenyan cultural patterns and contribute to the breakdown of the Kenyan family through the neglect of children, and to gender hostility that is linked to domestic violence. There is no question that traditional Kenyan gender roles have changed. Because of economic, political, and social changes initiated by Western colonialism, men have sought jobs in the city so that the responsibility for the maintenance of the rural family has fallen largely on women. On the other hand, economic opportunities such as "Freemark" and microfinance initiatives have created economic improvement for some women. Men have lost their traditional male roles, and are marginalized in the family. Kamaara and Omare therefore argue that actual or perceived injustice to men due to these patterns has created gender hostility and increased domestic violence. Furthermore, men's isolation and women's work patterns have resulted in the neglect of their children. The violence in the family and neglect has made boys and young men susceptible to radicalization by al-Shabaab. They suggest that the Christian response is the promotion of "gender complementarity" or gender segregation.

The primary question is whether there is a causal relationship between these three concerns, particularly regarding the changes in the role of women and their empowerment. The primary concern of the chapter is the effect of the changes in gender roles on the radicalization

---

2. Two studies have indicated that radicalization in Kenya correlates with exposure to radical networks in which peer relationships played a prominent role (Rink and Sharma, "Determinants of Religious Radicalization," 23–24; Botha, "Political Socialization," 915).

3. See, for example, Sowad, "Migration Affecting Masculinities," which explores the gender identity of migrant Bangladeshi men in the UK. This chapter provides an interesting comparison and contrast with Kamaara and Omare's interest in the effect of Westernization on masculinities in Kenya.

of Kenyan youth. A Kenyan study of in-depth interviews of ninety-five individuals associated with al-Shabaab in 2013 concluded that the individuals were recruited from a segment of society that was very conservative in their gender roles.[4] The vast majority of the recruits were raised in conservative Muslim homes—only 9 percent were converts to Islam before joining al-Shabaab,[5] and they were socialized by al-Shabaab after conversion. In families where both parents were present, the father made the rules in 100 percent of the cases, and in cases where the father was absent, a male relative made the rules in all but three cases.[6] Therefore, not only is there no evidence that the mothers of radicalized youth were empowered, but it is unlikely that the mothers of this traditional group would have been permitted to participate in progressive programs such as Freemark. Studies indicate that if men "make the rules" they will assume control over any credit that their wives obtain from microfinance.[7] Not only were the homes of radicalized Kenyan youth traditional, but the survey indicated that they had very close relationships with their mothers, which would argue against the assumption that male youth were susceptible to radicalization because of patterns of gender hostility in the home. That is not to say that there would not be rhetoric among this group against the empowerment of women, but that it would target those they would identify as Christians and or possibly those Muslims under the influence of what they would stigmatize as Westernization.

There is no evidence of neglect by mothers that contributed to the radicalization of Kenyan males by al-Shabaab. On the other hand, the radicalized Kenyan youth indicated that their relationship with their father was not as strong, so that even if the role of the father in the family was more influential, they were not successful in transmitting the values that would prevent radicalization. There is some indication that a weak, poor, or disrupted relationship with their father may well be a contributing factor. Furthermore, Kamaara and Omare's anecdotal evidence of the radicalization of the son of the prominent and well-respected chief for Bulla Jamhuria, Mandera County, indicates that radicalization may occur when an individual's father occupies traditional positions of power

---

4. Botha, "Political Socialization," 898.
5. Ibid., 905.
6. Ibid., 898.
7. Hunt and Kasynathan, "Pathways to Empowerment," 43–46.

in Kenyan society.[8] Instead, Muslim youth may be frustrated with their fathers' political compromise with or accommodation to or manipulation of the dominant Christian culture in the political sphere.[9] One might conclude that the European strategy of increasing the influence of women in the Muslim population would be a solution in Kenya, but Botha warns against it. [10] He suggests that though the mother would be the most sensitive to the signs of radicalization, attempts to enhance the influence of women in the Muslim community may "facilitate resentment towards the agency responsible for these initiatives."[11] If that is true, then similar resentment would surely be the result of any attempt on the part of churches or other Christian organizations to interfere in Muslim families or promote gender complementarity that presumably would differ from traditional Muslim gender roles.[12]

While neither Botha nor Rink and Sharma suggest a relationship between domestic violence and radicalization of Kenyan youth, the question remains as to whether there is a causal relationship between the empowerment of women and domestic violence as well as the other problematic patterns of male behavior that were identified by Kamaara and Omare. They seem to suggest that economic gains by women have denied rights to men and children, though it is not entirely clear whether they were distinguishing between perception (rhetoric) and reality.[13] The majority of loans and financing in Kenya and in the world at large go to men. The rationale for women's economic and social empowerment through initiatives such as microfinancing targets the problematic patterns of male behavior that were identified in the chapter. Studies indicated that men tend to spend income and/or loans on alcohol, tobacco,

---

8. Kamaara and Omare, "Gender, Women, and Children," 14.

9. Botha writes, "Because [the youth] are not used to the realities of political and economic participation, are more idealistic and reform-minded, resulting in being impatient with the 'compromising methods' of their elders. . . . Instead of accommodation or manipulation (the favorite tactics of the older generation), the youth favor confrontation." Botha, "Political Socialization," 910.

10. For example, see Fataliyeva, "Preventing the Radicalisation," 14, in which it was proposed to the Council of Europe that "dysfunctional family situations could be prevented if women were involved as the main "educators."

11. Botha, "Political Socializaiton," 898.

12. This is assuming that Kamaara and Omare would not define "gender complementarity" along the lines of traditional Muslim gender roles.

13. Kamaara and Omare, "Gender, Woman, and Children," 19.

their own interests, or further productive activities rather than on the household.[14] Evidence from a range of settings has indicated that when women control income, they tend to spend it on household consumption (particularly children's nutrition), security, land, and their children's education.[15] Therefore, microfinance programs were developed to alleviate poverty for the entire family through credit targeted to women because the whole family is more likely to benefit from it. This indicates that the negative patterns of male behavior reported by Kamaara and Omare preceded and were rather the root cause and presupposition behind the development of NGOs (non-governmental organizations) that empower women.[16]

Nevertheless, there are often unintentional outcomes of idealistic initiatives, and that has been shown to be the case in studies of the effects of microfinance. In some cases, the impact of microfinancing has reduced violence within the family, but in other cases, it appears to have contributed to violence.[17] On the one hand, it was found that violence was reduced when empowerment not only increased capital, but also correlated with or provided education/information and support groups for women.[18] On the other hand, violence could occur in patriarchal contexts in which a woman gives control of the credit to her husband or son. There is a case in which a husband beat his wife to force her to apply for loans.[19] This suggests that violence correlates with scenarios in which microfinancing does not have the intended effect of the empowerment of women, but rather places more capital in the hands of their

14. Hunt and Kasynathan, "Pathways to Empowerment," 46.

15. Vyas and Watts, "Economic Empowerment," 578; Hunt and Kasynathan, "Pathways to Empowerment," 46.

16. The financing for NGOs is raised outside of Kenya so that women's loans do not detract from any opportunity for men.

17. The study of the potential association of violence and the economic empowerment of women is the focus of Vyas and Watts, "Economic Empowerment." On the one hand, household assets and women's higher education tended to reduce violence, but the evidence was mixed. Their conclusion was, "These limitations highlight the need to bring together economic theories, which largely focus on the household, with broader sociological findings on the ways in which gender relations at a micro-level are affected by a range of cultural, institutional and political influences acting in different spheres of men and women's lives" (599). In other words, there is no "silver bullet" or simple solution for gender hostilities.

18. Hunt and Kasynathan, "Pathways to Empowerment," 48.

19. Ibid., 47.

husbands or sons and leads to further exploitation, which is consistent with some of the patterns reported by Kamaara and Omare. Therefore, one may conclude that attempts to empower women through cash loans alone may not always have the intended effects of the empowerment of women nor the alleviation of poverty for the family as a whole. Without accountability and further services, men may be the only ones who receive further financial gain for their own pursuits while women are vulnerable to further exploitation and children may be the ultimate losers.[20] Although it is a major stretch to claim that men are being victimized, Kamaara and Omare's observations indicate that when traditional patriarchy intersects with modernization and globalization, Kenyan men do not thrive, Kenyan women are exploited, and Kenyan children are neglected.

On the other hand, some loans benefit female-headed households in which women have been abandoned and widowed because of Kenyan social, economic, and political patterns. It has been shown that female-headed households in rural Kenya are far more at risk for poverty and starvation than male-headed households because of various forms of inequalities and discrimination against women.[21] Loans that target female-headed households are a tangible way to meet the biblical mandate of caring for orphans and widows. Care for the oppressed should never be balanced with commensurate advantages or gains for the privileged group in the name of justice. Similarly, a biblical sense of social justice should not include the expectation that loans that address inequalities and discrimination for wives, sisters, and mothers be balanced with commensurate economic advantages or gains for their husbands, brothers, and sons.

What might be the outcome if the church was successful in advocating "complementarity" in occupations along gender lines? If Kamaara and Omare's analysis of the dynamics of the traditional practices of church and Christianity are understood in the context of global patterns, it would indicate that gender segregation would most likely result

---

20. Kamaara and Omare suggest that there is a problem of negligence. However, Hunt and Kasynathan, "Pathways to Empowerment," 46, suggest that it may disrupt education and opportunity. If mothers are overworked, children, and particularly daughters, may be withdrawn from schools to assist in the workload.

21. "In Kenya, women contribute the bulk of the agricultural labor . . . but they have a poorer command over a range of productive resources, including land, information, and financial resources." Kassie, "What Determines Gender Inequality," 155.

in women being explicitly excluded from higher-grade and higher-paid occupations and contribute to further impoverishment of Kenyan families. Inequalities and discrimination against women in rural and urban contexts would be exacerbated. Furthermore, outside aid offered to Kenya by NGOs funded by Western sources that positively stimulate the Kenyan economy would either be withdrawn or not accessed.[22] We want to be aware of a knee-jerk reaction to symptoms that have predictable outcomes that are far more equivalent to patriarchal colonialism than they are to the reciprocity of the traditional Kenyan culture that Kamaara and Omare describe.

What can the church in Kenya do to address radicalization of the youth? I cannot presume to have a Kenyan solution to the complicated struggles that the Kenyan culture and family face as a result of colonialism, modernization, technology, education, and globalization. However, I believe that Jesus conducted his ministry in the context of an imperialistic empire that used terror as a policy, so that the Gospels and teachings such as the Sermon on the Mount can be particularly relevant to the Kenyan experience. Therefore, I also draw upon some aspects of a biblical post-colonial hermeneutic and some insights from critical discourse analysis that allow me to relate to a situation that is far removed from my own. Although all Kenyans suffer from patterns of oppression resulting from colonialism, Christians will want to consider the responsibilities and impact of their current political and social dominance in Kenya. I suggest that the church cannot and should not attempt to interfere directly in the gender relationships in the Kenyan Muslim communities, nor should they instruct Muslim parents on how to raise their children. Rather, the Kenyan churches might be proactive in addressing the Christian culture and considering how Christian behavior may have contributed to the perception of a toxic environment for some in the Muslim community. Christians could commit to listen to the Muslim stories of religious inequality and how Muslims feel threatened.[23] The churches could train members who have power and privilege to embrace Jesus' example and call them to self-sacrificial servanthood rather than giving credibility to the rhetoric of power and competition of any who are trying to protect their own advantages. Servanthood would be expressed by the biblical practice of hospitality toward the other beyond

22. Kenya is among the world's leading recipients of aid from Western sources.
23. Botha, "Political Socialization," 911–13.

tribal/local boundaries and an attempt to practice the Kenyan value of reciprocity in political, and social, as well as familial relationships. The church could pay attention to inequality and counter the believer's tendency towards discrimination in all forms and across the levels of society in gender, social, cultural, and religious relationships. If the church chooses to act for the orphans and widows and aid the reversal of the discrimination against women in business and social contexts as a strategy to address poverty, it will want to blaze a careful ethical path, not accommodating selfish and wasteful dissipation and promoting the lure of materialism, but avoiding an unbiblical wealth, health and prosperity gospel. Two additional services that the churches can offer the home are to "turn the hearts of the fathers to their children" (Mal 4:6; Luke 1:17) and to be a major agent of socialization for their youth, with a radical call to mission in which they are peacemakers. I would clearly distinguish the mission of the church from the goal of building a nation, but I have a hope that if the churches are able to recruit their members to a discipleship that is contextualized within the Kenyan culture, then it could be a basis of healing for the family and nation.

REFERENCES

Botha, Anneli. "Political Socialization and Terrorist Radicalization among Individuals Who Joined al-Shabaab in Kenya." *Studies in Conflict and Terrorism* 37 (2014) 895–919. http://www.tandfonline.com/doi/abs/10.1080/1057610X.2014.952511?journalCode=uter20. Accessed 6 March 2017.

Fataliyeva, Sevinj. "Preventing the Radicalisation of Children by Fighting the Root Causes." Council of Europe, Parliamentary Assembly, Committee on Social Affairs, Health and Sustainable Development. 1–15. http://website-pace.net/documents/10643/2221023/Preventing-the-radicalisation-of-children-by-fighting-the-root-causes-EN.pdf/a0286e9e-cc3d-41a3-a4f5-d4c5a1d0d183. Accessed 6 March 2017.

Hunt, Juliet, and Nalini Kasynathan. "Pathways to Empowerment? Reflections on Microfinance and Transformation in Gender Relations in South Asia." *Gender & Development* 9, no.1 (2001) 42–52. https://www.jstor.org/stable/4030668?seq=1#page_scan_tab_contents. Accessed 6 March 2017.

Kassie, Menale, Simon Wagura Ndiritu, and Jesper Stage. "What Determines Gender Inequality in Household Food Security in Kenya? Application of Exogenous Switching Treatment Regression." *World Development* 56 (2014) 153–71. http://www.sciencedirect.com/science/article/pii/S0305750X13002374. Accessed 6 March 2017.

Rink, Anselm, and Kunaal Sharma. "The Determinants of Religious Radicalization: Evidence from Kenya." *Journal of Conflict Resolution* (December 2016) 1–33. http://journals.sagepub.com/doi/full/10.1177/0022002716678986.

Sowad, Abu Saleh Mohammad. "Migration Affecting Masculinities: The Consequences of Migration on the Construction of Masculinities of Migrant Bangladeshi Men Living in the United Kingdom." In *Discourse Analysis as a Tool for Understanding Gender Identity, Representation, and Equality*, edited by Nazmunnessa Mahtab et al., 50–73. Hershey, PA: Information Science Reference, 2016.

Vyas, Seema, and Charlotte Watts. "How Does Economic Empowerment Affect Women's Risk of Intimate Partner Violence in Low and Middle Income Countries? A Systematic Review of Published Evidence." *Journal of International Development* 21, no. 5 (2009) 577–602. https://www.academia.edu/10737194/How_does_economic_empowerment_affect_womens_risk_of_intimate_partner_violence_in_low_and_middle_income_countries_A_systematic_review_of_published_evidence. Accessed 6 March 2017.

Wright, Nat M. J. "Preventing Radicalisation and Terrorism: Is There a G.P. Response?" *British Journal of General Practice* (June 2016) 288–89. http://bjgp.org/content/66/647/288. Accessed 6 March 2017.

16

A Response to Joseph K. Koech

WAFIK WAHBA

CHRISTIANS HAVE A RESPONSIBILITY to extend God's love and acceptance to the hurting and broken communities in today's world. Koech's chapter on missions to Muslims provides an insightful presentation on the mandate of Christian missions from a biblical perspective while highlighting the current challenges in reaching out to Muslims in Kenya. He presents several practical and helpful tools related to understanding both the current context and the church's role in ministering among Muslims in the face of increased terrorist activities.

Throughout the modern history of Kenya, Christians and Muslims coexisted relatively peacefully. However, the terror attacks carried by al-Shabaab have had a ripple effect on Christians across the country. Violence, such as the Garissa University massacre of April 2015 that left 148 university students dead and hundreds of others wounded, has created anger and fear among both Christians and Muslims.[1] While Kenyan Muslim leaders condemned terrorist attacks, Christians are becoming suspicious of Muslims who might express feelings of sympathy with such horrendous acts. This fear of Muslims poses a serious threat to Christian outreach to Muslims.

In response to the complex issues facing the contemporary world, and missions in particular, Christians have a responsibility to understanding the current dynamics of Christian–Muslim relationships in

---

1. *BBC News*, "Kenya Attack: Garissa University Assault Killed 147," 2 April 2015.

general as well as addressing the issue of injustices that often result in increased fanaticism. The level of hostility between Christian and Muslim communities is growing in Kenya and around the globe due to misinformed communication and political tension. Religious differences are often used to fuel such hostilities; however, establishing mutual respect and common friendship with Muslims can often minimize the mistrust and hostility between the two communities. A better understanding of Islamic religious beliefs and worldview might help Christians in forming better relationships with Muslims based on understanding differences as well as mutual concerns. Christians and Muslims strive to live in peaceful communities and to enjoy healthy relationships. However, differences in religious beliefs and worldviews should not be used to ignite tensions. Therefore, proper training of Christian leaders on Islamic theology, history, as well as on current social and political issues is paramount.

St. Paul University's Centre for Christian–Muslim Relations in Nairobi presents an encouraging model for future relationship between the two communities. The "diapraxis" model that provides "dialogue in practice" where Christians and Muslims work together in overcoming stereotypes while attaining a better understanding of their historical, religious, and cultural differences is vital for establishing healthy encounters.[2]

Facing hostility, mistrust, and even persecution, Christians in other African countries have demonstrated the capability for extending forgiveness and reconciliation. For instance, Kenyan Christians may well want to look northward to the Coptic experience in Egypt for direction. In response to several attacks by jihadists where hundreds of Christians were massacred and numerous churches were burned during the last five years, many Egyptian Christians responded by extending forgiveness to those who committed the atrocities. They wrote the words "We Forgive" on the ruins of their homes and churches. Such a response created significant respect and affinity between Christians and the larger Muslim community, while alienating the terrorists. This is not to suggest that terrorist attacks will cease or that jihadist atrocities will not occur again; however, the Christian response won the friendship of much of the larger Muslim community. And because of those positive relation-

---

2. Dr. Joseph Wandera, one of this volume's contributors, is the director of this center.

ships, Christian witness and mission will hopefully have a better chance of being realized.

The Egyptian experience also reminds Kenyans that the Christian experience of redemption, reconciliation, and mission includes suffering. Through his suffering on the cross, Christ brought redemption to humanity; Christians are also given the privilege of suffering with Christ in order to extend God's forgiveness to humanity (Phil 1:24). In the midst of the present turmoil in Kenya, Christians need to keep these truths in mind.

17

Reading from a Muslim Perspective
Forging the Way Ahead

Halkano Abdi Wario

In March 2016, Uhuru Kenyatta, the president of the Republic of Kenya, posthumously awarded Salah Sadow Farah the Order of the Grand Warrior of Kenya. Farah, a Muslim, received the distinguished honor for his brave, selfless action of shielding fellow non-Muslim passengers during a bus attack by suspected al-Shabaab. Farah is no ordinary hero. He was shot by the attackers for standing up to say that enough is enough and that they could not keep killing innocent civilians based on their religious affiliation. He succumbed to his injuries a few weeks later.[1]

Farah was among a few dozen bus passengers who on 21 December 2015 were travelling from Nairobi to Mandera. Muslim passengers swapped clothes with their fellow Christian passengers making it difficult for the jihadists to separate and selectively kill non-Muslims in the bus as they earlier did at Westgate Mall in Nairobi, at Garissa University College in Garissa, in Mpeketoni, and in Mandera. By carrying out these heinous acts, the militants hope to ignite Islamophobic backlash, suspicion, paranoia, and inter-religious violence, and force the withdrawal of the Kenya Defence Forces from Somalia. This kind of strife would have undoubtedly boosted their numbers as it would be easy for them to radicalize and recruit among disenfranchised Muslims, and would

1. See "Kenya Honour for Muslim Hero."

add to a growing list of grievances against the state. Al-Shabaab have increased attacks against Kenya in response to the presence of the Kenyan army and its role in stabilizing regional forces under the auspices of the African Union Mission in Somalia (AMISOM), forces known to support the internationally-backed transitional federal government in Somalia.[2] Despite ethnic divisions due to competitive multi-party politics since 1992, Kenyans have demonstrated remarkable resilience on matters of faith and commendable religious tolerance in the face of jihadist attacks.

To understand the problems of terrorism in Kenya, it is important to recognize diversities within Islam in terms of doctrinal affiliations, racial and ethnic belongingness, and geographical distributions. It is also useful to put into perspective the discursive nature of Islamic traditions and to take note of the debates over correct interpretations of its core Scriptures, its vast histories, and the jurisprudential expositions that have been ongoing since its advent in seventh-century Arabia.[3] Groups or individuals, whether on the fringe or mainstream, have appropriated for themselves the right to speak for Islam and about Islam and have attempted, with varying successes and failures, to reconstruct society and related polities using the faith as a blueprint.[4] The current rise of fringe jihadist groups who claim to represent the general Muslim populace is not an exception. Current groups of jihadists, including al-Shabaab and other politically charged groups, emanate from situations of state failures, as armed struggles against local authoritarian regimes, as reactions to international interventionism in regional and state affairs, and by advantages offered by globalization that facilitates free movement of goods, persons, and ideas.[5] These groups extensively misuse the Qur'an and Hadith (the corpus of compiled literature documenting traditions of the Prophet Muhammad) and other secondary literature to provide a front of legitimacy and authority. Across the globe the largest casualties of terrorist attacks have been Muslims. In areas where Muslims and Christians have resided for decades in peace, selective victimization of

---

2. See Mwangi, "State Collapse"; Hansen, "Golden Age"; Marchal, "Tentative Assessment"; Shuriye, "Policies and Views."

3. See Asad, *Idea of and Anthropology of Islam*, 23; Anjum, "Islam as a Discursive Tradition."

4. Zaman, *Ulama in Contemporary Islam*.

5. Vidino et al., "Bringing Global Jihad."

Christians and Muslims who are opposed to their propaganda has been on the increase.

Actions of jihadist groups like the so called Islamic State (IS) in Iraq, Syria, and also Libya; Boko Haram in Nigeria, Cameroon, and Chad; al-Qaeda in the Maghreb in the Sahelian region; al-Shabaab in Somalia; and a myriad of other groups in Afghanistan and the Indian subcontinent affect religious minorities as well as the majority of Muslims. The question is: What has been the response of Muslim scholars and leaders? Many Muslim scholars within the country and across the world have expressed concern, noting, for example, the illegitimacy of jihadist groups to speak for Muslims and on behalf of Muslims. They have also condemned the actions of such groups as not sanctioned by the religion, and denounced the inhumane and un-Islamic killing of innocent civilians. These scholars have attempted to demonstrate that Islamic Scriptures and traditions call upon Muslims to always exercise compassion, avoid extremes, respect members of other religions, acknowledge the sacredness of all human life, and show the illegitimacy of armed struggle with aims of creating supranational polities based on distorted understandings of pristine and medieval Muslim histories. Globally, one of most famous responses has been the "Open Letter to Abu Bakar al-Baghdadi"[6] (the leader of IS), signed by dozens of religious scholars and leaders across the world. A number of Muslim-majority countries (Saudi Arabia, Egypt, and Mauritania, among others) and even some Western countries like the United Kingdom, the United States, and Australia, have state-sponsored/affiliated programs to address youth radicalization and recruitment, reintegration of former jihadists into society, and training and support for Muslim organizations working among vulnerable groups.[7] In Kenya, Muslim scholars and organizations often distance the majority of their constituencies from acts committed by these radical fringe groups, organizations, they point out, not sanctioned by the faith. Moreover, they have also actively engaged in public relations campaigns seeking to demonstrate that these groups wish to plant seeds of suspicion, hatred, and violence between the Muslim and non-Muslim populace. There is a general understanding among Muslims and mem-

---

6. See bibliography.

7. See Holtmann, "Editorials"; Halverson, *Master Narratives*; Ashour *De-radicalization of Jihadists*; Ashour, "Online De-radicalization"; Heath-Kelly, "Counter-Terrorism."

bers of other faiths in Kenya that what joins us together is our common humanity, common destiny as members of same nation-state called Kenya, and the same need to pursue individual and collective dreams of bettering our lives and those of future generations.

There is, however, a scarcity of well-documented case studies and empirical data that identify what Christian leaders, scholars, and ordinary believers are doing in coming to terms with terrorist attacks, deteriorating security situations, the response of the state to these attacks, resultant theological and philosophical discourses, and shifting relations between Christians and Muslims in Africa—especially in frontline states like Kenya. As a Muslim scholar who is concerned about Christian–Muslim interactions and with an ongoing research interest in state-funded, donor-funded, and independent programs focusing on countering violent extremism within the country, I find the contributions in this volume timely and well researched. The book raised a number of questions for me, however. First, how do ordinary Christians respond to terrorist attacks and threats that make them likely victims and targets? Second, how does the response of Muslim scholars and leaders differ from those of their counterparts from the Christian religious traditions? Third, what are the similarities, if any, between the philosophical and theological argumentations derived from religious texts made by Christian scholars and those by Muslim scholars in response to the terrorism phenomena in Kenya? Fourth, how do jihadist threats and attacks affect and transform religious subjectivities and imaginations for both Muslim and Christian followers in recent times and in the future? Fifth, how do these attacks impact already strained relations between Christians and Muslims and within diverse Muslim and Christian communities in the country? Last, but not the least, are there collaborative interfaith activities addressing problems associated with violent extremism so as to offer sustainable solutions for the greater enhancement of peace and stability in the country? It is hence refreshing and eye opening to read such richly researched works that bring forth insightful articulations on the response of Christian groups to the terrorism in Kenya. I will offer a brief review of each chapter.

Newton Kahumbi compartmentalizes relations between Christians and Muslims in three historical epochs: colonial, postcolonial phase I (1963–1998), and postcolonial phase II (1998–2015). This chapter provides rich historical instances and periods, characterized by tolerance, coexistence, and uneasiness. 1998 appears to be a watershed in strained relations between the two faiths, following simultaneous bombings of the United States embassies in Nairobi and Dar es Salaam by suspected al-Qaeda operatives. While major national and global events are notable markers of relations between Muslims and Christians, perpetual scholarly concerns with "outstanding" negative happenings obscure everyday struggles and interactions of ordinary believers of these religious traditions in markets, educational institutions, public transport, residential areas, and even homes. Resilience and ability to forge ahead even in spite of apparently selective terrorist attacks have helped Kenyans of diverse religious traditions strive to live together in peace.

Joseph Galgalo offers a brilliant analytical and interrogative exploration of the push and pull factors contributing to the rise in the number of terrorist attacks in Kenya. He questions how Kenyan Christians should response to terrorism threats and actual attacks, what appropriate measures the state can carry out to address historical and contemporary grievances and marginalization claims in Muslim majority areas, and pursue jihadist groups and suspected individuals within the rule of law without subjecting individuals and communities to stereotyping, profiling and unlawful detentions, trials, or enforced disappearances. Galgalo's emphasis on the need for Muslim and Christian leaders and followers, the state, as well as international communities to work together to bring an amicable solution to the problem of terrorism is urgently needed, both now and for the future.

Joseph Okello tackles one of the most visible responses of Christians to threats and attacks of jihadists, pacifism. Okello offers analysis of four forms of pacifism, namely absolute deontological pacifism, absolute consequentialist pacifism, contingent deontological pacifism, and contingent consequentialist pacifism. He points out that Christian pacifism "is a commitment to Christ's way of nonviolent suffering love, entailing a rejection of, and a refusal to participate in, war owing to the moral repugnance of the violence it represents and that all indications seem to point to the possibility that many victims left themselves at the mercy of the terrorists and accepted their fate without resistance and should be considered contemporary Christian martyrs." Histories of both Christianity and Islam document varied interpretations of pacifism, waging of war and peace, and martyrdom. Perhaps the recent use of the concept of martyrdom by jihadist groups to celebrate those who carry out suicide bombings and engage in military activity on their behalf has eclipsed any other notion of war and violence by Muslims. Islamic teachings often call upon believers to obey just and impartial government and only call for opposition and armed struggle if a government fails to rule with justice or transgresses limits set by God in the governance of its citizens. However, in recent times, jihadist groups have fought against local regimes, and convinced recruits by using decontextualized interpretations of Qur'an and Hadith that their uprisings are justified and legitimate and that they should die in their causes—guaranteed paradise as martyrs.

Related to Okello's contribution is David Tarus's work that gives refreshing new Christian theological approaches to coping with and making sense of terrorist attacks and threats in Kenya. Tarus proposes "a contextualized theological anthropology rooted in the Christian theology of the image of God, the Christ event, and the African concept of *ubuntu* (community)." It is imperative to adopt African concepts of humanness, as well as the reasons behind the rise of such attacks and threats and how to proactively respond to them as citizens of a multi-religious state. Historical and contextual understanding of the rise of jihadist groups out of regional security conflicts and state failures, transnational flow of arms and ideologies, interventionist measures employed by the Kenyan state, its neighbors, and regional/continental security arrangements in protracted civil wars, and continual engagement by religious leaders and interfaith forums will yield more pragmatic outcomes. Different forms of pacifism and appropriation of African philosophical worldviews on shared humanity will go a long way toward averting retaliatory attacks, suspicion, and profiling of Muslim communities. There are also historical parallels of pacifism within Islamic traditions. Muhammad and his followers were an oppressed minority for thirteen years of his formative mission in the city of Mecca. Despite abuses, physical attacks against them, destruction of their property, boycotts, enforced displacements, and emigration to Abyssinia by some of them, and threats of assassination and murder against some of them, Muhammad did not command them to retaliate or fight back in any way. It was only after the migration to Medina that the right to self defense became plausible against possible attacks by polytheist Quraishy Meccans and their allies.[8] These commonalities should be explored by religious leaders and scholars of

---

8. Hodgson, *Venture of Islam*.

both religions to build a better foundation for harmonious relations in the face of rising terror attacks.

Joseph Koech explores the precarious nature of Christian missions when proselytizing in Muslim majority areas in the light of rising terrorist threats and attacks. Koech suggests that challenges posed by terrorist activities can be addressed by re-evaluating mission strategies including better training of missionaries on Islam and local Muslim cultural milieus, understanding the implications of the terrorism threats and attacks, and mutual inter-religious dialogue. Both Islam and Christianity share an immense urgency to proclaim the core message of their faith to members of other religious traditions in order to win converts, and both religions share a stance of exclusivity about the truthfulness of their respective doctrines and histories, and have competed for followers across Africa. Koech's contribution raises the challenges for Christian proselytization to Muslim majority areas, an endeavor risky and critical to the growth of the church.

Joseph Wandera examines the discourse of select church leaders who preside over extensive congregations and who wield significant influence and who have demonstrated the existence of competing and complementary perspectives on the problems posed by terrorism in Kenya. Citing an array of case studies, Wandera posits that tacit sectarian themes have characterized responses from some church leaders, which have the possibility of negatively impacting interfaith relations. The author's main argument is that religion plays the highly ambivalent role of exacerbating exclusion and jeopardizing cohesion in the various contexts.

Julius Gathogo's contribution highlights an ecclesiastical paradigmatic shift in the way evangelical churches have moved from aloofness and indifference to politics to active appropriation of public space within political discourses in Kenya—including fronting polarizing perspectives on how to respond to terrorist attacks and threats. Gathogo argues that evangelicals in Kenya no longer want to be seen as mere spectators but as participants in redeeming society from turbulent situations. The rise of evangelicals in the public sphere is a global phenomenon witnessed by their growing influence in the United State elections last year. Unlike mainstream churches that often filter their public statements and opinions through established leadership structures, evangelicals are quick to appropriate public spaces to express highly polemical positions that may further strain Muslim–Christian relations.

Kamaara and Omare link the rise of al-Shabaab recruitment in Kenya's informal urban spaces to dysfunctional families, especially absentee father figures and inequality. They propose that restructuring and support to functional families and societal structures may be one of the most viable means of addressing radicalization and recruitment of youth into jihadist groups.

In fighting jihadist ideologies, threats, and attacks, concerted efforts of Muslim and Christian scholars, leaders and followers, and state and non-state actors are urgently required. Terrorism thrives in a state of disinformation and ethnic and religion divisions and suspicion. What brings Muslims and Christians and members of other religious communities together is common citizenship and belongingness in a country called Kenya that provides each of them with the opportunity to pursue their dreams and aspirations in an atmosphere of peace and stability. It is thus an urgent goal of these faith traditions to call upon the state to equitably distribute national resources, address existing and emerging discourses of historical injustices and marginalization that may contribute to radicalization, and to be a willing partner to adhere to the rule of law in governance and pursuit of suspected individuals and groups linked to terrorism.[9] There is need for leaders and scholars of both religions to preach about citizenship as a sacred covenant between themselves and the secular state. Citizenship comes with rights and responsibilities. Critique of the state so as to provide checks and balances against excesses is necessary, as is readiness to defend each other against the aggression of terrorist threats, attacks, and propaganda. For Muslims, the lure of jihadist groups with promises of better lives under their rule outside the country or their influence within the country, their manipulation of existing strained relations between Muslim citizens and the state to render their grievances into a meta-narrative for radicalization and recruitment, and their interference and disruption of harmonious inter-faith relations must be resisted through relentless grassroots outreaches and through multiple media platforms.[10] It is this "us" verses

---

9. Kresse, "Muslim Politics"; Willis and Chome, "Marginalization"; Ndzovu, "Politicization of Muslim Organizations."

10. Holtmann, "Editorials."

"them" mentality that the jihadist groups wish to inculcate within the dissatisfied Muslim citizenry that must be resisted with all means.

As citizens with privileged positions, Muslim and Christian scholars and religious leaders need not shy away from matters with national and regional political ramifications. Security is one of them. They need a common front on behalf of their respective constituencies in regards to analyzing and critiquing activities of the Kenyan state. For instance, when Kenya is part of the AMISOM forces in Somalia, what is the feasibility of such interventions given our economy, the impact on national security, relations between ethnic and religious communities, and the resultant vulnerability of our borders to entry by jihadist groups? This type of analysis can only be done if common interfaith platforms are put in place that engage all willing religious communities in de-radicalization programs.

State security agencies have been mentioned time and again by human rights organizations as contravening the dictates of our new Constitution in pursuit of terrorism suspects. Enforced disappearances, extra-judicial killings, and extended detention without trial are counterproductive in the long term. Religious leaders from both traditions are best suited to stand up to such blatant abuses of power that facilitate recruitment of aggrieved members of suspect communities into the terrorist ranks. This will immensely strengthen civil society in the country.

In the past few years, there have been initiatives founded by Muslim groups that are attempting to wrest from the jihadist groups the right to speak about and for Islam, and to interpret concepts such as jihad. The Building Resilience Against Violent Extremism (BRAVE) Movement, led by Dr. Mustafa Ali, is one such effort. The BRAVE Movement ran a series of advertisements on national television and radio debunking the narratives of jihadists as false and dangerous, and showing that Islam does not sanction killing of non-Muslims, and that we are citizens of one country irrespective of our ethnic, racial, economic, and religious differences. This initiative extensively used the Qur'an and other Islamic literature in the construction of counter-narratives. Programs attempting to counter violent extremism need not ignore the importance of religious ideologies in addressing youth radicalization and recruitment. It is, however, important that Muslim and Christian religious leaders visit each other's places of worship and address their respective congregants about mutual coexistence and continuously build bridges of dialogue and collaboration so as to cushion the country against the adverse effects of terrorism threats and attacks.

REFERENCES

Anjum, Ovamir. "Islam as a Discursive Tradition: Talal Asad and His Interlocutors." *Comparative Studies of South Asia, Africa and the Middle East* 27, no. 3 (2007) 656–72.

Asad, T. *The Idea of an Anthropology of Islam*. Occasional Papers. Washington, DC: Center for Contemporary Arab Studies, Georgetown University, 1986.

Ashour, Omar. *The De-radicalization of Jihadists: Transforming Armed Islamist Movements*. London: Routledge, 2009.

———. "Online De-Radicalization? Countering Violent Extremist Narratives: Message, Messenger and Media Strategy." *Perspectives on Terrorism* 4, no. 6 (2010) 15–19.

Halverson, J. R., et al. *Master Narratives of Islamist Extremism*. New York: Palgrave McMillan, 2011.

Hansen, Stig Jarle. "The Golden Age of Al-Shabaab (2009–10)." In *Al-Shabaab in Somalia: The History and Ideology of a Militant Islamist Group, 2005–2012*, by Stig Jarle Hansen, 73–102. Oxford: Oxford University Press, 2013.

Heath-Kelly, C. "Counter-Terrorism and the Counterfactual: Producing the 'Radicalisation' Discourse and the UK PREVENT Strategy." *The British Journal of Politics & International Relations* 15, no. 3 (2012) 394–415.

Hodgson, Marshall G. S. *The Venture of Islam: The Classical Age of Islam*. Chicago: University of Chicago Press, 1977.

Holtmann, P. "Editorials: Countering Al-Qaeda's Single Narrative." *Perspectives on Terrorism* 7, no. 2 (2013) 141–46.

"Kenya Honour for Muslim Hero who Protected Christian Bus Passengers." *BBC News*, 31 March 2016. http://www.bbc.com/news/world-africa-35937314.

Kresse, Kai. "Muslim Politics in Postcolonial Kenya: Negotiating Knowledge on the Double-Periphery." *Journal of the Royal Anthropological Institute* 15 (2009) S76–S94.

Marchal, R. "A Tentative Assessment of the Somali Harakat Al-Shabaab." *Journal of Eastern African Studies* 3, no. 3 (2009) 381–404.

Mwangi, O. G. "State Collapse, Al-Shabaab, Islamism, and Legitimacy in Somalia." *Politics, Religion & Ideology* 4, no. 4 (2012) 513–27.

Ndzovu, H. "The Politicization of Muslim Organizations and the Future of Islamic-Oriented Politics in Kenya." *Islamic Africa* 3, no. 1 (2012) 25–53.

"Open Letter to Abu Bakar al-Baghdadi." September 2014. http://www.lettertobaghdadi.com/14/english-v14.pdf.

Shuriye, Abdi O. "Policies and Views of the UN and Western Nations on Al-Shabaab and Its Recruitment Strategies." *Review of European Studies* 4, no. 1 (2012) 220–28.

Vidino, L., et al. "Bringing Global Jihad to the Horn of Africa: Al-Shabaab, Western Fighters, and the Sacralization of the Somali Conflict." *African Security* 3, no. 4 (2010) 216–38.

Willis, Justin, and Ngala Chome. "Marginalization and Political Participation on the Kenya Coast: The 2013 Elections." *Journal of Eastern African Studies* 8, no. 1 (2014) 115–34.

Zaman, Muhammad Qasim. *Ulama in Contemporary Islam: Custodians of Change*. Princeton: Princeton University Press, 2002.

Appendix

Timeline of Some of the Terrorist Attacks in Kenya from 2011 to 2016

Appendix

Date (dd/mm/yy)	Nature of Attack	Place	Casualties	Attackers
24/10/2011	Grenade attack	Nairobi: Mwaura's Bar	1 killed, 28 injured	al-Shabaab
24/10/2011	Grenade attack	Nairobi: Machakos bus station	5 killed, 64 injured	al-Shabaab
27/10/2011	Grenade attack	Mandera: vehicle carrying high school exams attacked	4 killed	Suspected al-Shabaab militants
28/10/2011	Landmine	Garissa: vehicle carrying officers to Liboi hits a landmine	3 injured	Unspecified attackers
05/11/2011	Grenade attack	Garissa: East Africa Pentecostal church	2 killed, 5 injured	Unspecified
06/11/2011	Ambush	Mandera: Suspected al-Shabaab militants attack a border post	1 killed	al-Shabaab
24/11/2011	Twin grenade attacks	Garissa: Holiday Inn Hotel	3 killed	Unspecified
26/11/2011	Ambush/Raid	Arabia trading center near Mandera, local police station	No casualties, arms, ammunition taken	al-Shabaab
05/12/2011	Landmine	UN convoy at Ifo refugee camp hits a landmine	1 killed, 3 injured	Unspecified
19/02/2012	Ambush	Garissa, Hulugho: Attack on a police station	2 killed, 2 injured	al-Shabaab
10/03/2012	4 Grenades	Nairobi: Machakos Bus Station	6 killed, 60 injured	al-Shabaab
04/04/2012	Grenade attack	Mombasa: Church crusade in Mtwapa-Mombasa	2 killed, 30 injured	al-Shabaab
28/04/2012	Grenade attack	Nairobi: Church in Nairobi's Ngara area	2 killed, 14 injured	Unspecified
15/05/2012	Shooting & Grenade	Mombasa: Bella Vista Night club	1 killed, 2 injured	Unspecified
28/05/2012	Grenade	Nairobi: Sasa Boutique, Assanand's House, Moi Avenue St.	38 injured	Unspecified

Timeline of Some of the Terrorist Attacks in Kenya from 2011 to 2016

Date (dd/mm/yy)	Nature of Attack	Place	Casualties	Attackers
25/06/2012	Bomb blast	Mombasa: Jericho beer garden bar	3 killed, 30 injured	Unspecified
29/06/2012	Ambush	Ambush at Ifo Refugee Camp	1 killed, 1 kidnapped	al-Shabaab
01/07/2012	Gunmen attack	Garissa: Catholic Church and AIC Garissa Church	17 killed, 45 injured	al-Shabaab
18/07/2012	Grenade attack	Wajir: 2 hand Grenades thrown into a barbershop	4 injured	Unspecified
25/07/2012	Landmine	Wajir: Police vehicle runs over a landmine	3 officers injured	Unspecified
01/08/2012	Unspecified explosion	Nairobi: St. Theresa Catholic Church	3 killed; 5 injured	Unspecified
03/08/2012	Homemade explosive	Nairobi, Eastleigh: near Kenya Air Force Headquarters.	1 killed, 10 injured	al-Shabaab
28/08/2012	Grenade attack	Mombasa: Lebanon Round-about in Mwembe, Mombasa	3 policemen killed, 12 civilians injured	Unspecified
21/09/2012	IED/Landmine	Garissa: Police Vehicle runs into a landmine	2 policemen injured	Unspecified
30/09/2012	Grenade attack	Nairobi: St Polycarp ACK church, off Juja Road	1 boy killed, 6 children injured	Unspecified
30/09/2012	Gunmen attack	Garissa town: Ngamia road	2 killed	Unspecified
20/10/2012	Youths with crude weapons	Likoni, Mombasa	1 injured	MRC
25/10/2012	Shooting	Dadaab: Hagdera refugee camp	1 killed	Unspecified
04/11/2012	Grenade attack	Garissa	1 killed, 10 injured	Unspecified
18/11/2012	Explosion detonated	Nairobi, Eastleigh: Kariobangi-bound matatu (taxi) blown up	7 killed, 33 injured	al-Shabaab

APPENDIX

Date (dd/mm/yy)	Nature of Attack	Place	Casualties	Attackers
05/12/2012	Explosion detonated	Nairobi, Eastleigh: Joster supermarket	2 killed, 6 injured	Suspected al-Shabaab
07/12/2012	Unspecified	Nairobi: al-Hidaya mosque	6 killed, 20 injured (including MP Yusuf Hassan	Suspected al-Shabaab
04/01/2013	Grenade attack	Garissa: Dagahale area	2 killed, 7 injured	al-Shabaab
07/01/2013	Grenade attack	Garissa: Ngamia road	1 killed, 8 injured	al-Shabaab
09/01/2013	Grenade Attack	Mandera: World Food Program compound	No injuries	al-Shabaab
16/01/2013	Shooting	Garissa: Attack on a hotel	5 killed, 3 injured	al-Shabaab
17/01/2013	Attempted attack	Garissa	2 killed (the bombers)	al-Shabaab
31/01/2013	Explosion detonated	Daghalle town near Dadaab	3 police injured	Unspecified
02/02/2013	Greenade attack	Wajir, Wajir county	1 soldier killed, 2 policemen injured	Unspecified
05/02/2013	Shooting	Garissa	An administration police officer killed	Unspecified
18/02/2013	Shooting	Garissa: Kwa Chege Hotel	6 killed, 10 injured	al-Shabaab
21/02/2013	Gunfire/Ambush	Liboi, Garissa county	7 killed	Unspecified
04/03/2013 (General Election Date)	Grenades, Armed attacks	15 separate grenade attacks at different polling stations in Mandera and Garissa; 1 ambush at Kilifi and Mombasa Counties	12 killed, including 6 policemen in Kilifi and Mombasa counties. 1 killed 8 injured at attacks on several polling stations in Garissa and Mandera	"Armed Seccesionists" possibly MRC

Timeline of Some of the Terrorist Attacks in Kenya from 2011 to 2016

Date (dd/mm/yy)	Nature of Attack	Place	Casualties	Attackers
09/06/2013	Grenades	Nairobi; Eastleigh and church in Likoni, Mombasa	15 injured	al-Shabaab
21/09/2013	Shootings; Grenade attack	Nairobi: Westgate Mall	67 killed, 150 injured	al-Shabaab
13/12/2013	Blast	Wajir	1 killed, 3 injured	Unspecified
14/12/2013	Grenade attack	Nairobi: Eastleigh-Town bus exploded	4 killed, 36 injured	al-Shabaab
01/01/2014	Grenade	Mombasa: Tandoori Bar, Diani	10 injured	Unspecified
19/03/2014	Attempted attack through IED	Mombasa	No casualties	Unspecified
23/03/2014	Gun attack	Mombasa: Joy of Jesus Church, Likoni	6 killed, 18 injured	al-Shabaab
31/03/2014	3 IED Blast	Nairobi: Eastleigh estate	6 killed, 30 injured	al-Shabaab
01/04/2014	Improvised bombs	Nairobi: Eastleigh: 2 Cafes, barely 300 meters apart hit.	6 killed, 20 injured	al-Shabaab
18/04/2014	Gun attack	Garissa: Kwa Njenga Hotel, Garissa	6 killed	al-Shabaab
24/04/2014	Car bomb	Pangani police station	4 killed	al-Shabaab
03/05/2014	Twin attacks: Grenade and improvised explosive device	Mombasa	3 killed	Unspecified
04/05//2014	Homemade bombs	Nairobi: Thika Road: explosive device detonated inside commuter bus	3 killed, 87 injured	al-Shabaab
16/05/2014	Twin explosions	Nairobi: Gikomba market	10 killed, scores injured	al-Shabaab

Appendix

Date (dd/mm/yy)	Nature of Attack	Place	Casualties	Attackers
23/05/2014	Grenade	Mombasa: Grenade thrown at police vehicle	2 injured	Unspecified terror suspects
15–16/06/2014	Shooting, beheading	Mpeketoni, Lamu	48 killed; several kidnapped	al-Shabaab claimed responsibility; Government blames local politics
17/06/2014	Kidnapping	Maporomokoni village, Lamu	9 killed	al-Shabaab
07/07/2014	Gun attack/ Raid	Gamba town, Tana River county and Hindi town, Lamu county	20 killed	al-Shabaab or MRC
26/09/2014	Grenade attack	Garissa market	6 injured	al-Shabaab
23/10/2014	Grenade attack	Garissa	8 injured	al-Shabaab
02/11/2014	Attack on army barracks	Mombasa: Nyali	6 of the 15 attackers killed; 1 soldier killed	MRC
02/11/2014	Attack on Police Post	Malindi Town	No deaths	MRC
22/11/2014	Attack	Mandera: a Nairobi bound bus	28 people	al-Shabaab
02/12/2014	Quarry raid	Koromey area in Mandera	36 killed	al-Shabaab
13/12/2014	Gun raid	Kaloleni, Mombasa County police station	1 kilofed, 2 injured	MRC
13/03/2015	Gunmen attack	Governor and his team attacked, Mandera County	4 people killed (3 police officers and a senior chief)	al-Shabaab
02/04/2015	Gunmen attack	Garissa University College	148 killed	al-Shabaab

Timeline of Some of the Terrorist Attacks in Kenya from 2011 to 2016

Date (dd/mm/yy)	Nature of Attack	Place	Casualties	Attackers
25/04/2015	Police patrol ambushed	Yumbis, Garissa	1 police officer killed, 13 injured,	al-Shabaab
14/06/2015	100 Islamist militants attack	Lamu KDF Camp	2 soldiers and 15 terrorists killed	al-Shabaab
07/07/2015	Gunman attack	Mandera: Residential area	14 killed, 10 injured	al-Shabaab
21/12/2015	Gunmen ambush attack	Nairobi to Mandera bus	3 killed; 2 injured	al-Shabaab
15/01/2016	Gunman attack	KDF camp, El Adde, Somalia	Uncertain-perhaps 180–200 Kenyan soldiers killed	al-Shabaab
14/07/2016	Gunman attack	Kapenguria Police Station	7 police officers killed, several injured	Constable Abdiha-kim Maslah
11/09/2016	Petrol bomb and knife stabbing	Mombasa Police Station	3 female terrorists killed, 2 policemen injured	al-Shabaab
21/09/2016	Gunman attack	Garissa: Amei Police Post	Police officers shot at; weapons, police car stolen	al-Shabaab
25/10/2016	Gunman attack	Mandera: Bisharo Hotel	12 people killed	al-Shabaab

Subject Index

Afghanistan, 65, 66, 85, 207
Al-Haramain Foundation, 26
Al-Qaeda, 4, 21, 37, 49, 57, 65, 66, 83, 106, 133, 141, 207, 209
Al-Shabaab, 5, 6, 21–24, 27, 28, 30, 36–38, 44, 50, 78, 80–82, 85, 106, 107, 113, 133–49, 161, 178, 184, 193–5, 202, 205–7, 212, 216–21
African Union Mission to Somalia (AMISOM), 6, 77, 206, 213
Anglicanism, 19, 44, 72, 74, 76, 83, 110, 137, 176

Bethel Church, 20
Boko Harem, 106, 138, 207
Britain/British, *see England*
Building Resilience Against Violent Extremism (BRAVE), 213

Central Africa Republic, 106
Christian Religious Education (CRE), 15, 16
Christianity
  Church buildings, 5, 7–9, 19–22, 25, 27–29, 81, 137, 167, 203
  Clergy, 18, 22, 76, 82, 83, 117, 137
  Early Church, 41, 55, 61, 135, 136, 152, 169
  Education, 13–16, 29, 46
  Extremism, 115
  Great Commission, 153, 154
  Leaders, 7, 16, 24, 25, 30, 44, 47, 61, 76, 77, 79, 82, 83, 107, 108, 112–20, 128, 137, 163, 173, 175–7, 181–2, 186–8
  Missions/evangelization, 12, 13, 16–20, 110–13, 30, 124, 151–69, 177, 189, 200, 202–4, 211
  Peace efforts, 40, 45–48, 50–52, 57, 60, 62, 116–20, 123–31, 144, 157, 175, 202–3
  Reformation, 74, 95, 136
  Sermon on the Mount, 40, 84, 199
  Worship, 166, 188
Church Missionary Society (CMS), 110
Cold War, 4, 84, 106
Council of Islamic Preachers of Kenya (CIPK), 30

Daystar University, 17, 159

East Africa, 5, 13, 17, 19, 20, 33, 47, 75, 76, 78, 90, 110, 111, 137, 141, 156, 157, 177, 183, 216
East African Revival Movement, 75
Encyclopedia of Terrorism and Political Violence, 3
Egypt, 20, 29, 96, 203, 204
England, 12, 34, 59, 86, 176, 178
Ethiopia, 133, 163
Evangelical Alliance of Kenya (EAK), 114

French Revolution, 3
Freemark Initative, 140, 194, 195

Global Terrorism Index, 5
Good News Evangelical Centre, 79

Help Africa People, 26
Hinduism, 16

223

Ibrahim Abd al-Aziz al-Ibrahim Foundation, 26
International Relief Organziation, 26
India, 20
Iran, 20, 85
Iraq, 65, 66, 85, 106, 207
Islam
  Clerics, 6, 7, 27, 78, 115, 117
  De-radicalization, 81, 115
  Education, 13–16, 18, 26, 29
  Extremism, 6, 7, 12, 21, 23, 25–27, 31, 45, 73, 76, 78, 113, 115, 117, 133, 143, 144–47, 175, 193–6, 199, 200, 205, 207, 208, 212, 213
  Festivals, 15, 29
  Fundamentalism, 3, 144, 155, 156
  Hadith, 206, 210
  Jihad, 27, 28, 42, 81, 108, 114–16, 33, 88, 203, 205–14
  Leaders, 6, 7, 15, 16, 18, 20, 22, 28–31, 38, 64, 65, 107, 112–20, 134, 157
  Mihadhara, 19
  Missions/evangelization, 12, 13, 17–20, 30, 195, 210
  Moderates, 27, 166
  Muhammad, 18–20, 22, 114, 206, 210
  Mosques, 7, 14, 15, 17–19, 21, 27, 28, 81, 110, 112, 116–19
  Peace efforts, 23, 24, 116–20, 157, 202, 203
  Qur'an, 5, 22, 23, 27, 54, 114, 158, 166, 206, 207, 210, 213
  Radicalism, *see extremism*
  Ramadhan, 15
  Youth, 6, 7, 17, 20, 22, 28, 29, 45, 67, 68, 80, 81, 133, 144, 159, 193, 195–200, 207, 212, 213
Islamophobia, 24, 25
Islamic Party of Kenya (IPK), 21
Islamic Religious Education (IRE), 15, 16
Islamic State (IS/ISIL), 106, 207

Jesus Is Alive Ministries (JIAM), 137

Just War Theory, 39, 42–45, 52, 55, 58, 62, 63, 65, 79, 82, 174, 178

Kenya
  Colonialism, 12, 13, 33, 34, 139, 177, 179, 185–9, 194, 199, 208
  Constitution, 24, 25, 29, 38, 62, 78, 113, 213
  Economics, 124
  Education, 35, 47, 65, 68, 73, 76, 78,
  Extremism, 6
  Garissa Province/College, 6, 21, 22, 29, 35, 44, 54, 55, 60, 68, 113, 116, 117, 143, 144, 160, 162, 163, 165–7, 186, 202, 205, 216–21
  Government, 4–7, 21, 22, 25–29, 33–36, 44–47, 50, 51, 61, 69, 70, 73, 75–78, 80–83, 91, 107–9, 112–5, 117, 132, 133, 145, 155–71, 173–7, 210, 212
  Independence, 34
  Isiolo County, 14, 20
  Media, 5, 21, 50, 81, 83, 99, 100, 116, 118, 164
  Military, 5, 6, 21, 38, 50, 53, 61, 65, 67, 70, 74, 77, 79, 81, 83, 107, 133, 141, 166, 184, 210, 221
  Population, 4, 6, 16, 26, 34–36, 108, 133, 155, 158, 194, 196
  Post-Colonialism, 9, 13, 14, 111, 134, 138, 139, 141, 176, 199, 208
  Social Issues, 29, 124, 176
Kenyan Defence Forces (KDF), 6, 21, 74, 83, 133, 141, 166, 221
Kenya National Inter-religious Network, 30
Kenyan National Commission on Human Rights (KNCHR), 113
Khadi Courts, 24

Malaysia, 20
Mercy Relief International Agency, 26
Methodism, 17, 72, 75, 209, 210
Mombasa, 5, 14, 21, 27, 28, 30, 78, 79, 82, 86, 110, 115, 143, 157, 185, 216–21

Subject Index

Nairobi, 4, 5, 12, 15, 17–19, 21, 23, 26–32, 37, 54, 59, 68, 75, 112, 116, 140, 142, 159, 160, 203, 205, 209, 216–21
National Council of Churches of Kenya (NCCK), 73, 76, 78, 82, 113, 114, 116, 186, 187
National Imam's Council of Australia, 146
Non-Government Organizations (NGO), 26
Norfolk Hotel, 4, 37

Operation Linda Nchi, 6, 38, 107, 133

Pacifism, 39–42, 45, 46, 50–63, 65–70, 79, 84
Pakistan, 20
Paradise Hotel, 5
Pentecostalism, 20, 24, 72–74, 76–78, 82, 86, 113, 115, 177, 216
People's Commission of Kenya, 29
The Popular Front for the Liberation of Palestine (PFLP), 4
Portugal, 13, 110
Presbyterian Church of East Africa, 17, 137
Presbyterianism, 74–76, 83, 177

Quakerism, 123, 124, 130
Quraishy Meccans, 210

Roman Catholicism, 14, 18, 29, 41, 72–74, 114–7, 137, 138, 159, 217

Saudi Arabia, 17, 20, 207

Seventh-Day Adventism, 19
Sikhism, 16
Somalia, 5, 6, 21, 27, 28, 34, 37, 38, 50, 57, 70, 74, 77, 80–82, 85, 86, 106–9, 122, 132, 133, 141, 156, 166, 178, 205–7, 213
South Africa, 19, 90, 91, 109
Supreme Council of Kenya Muslims (SUPKEM), 18, 23, 30, 111, 157
Syria, 106, 144, 145, 207

Tanzania, 4, 19, 81, 91
Tel Aviv, 9
The Truth, Justice, and Reconciliation Commission, 35, 36, 49

Uganda, 4
United Nations, 6, 29, 133
United States of America
    Christianity, 81, 124
    Department of Defense, 132
    Embassies, 4, 12, 21, 26, 37
    Foreign Policy, 4, 27, 65, 85
    Terrorist Attacks, 3, 4, 84
    Government, 4, 84, 85
    Relations with Islam, 27
Ufungamano, 29
Union of Islamic Courts (UIC), 133
Upendo Spiritual Church, 83
Usalama Watch, 28

World Assembly of Muslim Youth of Saudi Arabia, 17

Zanzibar, 110, 157

Names Index

Akali, Joshuah, 82
Alessandro, Joseph, 116
Ali, Mustafa, 215
Aronson, Samuel, 4
Augustine of Hippo, 41–43, 79, 80, 135, 136
Ayanga, Hazel, 134

Bakari, Sheikh Salim, 7
Barre, Siad, 132
Barth, Christopher, 96
Basil of Caesarea, 136
Bosch, David, 152, 154
Braaksma, Debra, 159
Brislen, Michael Dennis, 157
Bujo, Benezet, 91
Bush, George W., 84
Buzan, Barry, 112

Calvin, John, 41, 96
Carter, Jimmy, 85
Chabal, Patrick, 184

Day, Dorothy, 41
Dor, Sheikh Mohamed, 117
Deedat, Ahmed, 19
Duquoc, Christian, 102

Faulkner, Mark R., 157
Francis, Pope, 30, 117, 122

Gatu, John G., 177
Gitari, David, 75, 76, 85, 177
Glasser, Arthur F. 153
Gifford, Paul, 7, 9, 184, 185
Gushee, David, 98

Hall, Douglas, 93
Hoekendijk, Johnannes, 152
Hooper, Handley, 175
Hussein, Saddam, 65

Ibrahim, Amina H., 142
Idowu, Bolaji, 89
Idriss, Sheikh Mohammed, 7
Irenaeus of Lyons, 94
Ismail, Sheikh Ibrahim Omar, 7

Jenkins, Philip, 8, 176
John Paul II, Pope, 43
Juergensmeyer, Mark, 3

Kagame, Alexis, 90
Kahumbi, Newton, 208
Kambo, Joseph, 136
Karanja, Peter, 73, 113, 114
Kariuki, Mark, 114
Kassim, Mohammed Sheikh, 7
Katongole, Emmanuel, 185, 188, 190
Kenyatta, Uhuru, 205
Khomeini, Ayatollah, 20
Kibaki, Mwai, 133
Kim, Caleb Chul-Soo, 156
King, Martin Luther, 65
Koech, Joseph, 154
Kuria, Archbishop Manasses, 19, 29
Krapf, Johann Ludwig, 110, 157

Lagho, Wilybard, 115
Laqueur, Walter, 4
Lewis, H. S., 157
Love, Maryann Cusimanno, 64, 66
Luther, Martin, 41, 136, 173–75

Names Index

Makaburi, *see Shariff, Abubakar*
Mbiti, John, 8, 82, 89, 91, 156
McGavran, Donald, 153
McKee, Robert Guy, 99
Middleton, Richard, 95
Moi, Daniel arap, 72, 74, 77, 78, 111, 177, 186
Mugambi, Jesse N. K., 82, 89
Mutiga, Murithi, 141
Mwakimako, Hassan, 26, 157

Njoya, Timothy, 83
Nyiramana, Cecile, 123, 124, 130

O'Dea, Janet, 134
O'Dea, Thomas, 134, 135
Odira, Charles, 114
Oldham, J. H., 177
Otabil, Mensa, 177
Otunga, Cardinal Maurice, 18, 19, 29

Phillips, David, 157

Ramsey, Paul, 94, 97
Reagan, Ronald, 85
Reynolds, Thomas, 96, 97
Rogo, Sheikh Aboud, 7
Rushdie, Salman, 20

Said, Sayyid,
Saleem, Sheikh Mohamadu, 146
Seif, Mohamed Seif, 29
Shariff, Sheikh Abubakar, 7
Stitcher, S. B., 139

Tablino, Paul, 157
Takar, Hassan, 22
Taylor, Charles, 184
Tutu, Desmond, 90, 92, 102

Waever, Old, 112
Wanjiru, Margaret, 77, 137
Weston, Frank, 177
Wilkins, Michael J., 153

CPSIA information can be obtained
at www.ICGtesting.com
Printed in the USA
LVHW052252120122
708310LV00017B/1905